What
MENNONITES
Are
THINKING
–2000–

Design by Dawn J. Ranck

WHAT MENNONITES ARE THINKING, 2000

Copyright © 2000 by Good Books, Intercourse, PA 17534
International Standard Book Number: 1-56148-300-1
ISSN: 1099-0704

What
MENNONIT
Are
THINKINC
–2000–

— Edited by —
Merle Good *and*
Phyllis Pellman Good

Good Books

Intercourse, PA 17534
800/762-7171
www.goodbks.com

This book is made possible
in part by the following sponsors—

Eastern Mennonite University

The People's Place

Mennonite Weekly Review

Goshen College

Good Books

*(Please read the sponsors' messages
on pages 325-330)*

Acknowledgments

"Racism in Canada?" by Brad Reimer is reprinted by permission from *Canadian Mennonite* (February 21, 2000).

"A Third Way Between Fight and Flight" by Richard A. Kauffman is reprinted by permission from *The Mennonite* (May 2, 2000).

"I Was a Mennonite Teamster" by Rosanna Landis Weaver is reprinted by permission from *The Marketplace* (July-August, 2000).

"Should Be More People Like Who?" by Robert Rhodes is reprinted by permission from *Mennonite Weekly Review* (March 2, 2000).

"Why Mennonites Aren't Usually Funny (in Writing)" by Maurice Mierau is reprinted from *Rhubarb* Magazine.

"A Modern Saul of Tarsus" by Jewel Showalter is reprinted by permission from *Mennonite Weekly Review* (June 15, 2000).

"The Nonswearing of Oaths" by Harold Sensenig is reprinted from *The Eastern Mennonite Testimony* (August, 2000).

"Some Things I Want My Children to Know" by Ron Adams is reprinted from *The Gathering, Words and Art by Community Mennonite Church of Lancaster,* by permission of the author and of Parrot Press.

"Minding Us Mennonites" by Phyllis Pellman Good is reprinted by permission from *The Mennonite Quarterly Review* (January, 2000).

"Man answers God" by Rhoda Janzen is reprinted by permission from *Christian Century* (August 16-23, 2000). © 2000 Christian Century Foundation.

"Overflow" is from *Tasting the Dust* by Jean Janzen, © 2000. Reprinted by permission of Good Books.

"Peace and Unity" by Levi Miller is reprinted by permission from *Christian Living* (June, 2000), Herald Press.

Acknowledgments

"Humility Is Valuing Others" by Ardie S. Goering is reprinted by permission from *Mennonite Weekly Review* (May 25, 2000).

"Toward a Culture of Global Understanding" by Pakisa K. Tshimika is reprinted by permission from MBMS International's *Witness* magazine (May-June, 1999).

"Mennonites and Music" by Isaac R. Horst is reprinted by permission of Herald Press from *A Separate People; An Insider's View of Old Order Mennonite Customs and Traditions.* All rights reserved.

"Closed on Sundays" by Arthur Bert is reprinted by permission from *The Marketplace* (April 2000).

"What Families Should Value" by John D. Roth is reprinted by permission from *Christian Living* (June, 2000), Herald Press.

"A Benedictine Mennonite: Prefer Nothing Whatever to Christ" by Arthur Paul Boers is reprinted by permission from *Canadian Mennonite* (March 20, 2000).

"Micah, My Twin" by Robert J. Baker is reprinted by permission from *Christian Living* (August, 2000), Herald Press.

"Living on the Iceberg: 'The Artist as Critic and Witness' 36 Years Later" by Rudy Wiebe is reprinted by permission of the author from *Conrad Grebel Review* (Spring, 2000). © Rudy Wiebe, 2000.

"Menno Simons Shares the Podium with Myron Augsburger and Tony Campolo at the Mennonite General Assembly;" by Leonard Nolt is reprinted by permission of the author.

"Menno Simons Sighs and Leans Back in His Seat" by Leonard Nolt is reprinted by permission of the author.

"Dickie Derksen" by David Elias is from the collection *Places of Grace*, published by Coteau Books, and is reprinted by permission of the publisher.

"Coat of a Visiting Nurse" is from *Eve's Striptease* by Julia Kasdorf, © 1998. Reprinted by permission of the University of Pittsburgh Press.

"Ice" is from *Tasting the Dust* by Jean Janzen, © 2000. Reprinted by permission of Good Books.

WHAT MENNONITES ARE THINKING, 2000

"Thinking of Certain Mennonite Women" is from *Eve's Striptease* by Julia Kasdorf, © 1998. Reprinted by permission of the University of Pittsburgh Press.

"A Traditioned Theology of Mission" is from *By Faith They Went Out: Mennonite Missions 1850-1999* by Wilbert R. Shenk. Reprinted by permission of the author and Institute of Mennonite Studies, 2000.

The book review by Bernie Wiebe of *The Journey Toward Reconciliation* is reprinted by permission from *Journal of Mennonite Studies* (Volume 18, 2000).

The book review by Kimberly Schmidt of *Women Against the Good War: Conscientious Objection and Gender on the American Home Front, 1941-1947* is reprinted by permission from *Mennonite Historical Bulletin* (January, 2000).

The book review by John A. Lapp of *Do I Still Have a Life?* is reprinted by permission from *Mennonite Weekly Review* (October 5, 2000).

The book review by Pamela E. Klassen of *Mennonites in Canada, 1939-1970: A People Transformed* and *Mennonites in American Society, 1930-1970: Modernity and the Persistence of Religious Community* is reprinted by permission from *The Mennonite Quarterly Review* (October, 1999).

The book review by Rodney J. Sawatsky of *Mennonite Education in a Post-Christian World: Essays Presented at the Consultation on Mennonite Higher Education, Winnipeg, 1997,* and of *Education for Peoplehood: Essays on the Teaching Ministry of the Church,* and of *Theological Education on Five Continents: Anabaptist Perspectives* is reprinted by permission from *The Conrad Grebel Review* (Fall, 1999).

The book review by Walter Klaassen of *Golden Apples in Silver Bowls: The Rediscovery of Redeeming Love* is reprinted by permission from *Pennsylvania Mennonite Heritage* (October, 2000).

Table of Contents

Table of Contents

Introduction

We are pleased to present our third annual collection for your consideration and enjoyment. Our goal has been to create an annual, containing some of the best current Mennonite writing and thinking.

"Mennonite" can mean faith, as accepted by certain groups of Christians who claim that name (Amish and Brethren are related groups). "Mennonite" can also bring to mind any of a variety of ways of life. This conversation/tension between faith and life forms the backdrop for many of the pieces in this collection.

Writings were selected on the basis of both content and style. For many pieces, this marks their first publication. All others, to qualify, were published since January 1, 1998.

Writers were eligible if they: a) are current members of a Mennonite-related group, or b) have had a significant interaction of many years with a Mennonite-related group, or c) deal with Mennonite-related material in a compelling way.

Please note that the Cumulative Indexes beginning on page 331 include both this year's collection, as well as *What Mennonites Are Thinking, 1998* and *What Mennonites Are Thinking, 1999*. (Copies of any of these three books may be ordered from your local bookstore or by calling 800/762-7171. Note the special order form at the back of this book.)

We hope readers of many backgrounds will enjoy this volume, including readers among our various Mennonite-related groups.

—Merle Good and Phyllis Pellman Good, Editors

Featured Articles, Essays, and Opinions, I

Racism in Canada?

by Brad Reimer

I have been on an interesting journey looking at racism in the Canadian context. It has been both a personal journey and one of coming to understand what it means to be part of the dominant culture in North America.

My main reason for the study was dissatisfaction with Mennonite Central Committee's anti-racism training called Damascus Road. At Mennonite Voluntary Service (MVS), we use Damascus Road at orientations for volunteers. My frustration is its overwhelming focus on the United States.

Because MVS is a binational program, we ought to have a presentation that addresses racism in both Canada and the U.S. I hope my study will help us create this. What follows is a summary of what I learned.

The differences between Canada and the U.S. are too many to mention, but here are some key differences:

- We have a deep-seated, historical concept of *two* founding nations: France and England. The U.S. does not.
- Our history of dealing with First Nations people is different. We carried out a slow and relatively nonviolent process of systematic genocide, whereas the U.S. had a much more blatant policy of cultural eradication and assimilation.

- Canada does not have one particular People of Color that makes a significant impact on the dominant culture. The U.S. has two—African American and Hispanic people.
- We have multiculturalism as a national policy; the U.S. does not.
- We bear the sociological impact of having the U.S. as a neighbor; the U.S. doesn't have such an outside influence.

I have learned that much of the history we are taught is questionable—those who "won the war" write the history. To better understand things today, we need to delve into the complex realities of immigration trends, native cultural trends, distinctions between groups of people, and the workings of systematic genocide.

For example, we never learn about the racism found in the speeches of our early prime ministers. We don't learn how the government set policies to keep people of color "under control."

Two founding nations: The reality is that all immigrant groups in Canada are measured against the French-English "norm." Even as this reality changes, these two "founding nations" still dominate the agenda of Canadian life. This may be one of the least-researched and most powerful influences on racism in Canada.

First Nations: In the United States, the practice was to eradicate the Indians to clear the way for European settlers. Canada did not experience such a massive European influx—we had no Kansas or Oklahoma land rushes. Here, government policy turned into a slow genocide of First Nations peoples.

So today, Canada is still deeply embroiled in land claims and native rights issues such as self-government. In the U.S., these are virtually nonissues. The native population in the U.S. appears to have assimilated much more into U.S. society. We are in very different places when it comes to First Nations peoples.

People of color: In the U.S., two dominant people of color carry a significant weight. The African-American population numbers about 32 million, the Hispanic 30 million (total U.S. population is about 267 million). In Canada, which has a population of 30 million, the largest people of color is identified as "East and Southeast Asian" at 1.27 million (1996 statistics). First Nations population is approximately 477,630.

Multiculturalism: In the United States, multiculturalism is a bad word; in Canada, it's national policy. How does this affect our thinking in Canada?

I was saddened to read that the multiculturalism policy in Canada was basically a Liberal government plan to appease immigrants and keep their votes. Most minority groups would say the policy is a failure, but not all agree. Speak to groups such as Ukrainians, Jews, Estonians, and the view is different. Has it been worth the journey?

U.S. as neighbor: As the U.S. sends a barrage of cultural ideas across the border, we in Canada find it difficult to discern what is distinct about our history and society. But most Canadians would say, "We don't have a problem with racism like they do in the U.S." This adds one more level of complexity to facing racism in Canada.

Racism in Canada?

One form of racism we have inherited from the U.S. is "hate groups." These groups would have taken root in Canada in some form even if the U.S. were not our neighbor. However, many of these groups are based in the U.S. Canada has a wide range of hate groups, including people known for their racist views, such as Ernst Zundell, Jim Keekstra, and Terry Long. Anti-Semitism seems to be a more prominent issue in Canada than other forms of racism. Hate groups spend most of their time on issues such as the Holocaust and Jewish conspiracies. Perhaps this is because the Jewish community challenges each accusation, making it more visible. Are other "minority" groups simply not as organized?

Economics and race relations: In my readings and conversations, I continually return to economics and its role in perpetuating racism. (One can use other words in place of economics, such as class or power imbalances.) The common thread is that wherever there is economic disparity or an imbalance of power, racist ideas seem to manifest themselves.

An example is the recent fishing dispute in New Brunswick. For many years, aboriginal and non-aboriginal fishers have worked side by side, sharing the sparse resource. The recent Supreme Court decision allowed aboriginal fishers to go out three weeks before the official lobster season. As soon as the native fishers headed out to sea, racial slurs and violence began.

Did this rapid imbalance of power manifest itself in racism? Would it have made a difference if the group given "special" rights had been Mennonite or Ukrainian?

Lingering Questions

I continue to wrestle with several questions and I invite readers to engage these questions as well:

- Did racism exist before colonialism?
- How does our simplistic understanding of history feed into our racism?
- How would Canada be different if we did not have an official policy of multiculturalism?
- How does one deal with a perceived power imbalance, especially when others fail to see the same reality?
- How does our Mennonite understanding of service play into a racist theology?

Brad Reimer, Winnipeg, Manitoba, is associate director of Mennonite Voluntary Service.

A Third Way Between Fight and Flight

by Richard A. Kauffman

Mennonites have not done so well at disagreeing with each other, despite our peace position. Rather than fight nice, we tend to take flight instead. Welcome to First Church of the Splinter over (fill in the issue). The question I hear repeatedly in the church now is: Can we avoid a church split over homosexuality and church membership, and who decides who is in and who is not in the new church?

We Mennonites like to think of ourselves as a people of the "third way" who try to hold together polarities that divide many other Christians. When we're at our best, we hold together evangelism and social concern, peace and justice, orthodoxy (sound teaching) and orthopraxy (faithful living). Can we, on this knotty issue, find a third way that avoids a contentious fight or an escapist flight?

If we can't avoid a church split, it will be like pulling up a blanket on a cold winter night to cover one's cold chin, only to expose one's feet to the chilly air—to borrow an image from John Updike. What have we gained if the General Conference Mennonite Church and the Mennonite Church integrate, only to splinter over homosexuality and church membership?

The homosexuality debate plays on two different Mennonite impulses, both of which are encoded in our spiritual beings, each with biblical roots. One is a concern for personal, moral righteousness, including sexual holiness. This is sometimes accompanied by a concern for the true church, a disciplined—and disciplining—church.

The other impulse is to be hospitable toward others, to care for the down-and-out, to advocate for the marginalized. This is often accompanied by a reticence to judge others.

These aren't uniquely Mennonite impulses. But we have held them in tension in a uniquely Mennonite way. I can't imagine any dedicated Mennonite seriously making a case for something other than integrity in matters of truth telling, promise keeping, fairness and honesty in business practices—and sexual fidelity. And I can't imagine any of us seriously advocating anything other than welcoming the stranger and providing justice for widows, aliens, and the orphans. But in dealing with homosexuality, some of us are prone to let one impulse trump the other.

Good people, usually with the best of intentions, are on each side of the homosexuality debate. I have friends and family members on each side; I have even been surprised by the particular positions individuals take. Sometimes having a gay family member or close friend who is gay tilts a person toward the inclusive side. But not always. Often, if a person takes a conservative (or liberal) position on other issues, they will follow suit on homosexuality. But not necessarily.

The other perspective: In relating to others with

whom we disagree about homosexuality, it would be a good discipline for us all to recognize a part of ourselves—or at least a part of our spiritual heritage—expressed in the other perspective. Maybe it's like the experience siblings often have: They see one or the other of their parents in each other, sometimes even parental traits they don't particularly appreciate, yet it's part of their family heritage. Of course, many of us find ourselves in the middle: To shift the image slightly, we're like children of divorced or separated parents who don't want to have to choose between these two impulses.

The time-honored way Mennonites have rightly dealt with issues like this is to ask what the Bible says on the subject. But we're never going to reach an acceptable resolution with each other on this issue by simply debating the texts that deal explicitly with homosexuality. The Bible has more to say about sexuality in general and our human relationships with each other before God than what its few texts on homosexuality teach us. Besides, we each wear our own pair of lenses when we read those texts.

We need to go deeper into the biblical themes of who God is, what God requires of us, the nature of the church, and how we understand grace. Here, too, there are at least two theological models or tendencies and polar opposites.

One tendency emphasizes the holiness of God. The church that tends to grow out of this is an exclusive one, and grace is seen as a life-transforming, recreative force.

The other tendency emphasizes the love of God. This can lead to an inclusive church, with grace seen as nonjudgmental forgiveness, pardon, and acceptance.

There's a saying that God loves us so much God accepts us just the way we are, but God loves us so much God doesn't want us to stay the way we are. How to hold these two impulses in tension is the challenge. Jesus was probably the only person who could hold together radical inclusiveness with the radical demands of discipleship.

There's still another distinction. On one side are those who say we need to listen to the voices of our spiritual forebears—to the tradition of the church, its teaching and practice. It would be arrogant for us to think we have all the answers in our modern, or postmodern, "enlightened" times.

On the other side are those who say the Lord has more light and truth to reveal from his Holy Word. The church has changed its mind on other issues, such as slavery or women as leaders in the church. Perhaps the Spirit is suggesting that new evidence about homosexuality should have its way with us.

Heeding wisdom from the past, being open to new light: We'd be fools not to do both. But how can we hold these two impulses together in creative tension? Is there a third way here, too?

Let me make four suggestions:

1. We need to commit ourselves to a discernment process and recognize that we are not engaging in a battle to win public opinion. Forming caucuses within or across area conference lines or engaging in petitions and ad campaigns will merely escalate the polarization.

Mennonites are learning about conciliation and mediation. Why can't we employ the best conciliation and problem-solving tools we have to deal with this issue? For starters, we should delineate what we agree on, then isolate real differences between us and the principles and issues behind them. Then we can look at the implications of our differences and what they mean for our life together.

We are dealing with boundary issues that are fundamentally identity issues. Who is in and who is not, by what criteria, and who decides—these questions focus the larger question: What kind of people do we want to be? I'm convinced that if the homosexuality issue hadn't converged with the creation of the new Mennonite Church, something else would have come along to force this question upon us. Do we look at the membership issue as a challenge, perhaps an opportunity even, rather than just a seemingly irresolvable dispute?

2. We need to be ready to make some tough, discriminating decisions—not easy for Mennonites, since we tend to think in black-and-white terms. This is as true of the open and welcoming side as of those wanting to hold the traditional line. Is either side open to considering shades of gray?

On the one side, there are some gay lifestyles that, morally speaking, are better than others. I have known people who have been in and out of numerous relationships, not always in a serial fashion. I have known others who have been in stable, committed relationships for decades. Is there not a moral distinction to be made here, a relative value judgment to be placed on these different lifestyles?

On the other side, there are people who think they are gay who might just be confused about their sexual identity. Or some may be at a point on the gay-straight continuum where they could—with communal support, appropriate counseling, and spiritual discipline—live a "straight life." There are some gays who don't want to be gay or who don't find liberation in accepting their same-sex attraction. Can we stand with these people, too?

To all I ask: Can we agree that, even though we don't really understand what causes homosexuality, it is part of the woundedness of God's creation? And can we agree that all of us are called by God, on the basis of God's suffering with us on the cross, to bear the wounds of those so inflicted—to make them our wounds? Likewise, can we agree that God's intention for sexuality is for lifelong, covenantal, monogamous, heterosexual unions and that whatever pastoral accommodations we make for homosexuals in our midst are an exception to the standard, not an equally normative model?

3. We may need to live with some ambiguity. Not everything can be resolved one way or the other. How much unresolved tension can we live with?

Tony Campolo is a dynamic evangelical preacher, sociologist, and political activist who has spoken at some of our churchwide Mennonite gatherings. On the issue of homosexuality, he makes no bones about where he stands: Homophobia is wrong, and gay bashing is a sin. But homosexual activity, he says, is also a sin, not befitting Christian disciples. What some people don't know is that Tony's wife, Peggy, belongs to an open and accepting mainline congregation where homosexuals in relationships may come just as they are and remain without ever changing. Tony and Peggy have vigorous disagreements and debates over this issue. But they've agreed to disagree, to keep talking, and to stay married in the same house in spite of it.

Can the Campolos be a model for us as a denomination? I'm on Tony's side on this issue, but the question I put to myself and others like me is: Can we live with the Peggys in the Mennonite church if, indeed, that means also accommodating a few congregations who, as part of their mission, welcome some noncelibate homosexual members? If so, then maybe we can consider accepting the concept of "congregations of refuge," congregations that, under certain conditions, are freed by their area conferences to welcome practicing homosexuals. Is there a third way here, too?

4. We need to recognize that we are not just doing problem solving on a human plane. It is the mind and will of God we seek. This calls for prayer, listening to the Spirit, fasting, and repentance. And in contexts where decisions must be made (congregations, area conferences, churchwide assemblies), alternative decision making procedures should be explored.

For instance, apart from the issue of homosexuality, there is a movement in some circles in the broader church toward dispensing with parliamentary procedures and using a process of spiritual discernment that joins discussion, prayer, silence, and listening to the Spirit—always focusing the question: God, is this your will? Rather than a parliamentarian overseeing the process, a "discernmentarian" helps keep the process on track. This proposed discernment process involves three interlocking venues where the will of the Spirit is prayerfully sought: the church, the home, and one's own prayer closet. (For more on this process, see *Discerning God's Will Together, A Spiritual Practice for the*

Church by Danny E. Morris and Charles M. Olsen,
Upper Room Books, 1997.)

One think I know for certain is that we can't be
absolutely certain about these matters. The people who
make me most skeptical and guarded are those—on
either side—who are so sure of themselves. And I've
sensed that there's more than enough self-righteousness
to go around.

If we can't find a third way and a church split
results, I don't know which group I'd want to join. I'm
willing to be part of a church committed to wrestling
with the issues, but I'm not willing to be part of a
church defined by homosexuality, either for it or
against it.

A measure of humility would help us all. We have
made mistakes before, perhaps especially when we've
been either immoderate or indiscriminate. For a long
time we froze out people who were divorced, regardless
of the situation or circumstances. Perhaps now we are
reaping the whirlwind of an indiscriminate acceptance
of divorce, not just as a way of dealing with bad marriages but as a result of people putting the search for
personal fulfillment ahead of maintaining covenantal
relationships. Either course should give us pause as we
find our way through the thicket of homosexuality and
church membership.

Just as individuals need to confess their wrongdoing,
so do we as a group. And to cry for mercy to the God
who saves us all. I may have this all wrong, or some
parts of it wrong. God forgive me—and correct me—if I
do. And you, too, reader.

*Richard A. Kauffman, Winfield, Illinois, is a member of
Lombard Mennonite Church.*

I Was a Mennonite Teamster

by Rosanna Landis Weaver

Mennonites were often startled to learn that I worked for the Teamsters. Many carried their own labor stereotypes, picked up from the media or from past encounters. They asked a lot fewer questions about the Teamsters than my Teamster friends asked about the Mennonites. I can't remember a Mennonite asking me, "What does the labor movement stand for?"

A popular union bumper sticker says: "The Labor Movement: The folks that brought you the weekend." Like it or not, the labor movement played a key role in creating a standard of living and ideas about work that have benefitted all of us. It helped eliminate child labor in this country and helped bring us eight-hour days, five-day workweeks, paid vacations, and safer working conditions.

My work with the Teamsters converged with my Anabaptist faith in several areas. One was the importance of justice. Most Anabaptists might not regard the labor movement in terms of justice. But the mission the AFL-CIO lists on its Web page, "to improve the lives of working families—to bring economic jus-

tice to the workplace and social justice to our nation,"
fits comfortably into my Anabaptist view of the
world.

Helping the Poor Gain Power

People use Scripture to support all sorts of things.
Labor supporters can look to verses like James 5:4,
"The wages of laborers kept back by fraud cry out, "
or Philippians 2:4, "Look not to your own interests,
but to the interests of others."

More important than scattered verses, however, is
my sense that helping the poor gain power is completely in line with the overarching story of the Bible.
The Old Testament prophets make it very clear, as it
says in Jeremiah, that justice will bring peace. Amos
decried the excesses and injustices of Israel's wealthy.
He pronounced the wrath of God on those who
"trample the needy and do away with the poor of the
land." The prophets themselves were from the working class. Jesus was born into the family of a crafts-
man.

My Anabaptist tradition speaks to a number of
workplace justice issues that the labor movement
actively confronts:

1. Shift to part-time. For several years now, corporations have been reshaping the full-time workforce
into part-time and contract employees—saving money
on health and pension benefits, workers' compensation, taxes, and the costs of obeying important workplace laws. In 1997, almost 30 percent of the U.S.
workforce was in nontraditional jobs—part-time, tem-
porary, independent contractor or on-call employees.
That isn't always bad. I work part-time now so I can

spend more time with my baby, and others choose to work part-time for various reasons. But the majority of people in these positions—59 percent, according to the Bureau of Labor Statistics—would rather work full-time.

2. Wage stagnation. If you count inflation, the bottom 80 percent of the American workforce hasn't seen a pay raise since the 1970s. From the mid-70s to mid-90s, the wages of a male high school dropout have fallen by 25 percent; male high school graduates by 20 percent. Unions make a difference. Union employees are paid an average of 34 percent more than non-union counterparts and are much more likely to have health and pension benefits. The gap between non-union and union wages is true for every demographic category, but it is largest in the most underprivileged sectors. Union membership makes the most difference for Latino women.

Many people don't see this problem because the poor are anonymous, according to Robert Reich, former U.S. Secretary of Labor.

"People at or near the top, or even in the upper tiers, simply don't see that much of the bottom half anymore," he says. "Separated geographically, economically, and culturally, the poorer members of society have all but disappeared. The people who produce or talk on the TV shows, who write the editorials and columns and who raise the money for political candidates have no reason to suppose that so many people in this country are still having a hard time of it. So it's easy to conclude that everything is going fine for everyone."

3. Wealth stratification. According to *Business Week*, CEOs now earn an astounding 419 times the

pay of average blue collar workers, up from 42 times
as recently as 1980. I care about this not just for
moral reasons, but also for selfish reasons because I
don't want a society where the wealthy live in gated
communities, and there is no middle class. I'm afraid
that may be the direction we're heading.

4. Corporate power. One important reason to support labor is to counteract—in favor of working people—the tremendous and growing power of the corpo-
ration. This may reflect my ideas about democracy
more than my ideas about religion, but there is something in my background, way back there with the
Anabaptist rejection of the Pope, that gets concerned
when an entity holds too much power.

Today in America public corporations hold a dis-
proportionate amount of power. Although we often
hear about the money individual unions give to political candidates, business interests vastly outspend
labor on every front. Fifty years ago corporations paid
35 percent of federal taxes; today they pay 11 percent.

Besides the struggle for justice in the workplace,
there are other areas of convergence between my
faith and the labor movement.

In the union, as in the church, there is a firm
believe that the value of an individual is innate and
not based on economic status. I saw this practiced in
a more real way in the unions than I have in the
church. It seems that even in the church we are
more and more sorting ourselves out by class. We
are more comfortable with those who are most like
us.

Another area of convergence that I never would
have expected at the Teamsters is that I often had a

sense that I was working in a community of faith. Several co-workers were Jewish and one was an Episcopalian, and we would sometime stay late and chat for hours about ethical issues. For a number of my co-workers, working in labor was a natural outgrowth of their religious faith. I heard much more talk about God, and many more references to faith, than I'd ever heard when I was a Mennonite volunteer in the peace movement.

Of course there also were areas of conflict. There were many times when it was difficult owing my loyalty to an organization that did things I disagreed with. I don't think that's unique to my job; others might have the same experience working for a public company where loyalty to shareholders might come before doing what is right.

Ends Justify the Means?

I also often experienced discomfort around the issue of whether the ends justify the means. I believe that sometimes the ends do justify the means. For example, I think folks who hid Jews from Nazis during the Holocaust were justified in lying to protect them. I think boycotts and disinvestment in South Africa were justified to end apartheid, even though some innocent people suffered economic injury.

But I don't believe the ends always justify the means. Which ends justify which means? It has to be decided on a case-by-case basis. And that is exhausting.

That exhaustion is one of the reasons I left the Teamsters last summer. I also was tired of having to defend the labor movement. I just wanted a job that I wouldn't have to explain or justify. I wanted to stop getting funny looks when I told Mennonites what I did for a living.

But even though I don't want to be engaged in these struggles on a daily basis, I still believe the labor movement is a justice movement—if sometimes a flawed one—and worthy of our serious and thoughtful consideration.

Rosanna Landis Weaver, Washington, D.C. spent seven years at the International Brotherhood of Teamsters, working in the area of shareholder activism.

In Casas Viejas

by Shirley Kurtz

With five of us and only four kitchen chairs for sitting up to the table, one of the rockers has to do. It's okay, though—I can loll while munching on Jennifer's beans and rice and salty, fried plantains, foods her Nicaraguan neighbors subsist on. Well, folks eat tortillas, too, and once in a while a bit of meat, here in this impoverished hinterland where our daughter and her husband are serving as relief workers with Mennonite Central Committee. Jennifer's been trying valiantly to keep our bellies filled.

She and John insisted on us visiting. "You must come for a month," Jennifer declared, so if she minds having her mom and dad and brother underfoot like this during the rainy season she's not letting on. The tile-floored adobe house, only one room and loft, is cozy with its books and lamps and a cupboard big enough to hold all our clothes, and even a rug to put down in the evening after we've swept the floor and bolted the shutters to keep out the night bugs and started supper on the little gas stove. It's too bad about the black plastic. Building the house, John roofed it with lovely half-moon clay tiles, but the night he and Jennifer moved in it rained, and gritty dirt sifted down and the water dripped and splashed—

they had to set out bowls. So that's why there's black plastic, now, lining the roof.

These nights, when it's time to sleep, John and Jennifer climb to the loft. Paulson unties the rolled-up foam for our bed on the floor downstairs, and Zachary stretches out on the sofa. It's not a real sofa, just a narrow, thin mattress laid atop a wood frame. Afternoons, somebody might lie there to read or snooze. A colorful sheet fits over the mattress and it's comfortable enough, for "missionary" life, anyway.

My sofa at home, I bought a few years ago. Upholstered in rich-hued floral tapestry, it's got deep tufts, plumpy pillows, and arms fat enough to sit on. I just love it. The only place in the living room it fits is in front of a window, so I do worry about sunlight causing fading. At least, due to the solid construction and sumptuous colors, you'd never guess all the jumping on it has endured and how many people's sweaty rumps. The other neat thing is, it belongs. Our house is old-fashioned, with dark woodwork and big creaky windows—not Victorian but close enough—and my sister once remarked that the sofa looks like the kind naked ladies recline on in Rembrandt paintings.

I don't know how many trips I made, hunting.

"We'll be visiting the neighbors," Jennifer has warned. "They're all excited about you coming." And one day John announces, "Doña Aurora's invited us all over for nacatamales." Indeed, one of Aurora's pigs has been butchered specially for us, so after dark we make our way up the path to Aurora and Humberto's.

In a gloomy corner of the kitchen, its dirt floor pocked and bumpy, a pot full of banana leaf-wrapped bundles is bubbling over the fire. Zachary and I sit opposite John and Paulson on old benches to receive the piping hot, greasy treats Aurora proudly hands round. All the time she's jabbering away in Spanish. Jennifer translates, perched on the adobe ledge along the wall, beneath the single, bare lightbulb's glare, and sometimes John helps out. Of course they have to translate our comments, too; we can't just be exclaiming "Rica!" or "Gracias!" as we spoon out the cornmeal mush and tidbits of chopped pork and potatoes. Even these words we bungle.

It's okay to eat the nacatamales; they've been boiled. We won't get sick. On account of the awful diarrhea one of our first nights here, after a meal in a grimy cafe, we're squeamish about anything uncooked.

The day Aurora comes over to our house for coffee, just Aurora by special invitation, she's dressed up and excited. She plops into a rocker, not the one by the table, and Jennifer slides a regular chair up close for a place to put Aurora's coffee mug and the little plate of cupcakes I made. We chatter and smile: Jennifer sitting primly, me down on the floor where I've a sewing project spread out, and Aurora like a queen in the rocker, savoring each sweet bite of cake.

I searched here, there, everywhere. Synthetic snaggy fabrics, ugh. Old padded flaps on the sofas' arms. Ugly boxy shapes, or too spare. Silly ruffles around the bottom, or a pleated skirt too rigid and formal. Nothing ever quite pleased me. I despaired.

Finally, at a store in Westernport, I spied the oversize flowers-and-tufts number.

It cost too much, though.
I brought home a picture to show Paulson, a bad pho-
tocopy—you couldn't really see. "Even the feet!" I
exclaimed. "Big round wood balls for feet, no dumb skirt!
Isn't it horribly expensive? Can you imagine something so
gorgeous?"
Paulson said the sofa probably wouldn't fit through the
door.

Doña Paula's living room, the morning Jennifer and
I trudged through a back field to visit her, holds tall
corn bins and maybe sacks of beans stacked, and
along the wall a set of orange plastic seats that look
like they came out of a restaurant booth or possibly an
old bus. In the kitchen I'm provided a battered wood-
slatted folding chair. Kitchen doesn't seem like the
proper word in any Casas Viejas dwelling; it smacks
too much of glossy wiped counters and gleaming plug-
in appliances and double chrome sinks with actual
faucets and water that comes out, whereas in Paula's
cooking room, rather, two green parrots swing and the
floor is the bumpy earth kind, same as Aurora's. Paula
shapes her tortillas one by one, pat-pat-pat, and cooks
them on her fired-up adobe stove and piles them
inside a gourd. Beaming, she hands me a little cup of
sweetened hot milk. "It's okay," Jennifer assures me,
right out loud in English. "It was boiled."

Another day over at Paula's, they're making cheese
out of a kettleful of raw milk that's been left to sit. I
know it's ridden with bacteria, because I watched
Paula one wet morning out with the cows, kneeling in
the manurey mud to coax some squirts into a dirty
plastic bucket. This is what she turns into cheese.

Sitting in her kitchen, I don't dare taste a bit of the
freshly shaped ball, all the whey squeezed out and a
little salt added. I'm still suffering the runs, off and
on, just from being here, I guess.

"Not the side door," said Paulson, wielding the yard-
stick, after he checked the sofa's measurements listed on
the paper. "Maybe the front door, if I remove the storm
frame. But then the staircase would be in the way, right
inside—the banister and big bottom post."

"What about the window?" I asked, meaning not the
front porch one but the oversize side window high off the
ground, facing the garden. I figured the delivery people
could drive their truck over the lawn and somehow hoist
the sofa through, maybe on ropes. The window sashes
would have to be removed first, and Paulson could crow-
bar the window frame loose. "No," he declared, "absolute-
ly not."

When I telephoned to explain the problem, the store
folks offered to bring over their love seat that matched the
sofa, from the set on display in the showroom, for a trial
run. "If it fits through your front door and our delivery
man is pretty sure there won't be trouble with the sofa,
we'll place your order with the furniture company," the
woman promised.

The love seat squeezed through! Just! So then, do you
think I rested easy? Waiting the next weeks for those
delivery men to return, till they actually jimmied my sofa's
fat arms past the door jambs, wedged it over the banister
post, and set it plop down on the floor? But at last,
euphoria. Maybe delirium. It had to sit there the rest of
the afternoon till Paulson could come home and help
heave it into place in front of the hearth.

27

WHAT MENNONITES ARE THINKING, 2000

*Finally I could go buy carpet to match and arrange
properly the chairs and lamps and tables and leafy potted
plants. The room wasn't supposed to look tropical, just
plush and inviting.*

At Cristela's, where the women are assembling to
mix up batter to bake into cakes to sell for a few extra
córdobas, I'm respectfully offered a dilapidated plastic
mesh chair, its broken sections restrung with twine or
maybe old shoelaces. For a little while I gamely hold
Paula's grandbaby Gustovo, but he's only thinly dia-
pered, no rubber pants, and when he suddenly leaks
onto my skirt I gasp and hand him back to his mother
Jeaneth. The others laugh. "To them it's just water,"
Jennifer says. Well, not to me! There's a sudden down-
pour of rain right when all the pans of cakes are ready
to come out of the oven, a large adobe structure shaped
like an upside-down bowl, built next to the house, and
the women relaying the cakes to safety under the roof
must hold umbrellas and splash through puddles.

I give up on cleanliness, going visiting, after this.
What is ever the use of setting out in a clean skirt?
Anyway, my long bold-patterned one with its gaudy
colors doesn't show the dirt. Now I just keep it balled
up in a corner of the closet, unwashed, to retrieve for
each new foray. I do still hold up the hem gingerly if
Jennifer and I are tramping through mud up some
trail or slogging across a creek. Angelina cheerily fixes
us sweet rice with cinnamon, generous bowlfuls. We
down the same thing at Silvia's. In Angela's smoky
kitchen, I'm hospitably served more hot sugared milk
("It's okay," Jennifer insists, "it's been heated") as four
hungry piglets circle a plate of scraps on the floor and

a hen and her chicks peck at some corn Angela has scattered atop the hard dirt. "We've got to get a picture of *this*," I hiss, scrabbling for the camera I usually carry along on these visits, and Jennifer steps back to the doorway to get a clear shot: pigs and chickens, and me in Angela's one wood chair with its back broken off, hoisting my skirt up around my knees.

It's in Maribel's house, though, where I spy the kitten.

Maribel's large, dirt-floor living room is bare except for the hammock strung up in the middle of the room and, along the wall, a bench where Jennifer sits. Maribel carries in an old chair for me. She's animated and talkative and pretty, combing and fluffing her bangs and spraying on underarm deodorant or maybe it's perfume (she squirts it right on her shirt), because we're going next to her mother-in-law's. I guess Maribel's morning chores made her sweaty—we found her down in the stream scrubbing laundry, and after she finished we hiked along up to her house and helped drape the clothes atop the woodpile to dry.

As for Maribel's cat, it's the ordinary, scrawny, Nicaraguan variety, a little yellow thing. It pads across the room and, over in the corner, paws delicately, the way cats do, then squats to do its business.

I couldn't get my fill. I feasted my eyes every time I passed through the room on my way upstairs. All our company exclaimed over the sofa, too, not just my sister.

Late one shivery night Paulson brought in one last load of wood for the stove and came upstairs to bed. Sometime in the wee hours, burrowed under the covers, I heard the yowling of a cat. We had two toms, so I supposed they were fighting out under the moon. I got up to go to the bathroom, then, and when I reached the door to the hall, an awful stench assailed my nostrils.

Descending the staircase warily in the dark, I heard more meowing. Suddenly, a cat leaped off the sofa.

"Paulson," I called out hoarsely, horrified. "Paulson!"

It must have sneaked in the door, past his leg when he was carrying in the wood.

A nightmarish few hours ensued. The animal had sprayed its tom scent all through the downstairs, and on hands and knees Paulson and I crept around sniffing carpets and furniture. We even found puddles on the kitchen floor and up on the table. We scrubbed and scrubbed, but at daylight the house still stank. A neighbor loaned me her bottle of Pine-Sol and I poured it on straight, thoroughly dousing the various damaged areas. So now the house really reeked. Exhausted and beside myself, I figured it was ruined forever.

Fortunately, I underestimated that Pine-Sol.

The other incredible thing, in case you wondered: the sofa never even got sprayed.

Thank God, life resumed it normalcy—my treasures intact after all, my house brimming with comforts, my heart laden with the all-consuming cares of this world.

The women came one afternoon for a get-together on Jennifer and John's porch, Jeaneth hauling along baby Gustavo. They clump together on benches and a chair or two I've dragged outside, but soon Jeaneth darts into the house and heads for the sofa. She's asking me for something, but it's all gobbledygook. "A plastic bag," Jennifer explains. "To spread under the baby, you know, in case." Why, of course. I hurry off to find one.

I rip open the bag so it can be laid out flat, to protect more area. Carefully I tuck it under Gustavo kicking his legs and grinning widely, his eyes huge pools, a dark liquid brown. So Jeaneth does understand, whew. She realizes the rules are different here on account of the fancy furnishings, more than enough chairs to put around the table (if you count both rockers), even a rug. She has some respect.

The night we arrive at the farewell meal the women have furtively planned, over at Doña Paula's, with us due to leave in a couple of days, we are astounded. Scrounged tables have been pushed together and spread with cloths, and benches set round. Paula must have asked the others to bring any dishes they own, for many places are set, each cheap mismatched plate with utensil laid next, and the food already ladled out. Bottles of soda crowd the tables, and motley so-so-washed cups. Everybody's gibbering happily.

"Drink the soda out of the bottle—don't pour it in your cup," we warn each other out loud, keeping bland looks on our faces, and "Better not eat the shredded cabbage." But we pick the meat off chicken bones and lick our fingers greedily and exclaim warmly, "Rica, rica! Gracias!" Angelina makes a speech and then Doña Paula; they're pleased we came to visit and prouder than roosters. I feel bad about the cabbage—I mean, leaving it on our plates. But what else to do? Even if the food here is washed, the water's teeming with germs. Getting diarrhea again would be too awful. There's too much at stake. But gracias, gracias! We can at least show our appreciation.

Back home again at Jennifer and John's, the shutters bolted, lamps lit, and rug unrolled, Paulson fixes

our bed and Zachary flops onto the mean little sofa.
Oh, sweet relief.

Sweet relief, but still the worry. Too much at stake.
Next it could be moths, or rust.

Shirley Kurtz is a writer who lives in Keyser, West
Virginia.

Should Be More People Like Who?

by Robert Rhodes

One thing our Hutterite community never lacks is visitors. Each year we probably get two dozen tour groups who come to see what we're doing—which isn't a whole lot sometimes.

We host schoolchildren, sewing circles, college classes, Lutheran aid societies, residents of a local nursing home who badly need a day out. Some genuinely desire to know us. Others are only curious.

Usually, our visitors have dinner with us in our communal kitchen and then take a walking tour of our barns and shops and perhaps one of the houses.

They are a hardy lot, these Hutterite watchers. Nothing seems to discourage them. They will walk as far as we ask them and endure with stoic stamina lectures about our "faith" and "lifestyle."

Then they will skitter across the ice or gravel in their high heels or Reeboks, moving from barn to shed until at last they start looking at their watches and toward the road and think of what else must be done that day.

The time of the world regains its gravity, and soon we realize our little moment of congeniality has ended

and lives must go on. They board their buses or climb
into their sensible cars and are gone, taking with
them whatever it was we could offer—and, we hope,
understanding something of our life together and how
it expresses our faith in Christ.

We are not the world's best tour guides or very
exuberant missionaries. But we try, and people seem
quietly satisfied.

• • •

Only one thing troubles me about all this.
Invariably, when our visitors are gathering themselves
and their purses to leave, one of them will come up
and say almost these exact words, striking at a deep
and tender root of my conscience.

I can see the words forming even before they say
them: "There should be more people like you."

The first time I heard this, I didn't know what to
say. It is meant as a compliment, but what does it
mean, really?

"There should be more people like you."

Well, actually, if you ask me, there shouldn't.

• • •

Why not? Are we not true in our belief? Are we not
striving to live a life of separateness, of plainness, of
genuine faith?

I fell this way mostly because we are humans and
not role models for anyone, unless they are willing to
live among one another's faults and differences and
hang-ups and to do so in community—in very close
personal and spiritual quarters.

But this is not what I mean either, for in this we
are not unlike a lot of people who try to share an
earnest life, even a common life.

I mean that instead, we should all strive to imitate Christ—who had no barns or shops or houses and whose community was one of the road.

Instead of people like us, who are lazy and take too much for ourselves, and always ask how our interests will best be served, there should be more people like the radical, trouble-making Christ—the one who turned tables, purged temples, and brought forgiveness and hope to the sorrowful. When have we last done this ourselves?

Christ felt no sense of entitlement to society's riches. He took nothing for himself. So why do we—and I mean all Christians, all followers of the Way—why do we perpetuate our sinfulness and defy the peaceful, fulfilling gift of Christ?

Because of our Anabaptist values, people look to us for something unique, even if they don't know exactly what it is.

In our case, they look at our communities, at our plain clothing, and believe they see something true and meaningful there.

But what is our plainness? Is it a virtue, a reflection of modesty and humility as it is meant to be, or merely an attribute? We should wonder.

• • •

When I first came to the community here, I told the brothers: "I have been looking for you for a very long time." I meant it then, and I still mean it.

I think others mean it as well, even if they don't say it. People most certainly are looking for us—for that which makes us different. It is an inescapable truth. In fact, even if we are not aware of it, the whole world is watching.

Let us remember that the difference they seek is not us, or anything we do. It is Christ. Let us offer no substitute.

Robert Rhodes is a former daily newspaper journalist. He lives with his family at Starland Hutterite Colony near Gibbon, Minnesota.

Why Mennonites Aren't Usually Funny (in Writing)

by Maurice Mierau

Mennonites are the funniest people in the world. They just don't know it yet. Why not?

It's the suffering thing. The descendants of Russian Mennonites in North America are still traumatized by the recent past. We are traumatized almost to the point of autism when it comes to creating comedy and satire, and preoccupied with the question of identity. Heirs of an inward-looking spirituality, we are comically self-absorbed but haven't spoken that joke just yet. There is some evidence that our rich vein of oral jokes and satire runs deeper in those who emigrated here in the 1860s, when leaving the old country was still voluntary. Less trauma, more laughs. But of course, they weren't serious enough to write it down.

It's also the comedy-is-evil, seriousness-is-holy thing. Read what Menno thought about the virgin birth and you'll be amazed that there ever was a Paul Hiebert, an Armin Wiebe, or even a Low German joke spoken out loud. We have a tradition of four centuries of self-repression. The reason so many of us are musical is because that was the only artistic outlet allowed by the little Ayatollahs who controlled most Mennonite communities. Literature and the visual arts were beyond the pale, worldly, reminders of the godless flesh. They could not serve as aural wallpaper before and after a sermon. And who would want to help the worldly laugh? They were going to hell anyway.

Then there's the save-it-for-the-after-life thing. Comedy, as Bakhtin reminded us, smoking all those cigarettes made from manuscripts that seemed eminently disposable, comedy is rooted in this world. Comedy overturns hierarchies, or at least seems to, it liberates us, maybe only for a while, allows us to transcend the shackles of our mortality, and even while we're crashing back to earth, we're laughing. On the way down we might enjoy some sex, some food, a hearty drink, a good fart, maybe even a smoke. To hell with our lungs.

But of course there are counter-examples. What about the Jews? Their history is one of constant persecution and suffering, and yet they have produced many great comedic writers, and virtually invented standup comedy in the last 50 years. They also have a dead language similar to Low German that has spawned so many imitators that Yiddish syntax shows up on TV more often than beer ads. Are we not as funny as they are? Dumber? Less disciplined? Congenitally grimmer? Smaller gene pool? Shorter history? Too many cold winters?

The big difference between us and the Jews is we've hardly suffered, compared to them. Naturally you can't quantify these things, but actually you can. And on the total suffering index, we're neophytes compared to the Jews. So we take ourselves too seriously. Self-parody is the beginning of comedy and satire. See Jane Austen, first book. Cultural self-confidence is also the beginning of comedy. See P.G. Wodehouse or Mordecai Richler.

That's why American Mennonite writers aren't generally that funny either. Like Canadians, they exaggerate the importance of their little brushes with death. Unlike Canadians, they lack our detached perspective on the culture of empire. Canadian Mennonite writers believe they've discovered the Sensitive Artist. Americans believe they've found Family Values. Both discoveries are banal, much more so than Norman Mailer's first or last novel.

My own poems are generally about death, suicide, rape, displacement, cultural dislocation, and other cheery topics. The closest I come to comedy is adopting a cutting tone while obsessively exploring this dark material. Fashionably bleak? Yes, depending how you read fashion.

But it's my feeling that young North American Mennonite writers, as they gradually become secularized in attitude and beliefs, have a unique perspective on the carnival of North America that could yet make us interesting writers of comedy and satire. If our center doesn't hold, we're already used to that. God has died quite recently for us, so we tolerate pain quite well, and as every new Rwanda or Bosnia or Kosovo unfolds we find the lack of divine intervention funnier. Even the disingenuous stupidity of mainstream media adds to the comedy, because writers remember.

WHAT MENNONITES ARE THINKING, 2000

We remember that the horrible things they did in the
1990s in the Balkans were like the horrible things
they did half a century earlier. We even remember
doing deals with the perpetrators of horrible things
back in the old country.

And we lived to do the same stupid things all over
again. Some of us survived. Some of us wrote about
the deaths, suicides, rapes, incests, family histories,
and some of us survived even further into a new century and learned to laugh because we were still alive.
Still bringing new children into the world where they
have a chance to be slightly smarter than us. Not
much smarter, because that would be embarrassing.
But smart enough to stop letting the preachers and
demagogues choke us into submission. Smart enough
to eat well, drink a bit, exercise too hard, and laugh.
Smart enough to write it down. Smart enough to
laugh.

*Maurice Mierau, Winnipeg, Manitoba, recently finished a
book of poems.*

A Modern
Saul of Tarsus

by Jewel Showalter

When the Integrated Mennonite Churches (IMC) of
the Philippines called Ambrocio Porcincula to oversee
their Laguna-Manila District and moderate the newly
formed board of bishops, they couldn't have chosen a
more unlikely man.

Twenty years ago, Porcincula, a politician and school
principal in Laguna, had bitterly opposed the Mennonite church planted near his home. He rallied his students to stone the building and disturb the services.

He hated the noisy prayers and songs that rang out
from the little church. Then one day, a pastor told
him, "Brother, the Lord needs you." His life was never
the same.

Luis Lumibao, newly-appointed missions director
of the IMC, remembers being inside the church when
Porcincula and his ruffians attacked. Today, it feels
much better having Porcincula on the same team, ral-
lying young people to carry the gospel to the ends of
the Earth. It's something the new bishop does with
unmatched zeal.

At the invitation of the IMC, Lancaster Conference
(Mennonite Church) bishops H. Howard Witmer and

Freeman J. Miller came to the Philippines April 10-13, 2000, to ordain four bishops—including the transformed Porcincula—and help inaugurate a new conference structure for Filipino Mennonites.

IMC's seventh annual Believers Conference met at Castaneda High School, seven hours north of Manila, and focused on "The Mennonite Understanding in Stewardship about Prayer, Giving of Talent, Resources, and the Great Commission."

Witmer and Miller each spoke three times: Witmer on the doctrines of God, salvation and nonresistance; and Miller on biblical simplicity, the Christian church, and marks of a true Christian.

"How do you teach biblical simplicity at an assembly of 40 Mennonite churches, when none of the pastors own cars and when the high school where you meet has only a trickle of tap water during some morning hours, where rice is the standard meal three times a day, and where mattresses are a luxury?" Miller asked.

But this year's assembly focused on Anabaptist doctrine, and this was his assigned topic.

Assembly participants totaled 212. Many others attended the dynamic youth-led evening worship services. The congregations represented were unabashedly Anabaptist, with names like Grace Anabaptist Church, Jesus Mennonite Church, and Christian Anabaptist Mennonite Church.

Miller said the highlight came Wednesday evening, when the four bishops—Adriano Fernandez, Ambrocio Porcincula, Jose Basa, and Romon Bansan—were ordained. They are the first Mennonite bishops in the Philippines.

"This was clearly a historic moment in the colorful history of Mennonite church development in this nation," Miller said.

Besides bishops, the IMC also ordained a new pastor and commissioned a new board of trustees, new youth officers and missionaries—an amazing feat for a conference that includes 16 dialects and stretches from south of Manila to the remote mountain tribes of the north.

IMC has come through the usual struggles of an emerging church, and this reorganization marks a new stage of development and positioning for future growth among the Mennonite churches of the Philippines.

In recent years, there has been significant growth through the planting of additional rural and urban churches and several plants in the capital city of Manila. Significant growth in membership and churches prompted the reorganization.

Lancaster Conference has had a relationship with Philippine Mennonites for more than 30 years through Eastern Mennonite Missions (EMM) funds and personnel. Miller serves as fraternal representative to Asia, a position filled earlier by Witmer and Ervin Stutzman.

On the final afternoon of the conference, the more than 50 pastors gathered with the new bishops and gave a report of last year's activities for each congregation. Most of the churches are growing and have many church plants planned or under way.

Bishop Basa, for example, baptized 100 people during the last year. The growing group moved six times, but their meetingplaces are still filled to overflowing.

They're now planning to start a daughter congregation.

Churches in many settings are expanding. One pastor hikes two to three hours into the jungle for Bible studies. Another has weekday Bible studies with business and professional people in downtown Manila and plans to start 10 new churches this year.

Although IMC stands at 1,750 baptized members, the congregations minister to three times that number during a normal week. Pastors frequently reported needing materials, larger facilities, and leadership.

While the growth is encouraging, it can't be fast enough to suit Bishop Porcincula. He's making up for lost time.

"Maybe in 10 years, we can host the Asia Mennonite Conference," he said. "Then, Mennonite World Conference!"

Jewel Showalter, Landisville, Pennsylvania, is a staff writer for Eastern Mennonite Missions.

The Nonswearing of Oaths

by Harold Sensenig

The oath is the strongest possible confirmation of
the truth of a statement. It is a solemn appeal to God
or to a sacred or revered person or sanction (as the
Bible, the temple, the altar) by way of attesting the
truth of one's word. The profane oath is a careless or
blasphemous use of the Name of the divine Being, or
anything divine or sacred, either by way of appeal or
as a profane exclamation.

The teaching of Jesus along with the teaching of the
apostles clearly gives us the New Testament position
on the nonswearing of oaths. "Again, ye have heard
that it hath been said by them of old time, Thou shalt
not forswear themself, but shalt perform unto the
Lord thine oaths: But I say unto you, Swear not at all;
neither by heaven; for it is God's throne; Nor by the
earth; for it is his footstool: neither by Jerusalem; for
it is the city of the great King. Neither shalt thou
swear by thy head, because thou canst not make one
hair white or black. But let your communication be,
Yea, yea; Nay, nay: for whatsoever is more than these
cometh of evil" (Matthew 5:33-37). "But above all
things, my brethren, swear not, neither by heaven,

neither by the earth, neither by any other oath: but let your yea be yea; and your nay, nay; lest ye fall into condemnation" (James 5:12).

Jesus' words bring into focus the difference in practice between the Old and New Testaments. Certain types of oaths were permissible under the Old Covenant. The profane oath was never allowed (Leviticus 19:12). The Israelites were instructed not to swear falsely. A blessing is pronounced on the one who has "not lifted up his soul unto vanity, nor sworn deceitfully" (Psalm 24:4,5). This implies that swearing was acceptable, but not with deceit. God's people were warned not to swear by false gods. "Thou shalt fear the LORD thy God, and serve him, and shalt swear by his name" (Deuteronomy 6:13). The lifting of the right hand, or both hands, and saying "as the LORD liveth," or "The LORD do so to me" seem to have been forms of an oath (Genesis 14:22; Judges 8:19; 1 Samuel 14:39; Ruth 1:17).

The hesitancy of the Jews to speak the Name of God led to their swearing oaths by things that in some way related to God. They swore by heaven, by Jerusalem, by the angels, by the earth, by the temple, by the altar, and by the sacrifice. This explains why Jesus addressed some of these ares in the Sermon on the Mount.

The New Testament position on the use of the oath is on a higher plane and, in this case, quite opposite from the Old. In the Old Testament the oath was commanded as a religious duty, but in the New Testament it is clearly forbidden. Jesus said, "Swear not at all . . . But let your communication be, Yea, yea; Nay, nay: for whosoever is more than these cometh of evil."

Jesus is teaching not only against swearing falsely but against swearing of any kind. The New Testament believer loves the truth, abides in the truth, and speaks the truth because truth issues from inward principle and not from outward pressure. The nonswearing of oaths is clearly not a neutral matter. The use of the oath comes of evil and will bring condemnation (James 5:12).

Tertullian, Origen, and Chrysostom, who were early church fathers, vigorously rejected the oath. Professing Christians began reusing the oath only after the state church was set up, and Christianity became a state religion. Augustine was instrumental in giving the theological foundation for the use of the oath. Since he was aware of the objections to the oath, he called for its use only in urgent matters. Nevertheless, he held that the oath contributed to the glory of God and was useful to the state and the neighborhood. This belief remained the basic position of the Catholic Church with increased emphasis upon the oath as a matter of divine law.

When the Reformers and the Protestant churches came on the scene they adopted the position of the Catholic Church on the oath. Martin Luther interpreted the passage in Matthew as forbidding the swearing of an oath on one's own initiative or out of custom but taught that the command of the state to render an oath must be obeyed.

This Protestant understanding and teaching concerning the oath generally remains among them to the present day. They claim that because of the imperfection of the human society and the general distrust of people toward each other, the oath is necessary even in a Christian society. It is evident that such an understanding fails to recognize and properly evaluate Jesus' direct prohibition of the oath.

The Anabaptists, in strict obedience to the teaching of Jesus, rejected and opposed the oath from the beginning. Their position was that our speech is simply yes and no. That this was the general rule among the Anabaptists is frequently attested in the trials, disputations, and confessions extracted by torture. In 1526, Andreas Castelberger requested the Zurich council to excuse him from the oath when he was to be exiled. On January 5, 1527, George Blaurock refused to swear the oath when he was expelled. The Schleitheim Confession of February 24, 1527, expressly refers to Christ's teaching, "who taught the perfection of the law and forbids Christians all swearing." In fact, all Mennonite confessions of faith have a statement on the nonswearing of oaths.

Mennonite immigrants, coming from Europe to the United States and Canada at various times (1683-1880), received full recognition for their position on the oath. The prior arrival of the Quakers, who had a similar position, paved the way for this acceptance. The federal constitution does not recognize the affirmation instead of the oath on grounds of conscience. But the religious freedom that it guarantees is understood to include this and has been so interpreted by the courts. Many state constitutions include provision for the use of affirmation in place of the oath, and generally there has not been a serious problem on this point in the United States or Canada.

Having statements that clarify our position on the nonswearing of oaths is a good way to help us to properly understand the Scriptural principles. However, our practice indicates what we really believe, irrespective of well-worded statements. *How can we maintain a practice that is in keeping with Scriptural teaching?*

1. We must understand that the clear command of Jesus is for us to obey today. It is not for some bygone era but for believers of this present time.

2. We must understand what to do instead of using the oath when an affidavit or declaration is required. Rather than saying "I swear," we must say "I affirm" to be speaking the truth.

3. We must understand what constitutes an oath. When we think of swearing, our thoughts often go to the courtroom, where the oath is commonly used. However, there are other, more subtle ways of swearing besides placing one's hand on the Bible and raising the other hand to solemnly declare to tell the truth. We must carefully read official documents before signing them. Some of them state that by signing, we are swearing that the information is correct. In some instances, the option may be given to swear or affirm. The word *swear* should then be crossed out. If to affirm is not given as an option, cross out *swear* and write *affirm* in its place. Simply raising the hand as a declaration of truthfulness should also be avoided.

4. We must understand that truthfulness is an integral part of everyday Christian living. The following is a quote from the *Mennonite Encyclopedia*: "The Christian should rather so live before God that His presence sanctifies heart and mouth; consequently, he does not willingly sin against God's commandment and always has God for a witness wherever he is and

whatever he does. Hence, the Christian does not make a special attempt to be truthful before courts and in extraordinary considerations but always seeks to live in the highest truth. The oath dulls this sense of absolute commitment and hence has a demoralizing rather than morally elevating effect. Jesus' prohibition of the oath is therefore not a literalistic, legalistic command but is grounded on a deep and solid religious and ethical foundation. The rejection of the oath binds one to absolute obedience to Jesus in full discipleship and always to live and testify in complete truthfulness."

The use of the oath has its origin in evil. It is not a neutral matter. The Christian speaks the truth from inner compulsion and not from outward pressure.

Harold Sensenig is from Smyrna, Delaware.

Reading Joshua Backwards from Exile

by James E. Brenneman

I.

The Book of Joshua has been read by many a liberation theologian as a political manifesto in support of the revolutionary politics of justice and liberation. In particular, the Book of Joshua is seen as the liberating climax of the Exodus story. Here then is a powerful historical precedent for throwing off the shackles of oppression in the name of God's liberating power. I wish it were that simple.

True, the Exodus story *has* provided great biblical leverage for understanding liberation. Still, there is the niggling raw data of the Exodus story that we sometimes forget. At the very beginning of the Exodus story (3:7-8), the Lord makes a startling promise to the Hebrew slaves. The Lord promises to "bring them up out of that land [Egypt] to a good and broad land, a land flowing with milk and honey . . . " This is the good news of liberation, the "freedom road" of Scripture. But the Lord also, in the same breath, promises to give them "the country of the Canaanites, the Hittites, the Amorites, the Perizzites, the Hivites, and the Jebusites." So, from the beginning, the *goal* of liberation was not merely liberation *from* Pharaoh. The ultimate *goal* was also the *conquest* of non-Israelites of every stripe and hue. And this conquest was mostly bloody and violent.[1] The book of Joshua, with its unrelenting brutality, is the climax of the Exodus story. Unfortunately, countless stories of liberation serve as direct historical analogies of this biblical story of liberation and subsequent conquest. One thinks of the Crusades or the brutal rule of the Christian dictator Ephraim Rios Montt in Guatemala some years back, claiming biblical precedent for his *coup* and subsequent reign of terror. Even now, today, one wonders whether such liberating texts feel all that liberating when read in Christian Palestinian congregations. So, what's a reader of Scripture to do? I would like to propose one way of reading Scripture that may serve to guide us in how we understand some of the violent texts we encounter between its pages. Of course, there are other readings as well that have helped in this task. I leave it to the discerning reader to help negotiate whether this option is or is not helpful to them.

II.

Let's take a journey back to the formation of Scripture *as Scripture.* The story of "how the Bible came to be" will help us to interpret the significance of those thorny questions of violence and conquest within its pages.

Long before there ever was a written document or any scrolls that came to be called Scripture, the ancient traditions of Israel were passed down from one generation to the next by word of mouth.[2] The Bible began as oral literature. We can discern those earliest oral components of the Bible from the final written form that we now have by way of certain criteria.[3] We'd expect these earliest oral elements to be formed in concise, poetic, or narrative units, attached to particular places, often worship settings, in which the events they describe include an unusual encounter with the divine or divine figures. There would likely be a missionary element as well, the passing on of Israel's faith traditions in an oral speech of some sort.

Using these criteria, several biblical texts stand out as very early kernels linking us to the origins of biblical faith. For purposes here, some examples include Deuteronomy 26:5-9; 6:22-23; Joshua 24; Psalm 78; Nehemiah 9:6f and, in the New Testament, Acts 13:16f. What is most apparent in comparing these oral traditions side by side is to notice the essential elements to the story of emergent Israel or the emergent church that were included in the telling and retelling of these stories. There are only three elements that every single oral tradition includes in their telling: something about the patriarchs or matriarchs, something about the Exodus, and finally, something about the "conquest" of the "promised land."

When looking at the final written Bible (OT) as we now have it, the Spirit-inspired compilers of Scripture divided their Bible into three component parts. The first section was traditionally called the Torah or Pentateuch (Genesis through Deuteronomy). The second section was called the Prophets, made up of the

Former Prophets (Joshua through 2 Kings) and the Latter Prophets (Isaiah, Jeremiah, Ezekiel, and the twelve Minor Prophets). The third section was called the Writings (Psalms, Job, Proverbs, Ruth, Song of Songs, Ecclesiastes, Lamentations, Esther, Daniel, Nehemiah and, finally, the Chronicles).

Given the outline of all the oral confessions of faith noted above, we might've imagined that Israel's first Bible, the Torah or Pentateuch, would have included in it something about the conquest of the "promised land." After all, all the earliest oral faith stories include the story of Israel's conquest of the "promised land" as essential to their telling and retelling. We might have expected, then, that Israel's first canon of sacred Scripture, the Torah, would have followed its oral predecessors and included the Book of Joshua in it. It doesn't. In Christian terms, it would be like the Gospel writers telling the story of Jesus, including in the Gospels his life, his death, but leaving out the most important part, his resurrection!

Throughout the Torah or Pentateuch, Israel is promised the land of Canaan as a gift of God. The final form of Israel's first Bible, however, leaves out the fulfillment of that promise as told in the book of Joshua. What happened in Israel's history that allowed its story gatherers to leave out of their first Bible (the Torah) the climax of the story must have been pieced together after the exile to Babylon.[4] And that makes all the difference.

In 586 BCE, the people of Judah witnessed the loss of their capital Jerusalem, their government, their "promised land," and their temple. This formative event demanded explanation. For Israel to survive under such persecution, it needed for its source of survival an indestructible element in society (unlike the Temple or any other religious icon) that would be commonly available, highly adaptable, and (unlike land) portable. Only a story could respond to all four criteria. Only the Torah and Prophets, now in scroll form, did.[5] So the exiles drew together whatever stories, laws, and other writings they had inherited from their past and produced their first Bible: the Pentateuch and the Prophets. The Writings were added later.

The Pentateuch begins with human choice. In the garden of Eden, Adam and Eve have within their power the power to choose for or against God. The Pentateuch ends with human choice also. The emergent "Israel" stands on the banks of the Jordan River (the Book of Deuteronomy) looking wistfully across the great Wadi to their yet possessed "promised land." For dispossessed exiles on the banks of the Tigris-Euphrates Rivers, such a story now paralleled their own experience of waiting to enter (in their case, return) to the "promised land." The Book of Deuteronomy lays out before the people of Israel through the speeches of Moses an open future: "I call heaven and earth to witness against you today that I have set before you life and death, blessings and curses. Choose life so that you and your descendants may live" (30:19).

Immediately following this choice-laden future at the end of the Pentateuch, the exiles pulled together a string of stories called the Former Prophets (Joshua-2 Kings). The Former Prophets end with Israel in Exile. Almost as if to respond to the open questions put

before Israel by Moses, the books of the Former
Prophets offer a negative example of the choices a
struggling Israel made that led them into exile and the
loss of land, temple, and the monarchy. As noted earlier, the exile had the effect of canonically displacing
the book of Joshua as the historical fulfillment of
God's promise of land. The stories in the book of
Joshua went from being the highpoint of the earlier
oral stories to its less-illustrious canonical placement
as the introduction of the Former Prophets, now offering a prophetic tale of a failed history ending in exile.
The Scriptural compilers in exile then placed all the
other prophetic books (the Latter Prophets) immediately after the Former Prophets as exhibits in their
new interpretation of old oral data. These Prophetic
scrolls provided additional evidence that God had
warned them that their wrong choices might lead to
exactly their present circumstance.

For the readers of Scripture today, it matters
whether we read the Book of Joshua a straightforward
history or canonically, *as Scripture.* Read as straightforward history, the Book of Joshua invites us to fulfill
the promises of God (especially for landed identity) by
means of violent conquest of native peoples. Reading
the book of Joshua canonically, back from exile as it
were, judges any theology that would choose to read
Joshua as legitimizing the way of violent revolution
and domination of "the other." Excising the most viru-
lent conquest book in the Bible, the Book of Joshua,
from its first canon (the Torah) and placing it as the
introduction to a failed history (Joshua-2 Kings) argues
in miniature what can be said now more generally. It
is a disservice to the Spirit-inspired makers of

Scripture to read Joshua *apart* from their placement of the book as the introduction to the failed history recounted in the Former Prophets. Just as we wouldn't expect anyone to fully understand the overall story of a great novel until the final chapter is read, we should never again read the Book of Joshua as standing alone without understanding its significance in light of 2 Kings (the end of the story). The final canonical form and function of the canon overwhelms the Bible's own violent tendencies, including its early ideological bias against non-Hebrew people groups.

All cultures, as evident in their canonical literature, have had to choose between confronting their violent measures in suppressing the opposition, on the one hand, and enjoying the camaraderie that such violence generates, on the other. What is unique to the Bible as canon, is that it is the first literature in the history of the world to grapple with the moral dilemma this choice represents.[6]

The canon-making community in exile chose to face this moral dilemma when it determined the extent of its first canon of Scripture and the form of its second component part, the Prophets. Any reading of the Bible's content, especially the Book of Joshua, must now incorporate the authoritative interpretation that the Holy Spirit-inspired final compilers of Scripture used in deciding on the morality of violence. Apparently they were critical of it. Such a canonical perspective insists on nonviolence as a first principle (rule of order) in deciding any canonical dispute between its covers and serves as a model for deciding the difficult differences inherent in human culture itself.

[1] I am aware of the historical reconstructions that argue for a more peaceful settlement of the promised land. However, such historical reconstructions do little to mitigate the way the Book of Joshua has been used repeatedly throughout history to endorse violent conquest.

[2] What we call "Scripture" (from the Latin, *enscriptura*, meaning "that which is written") is called by Jews to this day, *Mikra* (from Hebrew, *krh*, meaning "that which is read aloud"). This underscores the oral nature of the Bible in its original formation and in its current understanding among Jews. Hence, the emphasis they place on having the Bible read/sung by cantors as the centerpiece of their worship experience.

[3] For what follows see, Martin Noth, *A History of the Pentateuchal Traditions*, 1970, xxiii.

[4] This is further supported by the fact that only Nehemiah, clearly a post-exilic account, mentions the first mention of the Creation account in any of these early oral creeds. Presumably, Israel adapted the Babylonian creation accounts and converted them to their use when compiling their first Bible.

[5] James Sanders, *From Sacred Story to Sacred Text* (Philadelphia: Fortress Press, 1987): 19; Jacob Neusner, *Self-fulfilling Prophecy: Exile and Return in the History of Judaism* (Boston: Beacon Press, 1987); 5-17, 31--61.

[6] Gil Bailie, *Violence Unveiled: Humanity at the Crossroads*. New York: Crossroad, 1995), 44-45.

James E. Brenneman, Pasadena, California, is a professor of Old Testament and a pastor.

Some Things I Want My Children to Know

by Ron Adams

These are some things I want my children to know.
God loves you. God loves me. God loves us. We
don't always love God. We don't always feel God's
love. We don't always feel like we deserve God's love.
We don't always act like we love God. We don't
always act like God loves us. But God loves you. God
loves me. God loves us.

There is no place you can go where God is not with
you. Not the basement. Not the closet. Not the attic.
Not under the covers or even under the bed. There is
no place you can go where God is not with you.

There is no time of day when God is not with you.
Not when the lights are off. Not when the sun is shining. Not when you're the only one awake in the
whole house. There is no time of day when God is
not with You.

There is nothing that can take you away from
God's love. Not a crummy grade on your math test.
Not being sent to bed without a story. Not saying
things you don't really mean. There is nothing that
can take you away from God's love.

Sometimes things will happen that make you wonder whether God loves you. You may find a lot of money. You may lose your bicycle. Your best friend may get very sick. Your grandparents may die. You may be the class president. You may not get into the college you want. Your mom may lose her job. Your parents may split up. You may get everything you want for Christmas.

Good things and bad things will happen. When the bad things happen you may think God doesn't love you anymore. When the good things happen you may think God loves you again. You may wonder why you ever thought God left you. You may decide you don't really need God.

But God's love will never leave you. Not when bad things happen. Not when good things happen. God's love will never leave you. Even when you cannot even feel it, God's love will never leave you.

And you know how you can tell? Look around you. Your mom, your dad, your sisters, your brother, your classmates, your friends, your teachers, your mentors, complete strangers, all of them are here because God loves them. All of them are here because God loves you.

Nothing can take you away from God's love. Nothing. Not a thing. No thing. Nothing. Absolutely nothing. Not good things or bad things, not rainy days or sunny days, not sadness or silliness, not angels, not the president, not things in the present, not things in the future, not the devil. Nothing can take you away from God's love.

You could climb to the top of the highest mountain in all the world. You could stand on top of the tallest ladder on top of the highest mountain in all the world. You could stand on your tiptoes on top of the tallest ladder on top of the highest mountain in all the world. And guess what. God's love would be right there with you.

You could swim into the deepest cave in the bottom of the ocean. You could dig a deep hole in the deepest cave in the bottom of the ocean. You could curl yourself up into a tiny ball in the bottom of the hole in the deepest cave in the bottom of the ocean. And guess what. God's love would be right there with you.

Think of the scariest thing in the whole world. The scariest thing cannot take you away from God's love. Think of the most beautiful thing in the whole world. The most beautiful thing cannot take you away from God's love.

But what about when we die? Does God's love end when our life ends? No, God's love continues even after death. God will take us to a new place to live with God and all the people God lives with. And God will take care of our families after we die, so they won't be alone without God. And God will dry their tears. And God will watch over them. And someday God will bring them to live with us in the place God made just for us.

These are the things I want my children to know. Who will tell them? Who will say these things to them? Who will help them remember these things when bad things happen? Who will show them God's love?

We want our children to grow strong in their bodies and strong in their minds and strong in their faith.

And so we feed them. We educate them. And we tell them, we teach them, we show them what we know about God. We tell them about this God whose love is so great, so wide, so deep, so high, so strong, so much more than anything else we can think of or imagine.

But we need them to hear these things from someone other than just their parents. Because sometimes we forget. Sometimes we're too distracted. Sometimes we're too angry, or sad, or hurt to tell them these things. Sometimes we're just plain weak. We need help.

We need help. And so we help one another. We remind one another. We tell one another. We show once another this love that has no ending. And in the reminding and the telling and the showing, we are given the strength we need to share with our children these things about God. And our children listen as we tell each other that God loves us. They listen as we remind each other that God loves us. They watch when we show each other that God loves us. And so they know exactly what we're talking about.

Ron Adams, Lancaster, Pennsylvania, is a pastor and father of two sons.

Short Fiction, I

Aunt Liz

by Arlene Koch Holdeman

"When are we going?" wailed Sharon for the third time.

"Stop your whining or you'll have to stay at home with the boys," said Mother.

Sharon had been sitting with her jacket on at the kitchen table waiting for *hours* it seemed for Mother to finish preparing the macaroni and cheese casserole that Daddy and the boys would eat for supper. Now finally Mother slipped her apron over her head and hung it on the back of the basement door. She tugged her dress down smoothly over her rounded belly, then took out a hairpin and reset it, snugging her bun more firmly against her head.

"I'm ready now," she said as she put on her coat and pulled a plain black bonnet over her hair.

The phone call from Grandma Brubacher had come the evening before, asking Mother and Sharon to come for supper today because Aunt Lizzie and some man were coming from Toronto, and Grandma wanted help. Sharon didn't stop to wonder why Grandma, who could still do ten things at once, would need help. She was too thrilled about the chance to see Aunt Lizzie, who almost never came back home to Conestoga anymore to visit. Aunt Lizzie, the youngest of Grandma's large family, was twenty-five, pretty, and "worldly." Sharon wasn't exactly sure what that word meant, but she knew the voices using it were always heavy with disapproval. She, on the other hand, found it hard to disapprove of glamorous young Aunt Lizzie.

Heads lowered against the October wind, Sharon and Mother rushed along the sidewalk. Sharon skipped a half step to match her stride to her mother's. It was getting much easier to keep up since she had grown almost two inches in the past six months. Now at ten and a half she was already up to her mother's ear.

Grandma and Grandpa's house stood beyond where the sidewalk ended, among the scattered houses at the edge of the village. A narrow dirt path continued beside the street for the final two blocks. When they came to it, Sharon dropped back and followed, watching her mother's broad back moving determinedly ahead of her. Her mother's low shoes were wearing down at the heels, and a run in her dark stocking crept up out of one shoe.

As they approached the house, they spotted Grandma in her big garden, picking the last of the tomatoes from the nearly leafless vines. Her dark print dress brushed the tops of her black oxfords as she bent over. With her left hand she was holding up the bottom of her coverall apron to form a bowl into which she carefully placed the tomatoes. She wore a ragged brown cardigan and a kerchief knotted under her chin.

Mother called, "*Wie geht's,* Ma?" and Sharon said, "Hi, Grandma. Are they here yet?"

Grandma straightened up, gripping her apron tightly, and said, *"Zimlich gut. Wie bisht du?"* Then she added in English, "I don't know why they haven't come yet. Lizzie said they'd be here at 4:00." Sharon was happy when Grandma spoke English so she could understand. Most of the time she didn't remember unless Sharon reminded her.

Sharon ran ahead to hold the back door open for the women. The smells of freshly baked bread and a browning pot roast welcomed them, and Sharon wanted to go no farther than the rocking chair in the kitchen. But Grandma told her to go hang hers and her mother's coats on the coat tree in the front room. Sharon slowly headed to the big room at the front of the house, which always smelled faintly of the oil-burning stove during heating season. She was sure Grandpa would be there in his usual chair next to the stove and would insist on giving her a bear hug and a piece of horehound candy, fuzzy from his pocket. It was useless to try to evade him. But strangely, there was no sign of him.

After hanging up the coats, she returned to the kitchen to find Mother already wearing one of Grandma's big aprons and beginning to peel the potatoes.

She wanted to ask about Grandpa but didn't dare to interrupt the women's intense conversation. Their faces and gestures told her they were talking of something important, even though she couldn't understand their words. With a flash of insight, Sharon suddenly knew why Grandma asked them to come today: she wanted her favorite daughter to be here with her to face the Toronto man and Aunt Lizzie. Sharon began to set the table with the blue-flowered company dishes Grandma had put out on the counter. She coughed a little to remind them of her presense. It worked. Grandma smiled at her and switched to English. They were talking about Aunt Lizzie and the man, as Sharon had suspected.

"What do you think this man will be like? It's high time she's getting married, but I'm worried about what kind of man this is." She put a spoonful of lard into the hot iron skillet on the stove and added, "I wish she'd come back here and settle down with one of our young men from church."

"I don't see why she can't be satisfied here," Mother said. "All of her friends from school are settled down and happy here. What's so different about her?"

"Oh, I wish I knew," said Grandma.

The hot grease sputtered as Mother slid sliced potatoes into the skillet. She turned down the heat below the pan and said, "Do you understand what this job she has is all about? She says she's a librarian, but how can that be if she works for a bunch of lawyers?"

"Ach, I don't know. The world is changing so fast since the war. I just can't keep up," said Grandma.

Mother's flying knife had produced another heap of sliced potatoes. She added these to the ones already beginning to fry and said, "I wonder what else Lizzie's doing in Toronto. I'm worried about her. Is it true Pastor John came to visit her last time she was home?"

Catching sight of the listening Sharon, Mother switched again into Pennsylvania Dutch, followed by Grandma. So it went every time things got interesting, thought Sharon. As she quietly placed the silverware next to the plates, she strained to pick out words she knew, but could understand only the names Lizzie, Pastor John, Dad, and something about crying. Oh, it was frustrating to be allowed only glimpses into the secrets of adults! At times like this she wished she had tried to learn more Pennsylvania Dutch, but she was afraid of being laughed at. A lot of the kids at school made fun of the Dutchy accents of the ones who spoke it, even when they were speaking English.

When she finished setting the table, she sat down in the rocking chair, out of the way of the women. She was tired of trying to make sense of their conversation. Now she let their talk wash over her along with the other kitchen sounds, the loud ticking of the pendulum clock on the wall behind her and the twittering and whistling of Grandma's parakeet in the cage above her. The smell of the potatoes frying, added to the just-baked bread and roasting meat, made her ravenous. If only Aunt Lizzie and her new boyfriend were here so they could eat. She got up to snitch a pickle from the plate of relishes already sitting in the middle of the table.

But just then she heard a car door slam and half a minute later the front door opening. Aunt Lizzie called, "Yoo-hoo, anybody home?" Grandma and Mother hurried to the front room, Grandma wiping her hands on her apron as she went. Sharon hesitantly followed. In a large extended family with many adults, she know her unimportance. Besides, she felt shy around Aunt Lizzie, whom she rarely saw. But she was also fascinated by her, the only one of the family to have left their little town to move to a big frightening city.

As she approached, Sharon could hear Mother's *"Wie geht's?"* and Grandma's *"Wie bisht du?"*

"I'm fine, Mom," Aunt Lizzie replied. "I want you to meet my friend Rob Woodhill. He doesn't speak German. Rob, this is my mother, and this my sister Mabel, and this my niece Sharon." She ended by pointing at Sharon where she stood just inside the door to the room. "She's the one I told you about who looks like me."

"Sure enough, almost as pretty," he said, smiling at Sharon, white teeth flashing below a dark mustache.

Sharon could feel the blood rushing to her face as everyone looked at her. She felt exposed, but pleasantly so. She had thought she was nearly invisible to most adults and was surprised that Aunt Lizzie had told Rob about her even before they had arrived.

He shook hands with Grandma and Mother and then moved toward Sharon. The hand he extented was slim and long-fingered, and his dark eyes looked down at her from what seemed a great height. Sharon was almost too dazzled to remember her manners and shake his hand.

Aunt Lizzie was mesmerizing, too. She stood in the middle of the room in her bright red coat, her short blond hair curling around her face, black patent leather shoes adding almost three inches to her height. Gleaming lipstick and fingernail polish exactly matched the red of her coat.

"My, my, aren't you looking bright today, everything red and shiny," said Mother with a little laugh.

Lizzie smiled tightly and said, "Well, Mabel, a little bright color here and there wouldn't hurt you any, you know." Looking around, she added, "Where's Dad? I thought he'd be here. I want him to meet Rob, too."

"He's just taking a short walk. He'll be back soon," Grandma said.

Now Sharon understood why Grandpa hadn't been there when she arrived. She should have known: he was out smoking. Although everyone pretended that Grandpa liked to go for walks, even she knew the truth. She had often heard at church that smoking was a sin, so she was horrified when she had come upon Grandpa smoking behind the barn one time when she dashed around the corner, her brother in hot pursuit. He had quickly tried to hide his pipe, and she pretended not to have seen. When she questioned Mother later, Mother had explained that God would understand that Grandpa could not give up his pipe no matter how hard he tried. And he had tried, she insisted. He never smoked in front of his children or grandchildren, but the smell lingered in his clothes and hair. Sharon liked the fruity aroma from a distance, but up close when he hugged her against his rough wool coat, it was overpowering. It was nothing like the faint cigarette smell she now noticed emanating from Rob's coat. She wasn't sure if she liked it or not.

Rob reached for Aunt Lizzie's coat while she untied her belt and undid her buttons. When he slid it off her shoulders, his hand gently brushed her neck, and Sharon's own neck tingled as she watched him hang up their coats.

"Oh, I must check the potatoes!" said Grandma, and she moved toward the kitchen at a half run. "Rob, you sit down there and make yourself at home. Mabel and Lizzie, would you come help?"

"Mom, I've asked you before to please call me Liz. I'm not Lizzie anymore."

Mother followed Grandma, but Aunt Liz said to Sharon, "Sit down here with Rob and me. I'm sure they can manage without us." She sat down on the green prickly sofa close to Rob. When she crossed her legs, Sharon saw how her slim pink skirt pulled up, revealing shapely round knees. Sharon perched on the edge of a straight-backed chair against the wall. She wouldn't dare sit in the soft chair nearest the stove; everyone knew that was Grandpa's chair.

Rob said, "Well, Liz, your mother won't let your father smoke in the house, is that it?"

Sharon couldn't believe her ears--Rob talking out loud about Grandpa's smoking? Aunt Liz must have told Rob all about them.

"Oh, don't fool yourself, Rob," replied Aunt Liz. "Dad does anything he wants to in this house, doesn't he, Sharon? No, he's ashamed of his smoking. That's why he goes out."

"He sounds like an interesting old chap. I'm eager to meet him," said Rob as he put his arm on the back of the sofa, resting his hand on Aunt Liz's shoulder. He turned his attention to Sharon: "What grade are you in this year? Would it be fifth?"

"Yes," Sharon replied, and didn't know what else to say to this strange man from the city. Finally she added, "My teacher is Miss. Hadley. I really like her."

"My little girl is in fourth grade and my son in second this year," said Rob.

Aunt Liz looked hard at Rob, pressed her hand on his leg, and said sharply, "Rob!"

"Oh, oh," said Rob.

Sharon was speechless, but thoughts whirled through her mind. How could Aunt Liz's boyfriend have children? Sure, she knew about divorce, but she didn't know anyone who was divorced. Besides, wasn't divorce a sin? And wasn't even marrying someone who was divorced? What if Aunt Liz married this man? What would happen to her?

Aunt Liz turned back to Sharon and said in her normal voice, "Rob has two children who live with their mother. He was divorced a couple years ago, long before we met."

"Oh," Sharon said. She stared at the low flame that glinted blue through the small window in the front of the stove. For a few seconds there was silence. Then Aunt Liz stood and said to Sharon, "Come up to my room for a minute. I think I might have something for you." Even though she had moved out years earlier, her bedroom had remained just as she left it, even to some clothes she had left hanging in the wardrobe. Poking around in the room was one of the few things to do at Grandma's, so Sharon was familiar with the small room, its narrow mahogany bed, the fragrant cedar chest, and the dressing table with a fabric skirt that matched the frilly curtains Aunt Liz had made as a teenager.

Sharon followed Liz up the steep stairs, watching how her hips swayed under the tight pink skirt. When they were standing on the rag rug in the middle of Aunt Liz's room, Liz put her arm around Sharon's shoulder and said, "Now, I don't want you to worry about me and Rob. He's a very good man, and I think I'm really in love with him. It was his wife who left him. How can you blame him for that?"

Sharon was moved and flattered by Aunt Liz's confiding in her. Without hesitation, she answered, "I don't think you can blame him."

Aunt Liz squeezed her shoulder. "I thought I could count on you," she said. Moving to the chest, she said, "I think I have an old sweater that might fit you." She stirred through piles of embroidererd towels and pillowcases and finally pulled out a fuzzy pink angora sweater that closed at the neckline with two buttons that looked like little pearls. It was very different from Sharon's sweaters, scratchy stiff wool cardigans handed down from her older cousins or bought at the used clothing store.

"What do you think?" said Aunt Liz.

"Oh, it's beautiful! But don't you want it?"

"No, I wore it for a couple years. And I think you've grown enough that it'll fit you now."

It took Sharon only fifteen seconds to strip off her homemade blouse and pull the soft pink cloud over her head. She fumbled with the two little buttons, but her hands were shaking, so Aunt Liz buttoned them for her. She turned to look at herself in the mirror and was stunned by her reflection. Her shining eyes and the pink fuzzy sweater transformed her.

"Thank you, thank you," Sharon whispered.

Aunt Liz laughed. "It's nothing. I wasn't wearing it anyway. It looks good on you."

The thumping of Sharon's heart was so loud she could hardly hear what Aunt Liz told her about her life in the big city, the parks and the tall buildings and the bus she rode to her job right down in the center of town.

They heard Rob calling from the foot of the stairs, "Come on you two. Dinner's ready."

"We better go down before Grandma has a fit," Aunt Liz said. "Why don't you leave the sweater on."

Sharon hesitated, worrying about her mother's reaction. Would she say this sweater was worldly? But, emboldened by confident Aunt Liz, Sharon decided to risk it. She hurried down the stairs ahead of Aunt Liz. Near the bottom she tripped on a hole in the threadbare carpet and pitched forward. She put her hands out to break her fall, but Rob, who was waiting there for them, caught her and set her on her feet. "Whoa. Someone's hungry," he said. Looking closely at her, he added, "My, you look pretty in that pink sweater." Sharon, flustered from his touch and his look, didn't respond, but she followed the two adults as they moved toward the kitchen. When she saw Rob gently squeezing Aunt Liz's bottom, she quickly averted her eyes, embarrassed, but also vaguely thrilled. Would any man ever do that to her? Sometimes she hoped so, but most of the time she felt sort of sick at the thought.

In the kitchen, Grandpa was seated in his chair at the head of the table, and Grandma and Mother were placing bowls of steaming potatoes and corn next to the platters already in the middle of the table. Mother looked at Sharon, frowned, and said, "Sharon. . ."

But Grandpa's voice drowned out Mother's. "Well, Lizzie, it's about time you're showing up. Where were you off gallivanting this time? You should have been here to introduce me to your young man. Or maybe he's not so young."

Sharon cringed. She was relieved to escape her mother's comment, which likely would have been something about the sweater, but she wished Grandpa would be more polite, especially to company.

While everyone but Grandma found seats around the table, Grandpa continued, "He says he's an engineer, but not the kind that runs trains. Now I ask you, what other kind is there?" His snorting laugh signaled that this was a joke, and everyone else joined in half-heartedly.

As the laughter died, Rob said, "I'm an electrical engineer. I design motors for manufacturing equipment. I don't know much about trains, I'm afraid, although I have ridden on them."

"Yes, I know, I know." Grandpa impatiently responded. "I was just trying to make a joke. I'm not quite as dumb as I look. We had an engineer at the factory where I worked for twenty-five years."

"What kind of work did you do there?" asked Rob.

"Oh, I was just a peon running a drill press."

"That takes skill, too. We engineers would be useless without you people who run the equipment we design."

"Well, yah, I guess," said Grandpa, sounding unconvinced. "Ma, come sit down before everything gets cold."

Grandma made room on the table for the gravy boat and sat down in the empty chair next to Sharon. Grandpa said in a deep voice, "Let us pray." Sharon bowed her head but peeked from under her lowered lids to watch Rob's reaction. He bowed his head, too, but she could see him glancing secretly at Aunt Liz as Grandpa went on and on, praying for all his children and grandchildren by name, including Lizzie, and even Rob. Then he started on the widows and orphans of the world. He prayed that the sinners might be saved and the righteous be blessed. The fried potatoes no longer steamed and the gravy had a trace of a skin on top before his Amen rolled out.

Even so, everyone piled their plates with food as each platter and bowl was passed around the table. Mother got up and began to pour coffee for the adults while Sharon picked up her fork, finally done with passing dishes and eager to begin eating. Just then Grandpa said, peering at Aunt Liz through his thick glasses, "Well, Lizzie, I see you've been busy buying out all the stores in Toronto. Do you think that's necessary to attract a man, eh?"

"Dad!" Aunt Liz and Grandma protested in unison.

But it was Rob Grandpa was watching. Sharon saw Rob's jaw clench. Then he coldly said, "Of course it isn't necessary. Liz is beautiful in anything. But I do find her especially eye-catching in this cream and pink outfit, don't you? It sets off her coloring perfectly."

"Humph! Vanity, vanity, all is vanity," Grandpa muttered.

"You used to enjoy seeing me in new clothes," said Aunt Liz.

"That was before you got so *worldly.*"

"She looks just as appealing in her jeans," said Rob.

"Jeans!" said Grandpa. "Pants! On a woman! She didn't learn that in this house."

Sharon was prepared for an angry retort from Aunt Liz, but watched her instead coolly ignore Grandpa as she turned toward Grandma to ask about her old school friends. "What are Ruth and Mary doing now? I think I heard that Ruth had a second child, is that right?"

Mother eagerly stepped in: "They *both* have two children already. They're doing real well. Did you know Mary and Thomas took over her parents' farm? And Ruth and her husband moved into that old house two

doors down from where Fred Butlers live and they've
fixed it up *real* nice. You should see it! The Millers who
used to live there I think moved to Elora, isn't that
right, Dad? I think it was either Earl, or maybe Glenn.
They didn't live here very long. You remember they're
the ones with that boy who was crippled about three
years ago from that accident on Snyders' Road, or
maybe it was on the Conestoga Road, let's see, it was in
May of 1950, I think. Do you know who I mean?"

"No, but that's all right. You don't have to explain,"
Liz said.

Grandma said, "Oh, I know. It was Earl. He's the
one with that sister that never did get married, you
know, the one who used to work in the drugstore?
Loretta I think was her name."

Sharon saw the blank look on Rob's face and knew
how bored he must be. Desperately she blurted out
the only thing she could think of to include Rob in
the conversation: "Mr. Woodhill, what is your daughter's name?"

The twittering of the parakeet and ticking of the
clock were loud in the sudden silence. The swinging
pendulum slowed intolerably as Sharon registered the
dismay on Aunt Liz's face and the puzzlement and
then growing anger on Grandpa's. Rob opened his
mouth as though about to answer, then closed it
again. Sharon's face burned, and she prayed to be
transported ten thousand miles away.

Grandpa broke the spell as he glared at Rob:
"What's this she says—you have a daughter?"

"Yes, and a son, too, Susie and Jeff," Rob said calm-
ly. "They live with their mother. We were divorced a
couple years ago."

Sharon heard Grandma beside her saying weakly.
"You're divorced?" but she was watching Grandpa,
horrified as his face grew red and his mouth hard-
ened. She could see the ridges moving under the skin
of his jaw. Once he had blown up at her when she hit
a ball through the kitchen window, and she recognized the signs.

Now he jumped to his feet and shouted, "No
daughter of mine will ever marry a divorced man!"
His cheeks quivered and his index finger hammered
the air as though he were nailing each word in
place.

Sharon saw such a look of hatred flash across Aunt
Liz's face that her heart stood still. Rob shook his
head in amazement.

"Is that clear, Miss Lizzie Brubacher? Do you
understand, Mr. Rob Woodhill?" Grandpa continued,
leaning across the table toward them.

"Have we said anything about marriage?" said Rob
in a tight voice.

Liz, her face a mottled red, slammed down the
knife and fork she had been holding suspended above
her plate. "I'm not your child to be ordered around
anymore. I'll do whatever I please. You ran my life
long enough with all your rules and regulations."

"Now wait a minute, just wait a minute. Let's calm
down," said Grandma.

"No, I won't calm down, Mom. It's time for some
rebellion around here." Aunt Liz's voice was shaking.
"We've had too much shushing and too much calming
down." She glared at her father and said, "You've
always tried to run my life, to make me live by your
stupid rules, but no more. From now on . . ."

"And you've *always* been a bad girl, since you were little," Grandpa broke in "Disobedient! Rebellious! We took you to church and we tried to train you up in the way you should go. But you've departed from it. You've taken the wide road that leads to destruction. You'll never get to heaven at this rate."

"I wouldn't *want* to go if people like you and your damned busybody minister were there. Hell would be a lot more fun," answered Liz.

Sharon heard Mother suck in her breath with a loud "Oh!" and she saw Grandma cover her mouth and shake her head. She expected the voice of God to break through the ceiling above their heads, but it was only Grandpa who thundered, "Blasphemy! I won't have such language used in my house." He pointed a shaking finger at Aunt Liz. "You're a Jezebel. You get out of my house."

Rob leapt to his feet, pushing over his chair, and pulled Aunt Liz up beside him. "Come on, Liz, let's get out of here," he said, tugging her toward the door.

Grandma stood up, too, and took hold of Liz's other arm, crying, "No, no, you can't go. You're my daughter. This is your home." She looked angrily at Grandpa and said, "Peter, what do you think you're doing? Don't do this."

"Don't go, Aunt Liz," Sharon said, but Grandpa and Aunt Liz were focused only on each other.

"Go! Go! And don't come back," shouted Grandpa.

"Gladly! I've tried long enough to get along with you. I give up!" she shouted back. She shook off her crying mother but said gently, "Mom, I'll write to you later."

She and Rob disappeared through the doorway leading to the front of the house. Seconds later the outside door slammed; then a car roared away. Sharon could hear the coat tree still rocking in the resounding stillness.

She sat motionless, unable to comprehend the explosion she had set off. Numbly, she watched Grandpa sit back down and pick up his fallen fork from the floor. Now he was stabbing a pickled beet on his plate until it ran red and saying, "She deserved it. She deserved it. How dare she make light of heaven and hell. Saying hell would be more fun. Not in my house!" Grandma stood at the sink crying into her handkerchief, and Mother stood beside her with an arm around her.

Sharon pushed back her chair and was out the back door before anyone could say a word. Sobbing, she ran to the outhouse, closed and locked the door, and sat down on the toilet lid. A wave of nausea swept over her. She had heard arguments before, but never had she heard her family say such awful words to each other. She swallowed hard and brushed the tears from her cheeks. But they kept coming as every harsh word and gesture played over and over in her mind.

Finally the flood of tears slowed, and she looked around at the familiar little cubicle, hoping to soothe her mind. The last rays of sunshine shone through the cracks between the boards, illuminating the spider-webs filled with dead flies and moths. She glanced at the winter scene on the Miller Hardware Store calendar hanging from a nail on the wall, the same one she had been looking at for years. Then from the stack beside her she picked up one of the pages torn from an old Sears & Roebuck catalogue to be used as toilet paper. As she peered at the page in her hand, she saw models wearing slim skirts and pullover sweaters. In the dim light one even looked like Aunt Liz. Into her mind flashed a vision of herself standing joyfully in the middle of Aunt Liz's bedroom with Aunt Liz's arm around her, and she heard her saying, "I knew I could count on you." But fresh tears welled as she realized she had let her down. She was a blabbermouth and had spoiled everything. She didn't deserve the beautiful pink sweater. Would she ever see Aunt Liz again?

She wished desperately that she could reverse time and take back her thoughtless words. She could have asked some questions about Toronto. Why did she have to mention his daughter?

Some time later, Sharon heard Mother calling through the growing dark. She was not ready to go in, so she remained silent and unmoving. But her thoughts and emotions churned on. Suddenly one question sprang out clearly from the muddle and led to a new train of thought. Was Grandpa right? Would marrying Rob mean Aunt Liz would go to hell? Would God do that? Aunt Liz had said she loved Rob. He seemed like a nice man who loved her, too. Grandpa had called Aunt Liz bad. What did that really mean? Mother and Grandma were always telling Sharon what a good girl she was, such a helper, so obedient. She rubbed her hand over the soft fur of the sweater and wondered about bad girls and good girls. She prayed for it all to make sense.

Finally, shivering in the cold, she answered, "Coming," when Mother called again from the back steps. She followed the path her feet knew through the dark and entered the kitchen where Grandma, red-eyed, was washing dishes and Mother was drying.

Grandpa had disappeared. The lingering food odors turned her stomach, still queasy from her crying.

Mother said, "Sharon, we need to go as soon as I finish here, so you go up and put Aunt Lizzie's sweater away."

"No, Mother, this is my sweater now," Sharon said. "Aunt Liz gave it to me."

"Sha-a-ron," Mother said. "You do as I say."

"But why can't I keep it?"

"Because I said so. Now, don't make trouble. Be a good girl."

Sharon turned and walked into the front room. She slowly climbed the steps to Aunt Liz's room. There she picked up her blouse from the bed where she had flung it in her eagerness to put on the pink sweater. She walked to the window and stared out at the dark empty street below as she held the blouse in her hands. She absentmindedly fingered the lace Mother had carefully sewn around the edges of the little round collar. Abruptly she wrapped the blouse into a tight little ball and headed out the door and down the stairs. Back in the front room, she slipped the bundled blouse into her jacket pocket. Then she took her jacket from the coat tree, put her arms into the sleeves, buttoned it to her chin, and sat down in Grandpa's chair to wait for Mother.

Arlene Koch Holdeman lives and writes in Bloomington, Minnesota.

The Riotous Walls

by Diana Reneez

I'm one of those unlucky people who gets really ugly when I cry. If I cry even two tears my nose gets thick, my eyes get fat and squinty, my face turns red, and I look disgusting. If I happen to see myself in the mirror while I'm crying, it makes me cry even more. I feel so sorry for anyone who looks that miserable.

After what Beth said to me, I cried for ages. I cried all night and for the next two weeks every time I thought about it. I thought that was the end, that I, on top of being white, had proved myself to be against her struggle to discover her black self. I finally proved what a thick-bodied, thick-brained, head-in-the-sand Mennonite girl I am. I knew she just couldn't love me anymore. Everything about me was wrong.

The first time I saw her was the first period of the first day of our second year of high school. We had gym class—a misfortune for a fifteen-year-old who just spent a half-hour in the clutches of a curling iron.

I don't think I even noticed she was black. I noticed her because of her outfit. I'd never seen anybody wear a combination like that and I didn't know anyone who would. She put a bright yellow blouse under a scarlet red jumper—or maybe the other way around—anyway, the effect made you squint but keep looking. And she had giant pink-tinted glasses. To be fair, I should confess that I wore a calf-length red, white, and teal striped skirt with box pleats that I made myself in honor of the occasion of beginning tenth grade.

I smiled at her. This was obviously a new girl.

"Hi. I'm Beth," she said, like this would be the best news of my life.

It was.

She told me that her dad was from Nairobi, her mom from Ontario and that they lived in New York. She was staying in the dorm. I didn't know anyone from any of those places but it explained to me why she had the best tan in the world all year long and uncontrollable hair. I envied her fervently, her body built around the long bone structure of her east African cousins; she ate anything she wanted and was always skinny, skinny, skinny. I felt like a rosy pink pig next to her long dark exotic sort of beauty.

I wished a person could die of remorse. It was like the time I tripped my friend Sam Cotes in the college cafeteria. It's a rowdy place, and as he passed by my table I stuck my leg out into the aisle at knee height. I meant to stop him the way those bars come down and stop cars when there's a train coming. It was totally obvious. I was sure he saw me and I thought he was faking until he fell flat on his face on the tile. I wanted to die then, too. Sam was a music major—probably lost in some sublime inspiration too lofty for me to attain. Not even those super-jocks would trip a music major. That's how I felt on the day that I told Beth she would end up like Kerry. It was another horrible thing I did by accident.

Now I know she was mortified. Now I know she would have given anything to look like me—like nobody, like everybody, like any other fifteen-year-old girl with two hundred and fifty years of history in Pennsylvania. Now I know she was petrified, paralyzed, and confused by this religious school her mother sent her to—this Mennonite high school built on the somber principles of our Swiss and German ancestors where girls wore only dresses in 1987, and no rock music was allowed or lipstick or jewelry or dancing, and kissing could jeopardize your soul. Now I know she felt like she landed on Mars. I think she told me then, too, but I didn't understand. I believed her, but she had stumbled into the only world I knew.

By August, our patience with everything wore thin and restlessness grew like a cancer. A thousand muggy days had slumped by with a thousand more to come. Every day, the apartment shrunk smaller and smaller. The riotous walls closed in on us, their beautiful flowers choking in weeds of graffiti, until it felt like a pen for wild animals. I shrink, too, when it gets like this. I get smaller and smaller until I barely speak, barely move, barely breathe any air. If you are perfectly still and perfectly quiet, it's just as if you weren't even there.

Beth was talking and I wasn't, the way it had gotten to often be. She didn't seem to mind small spaces;

she just stayed the same size and filled up the whole house at once. Everyone else was discussing racism on which, even shrunken down, barely breathing and not making a peep, I am a glaring representative of the wrong team. I just sat hiding on the couch, my fingers busy making colorful clay beads, my mind busy trying to stay blank. Nina is white, too, but I guess she was already miserable enough.

"I really need to get a subscription to *Newsweek*," Beth said, expressing her new and deepening enthusiasm for events in Africa and African American communities. Of course. Why not? It's a reputable magazine. Millions of people read it.

"If you start reading that," I said, clawing for something that might spark, in the new Beth, a flicker of my old Beth, "you'll get like Kerry."

It was stupid, ok. It was stupid, stupid, stupid of me. Dumb, dumb, horrible, idiot-girl. Kerry is my sister. She's always been one hundred percent perfect in every way and that summer she embodied everything we swore we would never be.

"That's not funny, Jackie!" a complete stranger lashed at me. "I am NOT going to get like Kerry. Just because someone reads *Newsweek* does not make them a Miss Priss like HER."

She forgot that I was her best friend.

"If you don't care what's going on in the world that's your problem, but some of us do. You just go off with Tom and be a hippie if you want. But these are my people and I care about them, ok? So do NOT make fun of me!"

She forgot it was me who yanked on her arm to set her jammed elbow back in place when we worked at summer camp. She forgot she's the one who taught me to spell "sense" and "receive."

She taught me to dance. I taught her to do hand-springs. She taught me to put on makeup. I taught her to drive the 4-wheeler. She taught me to flirt. I taught her to fish. I let her drive the car around the parking lot of K-Mart one night and she told me what it was like when Mike kissed her. We were the best best-friends in the world. We gossiped, we studied, we wrote funny songs, we stayed up all night, we camped out, we played sick, we zipped two sleeping bags together to make one big one so that she wouldn't keep stealing all the covers when she slept over. I suffered with her the nervousness of her first date. She suffered with me my first heartbreak. We went to college together and shared our first apartment.

Suddenly, she was black and I was white. I went away to South America for three months and when I came back she was black and I was white. I was shocked. I was heartbroken. My Beth, my dear, my only Beth. I would have cut off my arms to keep from hurting her and suddenly I had wounded her terribly—had been hurting her all along by thinking she was just like me. I had no idea what to do. It never mattered to me if she was black and suddenly that was the wrong answer. I had no idea what to say. I was utterly speechless.

Diana Reneez, Santa Cruz, Costa Rica, teaches drama and literature.

By the Editors

Minding Us Mennonites

by Phyllis Pellman Good

I think of us Mennonites as a rather muscular
group—small, scattered, varied, but still making some
difference in the world. So I was a little sobered the
other night while catching "Jeopardy" on TV. I had
just remarked about how intelligent the contestants
seemed. But they all got stumped on the next question. The category was "Protestantism." The answer,
for which they were to provide the question, was,
"The group related to the Amish, named for one of
their leaders, a Mr. Simons." None of the three players
knew. Kind of humbling. Kind of funny.

Clearly the game-show brains who wrote the set-up
assumed the contestants and their audience had some
idea about who the Amish are. They were the reference point. Of course, we (smug) Mennonites know
why. If the Amish weren't so visually obvious, they'd
be no-names, too. And then we go on, explaining why
we're so small and nearly invisible, usually having
something to do with our tough discipleship standards
and our self-effacing, servant-like practices. Oh, yeah?
When and where and who, I'd have to ask, if it were
any other group claiming such a mix of sulky self-
analysis, tinged with a strain of self-pity and -right-
eousness.

Anyway, I was reminded that while we have our own self-perceptions, others may have a somewhat different view of us—if they have any, that is.

Who Is "Us"?

At the invitation of the editor of *Mennonite Quarterly Review,* I agreed to reflect, in a "highly interpretive" manner, on what Mennonites are presently facing, to give a sort of window into Mennonite life at this moment, as I understand it.

In an effort to be frank, I've imagined that I'm talking to my mother or to my daughters—and so I will be personal and candid. No footnotes, no documentation, no results of careful studies.

I will limit my observations, confessions, and questions primarily to the band of North American Mennonites of which I am a part. Once the "mainstream" among Mennonites, we of European origins and long histories in the peoplehood, are a shrinking percentage within the global Mennonite church. More than half the Mennonites in the world are now Africans, Asians, and Latin Americans. Within North America, Old Order and conservative groups will likely surpass us in numbers within a few years. And there are a rising number of charismatic Christians joining our church. In addition, more and more people groups are now also North American Mennonites. Clearly, we no longer have a lock-hold on the typical, or "correct," theological-historical-sociological mix that makes a Mennonite.

That's on top of our many other, well-documented sociological shifts, some peculiar to ourselves, others shared with the rest of North American society (such as giving up farming for professions and business, leaving the rural world, seeing women go to work, reducing the sizes of our families, becoming educated, specialized, and highly scheduled—all within a single generation).

So what kind of church are we now? I will suggest a few facts, name several myths and family secrets, and end with some questions that continue to follow us.

A Few Facts

1.) We Mennonites were never monolithic, but I believe the differences among us are more pronounced than ever before. Our varying, and sometimes tension-producing, theological streams are well known. They haven't gone away or subsided. Instead, they keep taking new shapes, often influenced by the political-theological currents of the day, whether we lean to the left or to the right.

But more and many-fingered fissures stretch out among us, and we don't know yet how wide nor how deep they will turn out to be.

Our incomes and our education separate us. Our urban or suburban or rural mindsets mark us. Our politics put us in camps. Our professions require us to hold confidential knowledge and to make private decisions that often have moral or ethical implications.

Some of us are prepared to permit the church community to have a strong interest in our daily lives and decisions. Others of us believe that our fellow church members understand too little about our worlds, and therefore have not earned the right to have moral authority over us.

Some of us are drawn to public life and activity, believing we ought to make a contribution there. Others of us are convinced the risk of compromise is too great and prefer to live quietly, hoping to be witnesses by our character and integrity.

We live increasingly independent, "unobserved" lives. We see comparatively little of each other. Sunday morning worship services and bimonthly small group meetings are no match for the tumble of decisions we each regularly make. They give us thin companionship in managing the overall tone and direction of our lives.

Our congregations are no longer the local parish; we are no longer each other's neighbors. Gone is the natural accountability of living near each other.

2.) The Past sits among us, throwing shadows that unnerve us, providing occasional comfort.

Sometimes the Past sounds like a Story of Crimes. The church was "authoritarian, restrictive, abusive, oppressive." It used weapons—words and enforced practices that whipped its members into dark, straight lines. "Nonconformity," "revival meetings," "prophecy," "Preparatory Services," "Council Meetings," "following Jesus," "Bible memory verses," "coverings/capes/plain suits."

Along the way we foisted off a lot of this "baggage." We may feel less burdened. But we aren't free of the Past. In fact, we're pretty skittish about authority; we're in a fog about defining lines; we can't be sure how firmly to set membership standards. Might we, by our nervous tiptoeing, be doing as much damage as the old preachers of the Past did? Only differently.

While the church has dithered around, trying to give "sensitive, enlightened" leadership, some of us have lived off the memory of the clear images that filled the Past, its unmistakably defining practices, the people who embodied what the church meant to be. Some find comfort in that old clarity.

3.) Authority is suspect. If we do agree we need it, we can't always agree on where it should lie or how firmly it should be held.

Ordination used to do the trick, although not automatically so. Collective wisdom usually kicked in, bestowing true authority on those leaders who most deserved it. Now we're more likely to vote for a professional who was credentialed in another world; we seem to find comfort in the training that backs up the degree. Or we choose a successful business person, seeming to reason that what works in the world of enterprise should carry over to the church. But we watch carefully, ready to withdraw our support if we perceive an empire being built or heavyhandedness setting in.

Does the church have any real authority over our lives and over choices of ours that matter? We each decide how much to yield, which piece, to whom, and for how long.

Several Myths

Some things are undiscussable in families. Among them are myths, held too sacred to be challenged. Or too fragile to be examined. Usually we determine there's more to be lost by picking them apart than by letting them stand. It can require a lot of energy to move in on a myth. But in the interest of good family health, and knowing that a written page can be more easily ignored than a voice in a circle, here are myths that I believe bear some respectful dissection.

1.) "Mennonites are good at conflict." We mean that because we are committed to making peace (and building and keeping it—and whatever other verbs are proper to include), we are good at helping other people resolve their conflicts. That is often true. But an extrapolation tempts us here. It is not necessarily true that Mennonites are good at resolving conflict among themselves.

That is the painful truth that wants to hold hands with the myth.

Because we Mennonites love peace (who doesn't, to be fair?), and have come to be so identified with efforts at peace-building, we are especially appalled by our own anger and disappointed in our inability to be direct about a situation or person who upsets us.

We are capable of savagery. Sometimes I wonder whether, in spite of all of the training and seminars, degrees and titles in peacemaking and reconciliation, we're any better at handling conflict, reconciliation, and Christian peacemaking than we were before we became "professionals" at it.

2.) "We have progressed to being quite broad and very inclusive as a church." We want to be a people of love. We would like to extend mercy without bounds.

Our recent history is full of discipline, often carefully adhered to, sometimes doggedly enforced. We'd like to right those wrongs; we blanch at being thought too restrictive, by insiders or by onlookers.

We want to invite others to join our fellowship, our faith family. We see some image, we have some bodily form in mind, when we express that wish. But how will the church keep its shape and its identity when we want to welcome everyone, when we want to exclude no one, despite their behavior?

Those of us who are most concerned about not eliminating anyone from becoming part of us seem to find it particularly difficult to embrace those who have more conservative theological or political points of view.

Our broadly "inclusive" impulses seem to cut mainly in one direction.

3.) "We modern Mennonites are on a faithful continuum with the Anabaptists of the 16th century." We perceive ourselves to be the staunch and loyal ones, having capably selected the proper path, securing the essentials, dodging the distractions, inconveniencing ourselves, and even sacrificing whatever was necessary.

We don't mean to overdo it, but often a subtle tone of judgment can creep into this softly spoken assertion. The target of our judgment is less often our Christian sisters and brothers of other communions and is more likely to be our own "cousins," those Mennonites or Amish whom we believe put the emphasis on minor points or have strayed toward fundamentalism.

We seem to hold some abstraction in our minds that represents the defining points and practices of early Anabaptism that we now, too, live by. It may be worth pulling out the Schleitheim Confession and comparing its statements with our behavior and beliefs. We may be surprised to see who's drifted—or how impractical, and possibly uninspiring, the old documents are.

Some Family Secrets

When I was growing up, my parents would occasionally entrust my brother and me with some information or opinion they thought we ought to know. Sometimes we already knew. The point was that this was material for insiders, not to be broadly shared.

I'm not bringing any news here. Instead, I mean to make a few observations that are probably obvious, if not often acknowledged.

1.) We worry about being thought to be too narrow. This is closely related to our fears about being thought to be backward.

We believe we'll suffer for the important things if need be, but we hate to be embarrassed.

Somehow we're convinced that we would choose jail or exile and give up our bank accounts and investments if we were asked to violate our faith. But we find it nearly impossible to say no to a membership applicant to our congregation or to refuse to participate in a neighborhood effort that compromises our principles. Many of us are simply fed up with being odd.

2.) Our church agencies can behave like principalities. Nervous about how to handle power, how to maintain their market share (if not increase it), and how to keep their funds flowing (if not grow them), these institutions can by heavyhanded, manipulative, public-relations-conscious. Congregations, schools, retirement communities, mission boards, insurance and mutual aid organizations, district conference and denominational apparatus. They do plenty of good—and, now and then, some harm.

3.) We have a seepage problem. Some of our people are drawn away to churches that offer a more outspo-

ken piety, often flavored with conservative politics.
Others feel the squeeze from the church if they
become highly successful in business, and so they
drift off. Many of our kids never become members, or
they grow quietly distant and drop out. They may be
lured by the promise of prestige, power, and prosperi-
ty beyond; they may be disillusioned by the little passion they perceive within the church; perhaps we
haven't sufficiently called them.

Despite all our efforts at missions, we haven't
found a way to stem the loss from within.

4.) We have the ability to be distracted by the
wrong things. Structures and details have nearly con-
sumed some wings of the church recently. Focusing
on too small a sphere can have us putting too much
energy on too little a scope. The neighborhood and
the congregation are primary, but they're not the
whole. The Mennonite church is increasingly a global
body, and we have family responsibilities to each
other. And privileges and resources from the same.

This family we have outside the West may have
some thoughts about where we should be putting our
energy these days, about what is central and what is
peripheral. We may be a bit lost right now; we seem
not to be fully certain about what really matters. It
may be time to seek some counsel from our sisters
and brothers elsewhere in the world, many of whom
live against the hard bone of inhospitable settings.

5.) We're more apt to agree about the questions that
swarm us these days than about their answers.

It must mean that certain classic stakes have been
driven deeply into many of us, such as: there is an
essential connection between what we believe and how

we live; we need the company of God's people in order to be faithful; our loyalties so shape our lives that we are of necessity different from the world we live in.

But what is the proper mix of these elements? How do they work themselves out within each of us, and in our life together? Who decides how it shall all come to be? About this we have unending debates.

In other words, if we were to plan a seminar about how to live as faithful Mennonite Christians, we could probably agree on the agenda and the subjects of the main addresses, but it would be hard for all of us to accept the same conclusions.

Questions We Haven't Yet Answered . . . To Our Own Satisfaction

1.) What beliefs and behavior should finally define us?

2.) Is "love," in the end, our only ethic? Should all our other principles and convictions flex before it?

3.) Where should our borders be? How elastic should they be?

4.) How do we have engagement with the world without becoming it? What safeguards do we have in place?

5.) How much diversity can we bear and still be a people?

6.) Are there sufficient theological and praxis solutions in Anabaptism to cover the realities of professionals' lives? Can our theology and praxis stretch to include the major institutions the church has built?

7.) Will we find a way to have our racial and our gender differences enrich us rather than anger and fray us?

8.) How do we cultivate a vital sense of the Transcendent God, of the redeeming activity of Jesus, of the enlivening place of the Bible, in our prosperous and secular settings (where thoughts of sacrifice and suffering seem not only archaic but meaningless)?

It's the Troubles that elbow their way to the front when one thinks about the well-being of the church at an historic moment, like the turning of the century. But the church's buoyancy and health, often expressed in unexpected places, cannot be denied, dare not be overlooked. A mix of diligence—and of surprises we can't quite imagine—may carry us through.

In a recent churchwide convention we discovered again that we can't always find satisfying resolution to our differences by endless discussion. Despite the employment of our best minds, intentions, and strategies, sometimes we can't reach agreement. But we can, even in those moments of utter exhaustion, still sing together. I don't find that an easy escape or a denial of our differences. Instead, it's reaching for a substantial prop we've been given to help guide us along the way.

Some years ago when we lived in New York City as students, a bunch of young-ish people, born into Mennonite families whom they had fled, ended up in scattered apartments within a few blocks of each other in the Village. In their chosen exile from their faith commuities, they had nearly formed a new one. Not only did they live fairly close to each other, they'd also get together now and then to sing from the *Mennonite Hymnal*.

Maybe it was just their version of going dancing like homesick Irish or eating goulash like farflung Hungarians. But the hymns they sang had texts, preachy words, here and there condemning words, words of faith and belief. Those songs offered them a foothold until they figured out where to step next. We may find it helpful to let our treasure of music do the same for us.

Recently, a group of seven Mennonites, gathered from around the globe, found they shared a remarkable amount of common ground. These Mennonites spent a week talking with six Roman Catholics in Venice about their churches' often ugly past and a possible future of forgiveness and shared witness. Neal Blough, one of the participating Mennonites who has lived in France for many years, reported that the Mennonites discovered they had considerable "commonality of convictions, in spite of our very different origins." (The Mennonites were one each from Congo, Guatemala, Germany, Canada, and the U.S., and two expatriates from France.) "Yes, there is a worldwide recognizable Mennonite identity," he reflected.

A part of the Mennonite contingent, Nzash Lumeya from Congo observed the Mennonites uniformly referring to the Sermon on the Mount as primary source material for their theology and ethics.

That looks hopeful.

There may be a lift for us if we pause long enough to allow ourselves to be ministered to, especially by our sisters and brothers beyond our borders, if we vulnerably confess our differences, if we allow music to displace talking for a while.

WHAT MENNONITES ARE THINKING, 2000

The problems and the imponderables won't disappear, but we may get a reprieve—we may even be saved—from cynicism and despair.

Phyllis Pellman Good, Lancaster, Pennsylvania, is a writer, editor, and co-editor of this collection.

Who's Not Borrowing?

by Merle Good

One doesn't have to hang around the fringes of
Mennonite discussions very long before the accusation
emerges. It may be offered with condescending compassion, but more often it is a heated, rather blunt put-
down. Those being criticized consider themselves to
be Mennonites, but those issuing the critique believe
themselves to be "more authentic" Mennonites.

So we're like the rest of the world. No surprise
there. Within all groups around the world there is an
ongoing debate about what ideas or emphases most
authentically represent the spirit of that group, its
past, and its future.

What's especially interesting about Mennonite conversations is not the debate. That's to be expected; it's
only human. For Mennonites, however, the big betrayal seems to be the "borrowing." As in, "Leader A bor-
rows a lot of his ideas from Group X." Or,
"Congregation B seems to borrow their theology from
Suspect ISM Z."

One could be tempted to find full-time entertainment observing this earnest interplay.

"She's not a real Mennonite, you know. She went
away to one of these liberal colleges and has totally
adopted their ideas. It's really sad." Or—"That congre-

gation has really lost their way. They borrow so many of their ideas from Fundamentalism. It's painful to observe how far they've wandered. And though they still call themselves 'Mennonite,' we all know they're not really authentic."

These conversations assume that there now is or once was a coherent theological core called "Mennonite theology." That's perhaps where the problem begins.

Mennonites of all authentic stripes (from Old Order to the most progressive) have always been more centered on practice than on theology. We are a practical people, and our debates and splinters through the centuries have mostly been about how we live our lives, rather than about a finely tuned theological debate. There are exceptions to this, but it seems fair to say that we have never been a big enough tent to muster a full-blown theological system and core.

This acknowledgment may be upsetting to some among us, but my guess is that most of us sense instinctively that we've never been known for our theological system. True, some Mennonites have invested their advanced degrees in trying to create such a system, and their efforts are appreciated, I'm sure.

But let's be honest: "Let her or him among us who has not borrowed cast the first stone."

Not that borrowing is wrong. It's the only option. When one has "a network of emphases and reactions" as your history and identity, no one can survive without borrowing from some place to give more coherence to the life of authenticity one wishes to live. Our history overflows with examples of borrowing. There was no other way to survive.

What's the point? Only to note that we all borrow, of necessity. And heated denunciations of other Mennonites because "they borrow their ideas or emphases" (as though we don't) aren't all that helpful.

One week, one may hear someone quote Henri Nouwen in one breath and, in the next, accuse other Mennonites of "borrowing from Fundamentalism." The next week, one may catch someone else quoting from *Christianity Today* in one breath and, with barely a pause, point a finger at some other Mennonites and accuse them of "borrowing" from Liberalism.

The Old Order groups have been said to have borrowed a great deal from German culture which may not necessarily be "authentically Mennonite." But are those who see life primarily as a struggle around "peace and justice" issues any less influenced by extra-Mennonite influences?

Being a Mennonite in today's world can be a joyful journey. We can all learn from the whole family of faith, in North America and around the world, tiny and inconsequential as we are.

It's a fact that we all borrow from other Christian streams. But being "authentic Mennonites," we may not want to say so out loud!

Merle Good of Lancaster, Pennsylvania, is a writer, dramatist, publisher, and a co-editor of this volume.

Poetry, I

Man answers God

by Rhoda Janzen

Maschine Zur Vertilgung Der Heuschrekken
—Johann Braun Archive, Kiev

They were working on a machine
that would inhale and annihilate
the locusts. Even on paper
it looked ominous: creaking wheels,

gears, penciled arrows to chart
wind movement, the funnel
with the sucking power, the black
rubber belt imported from

Germany. You would hear the tic
of contact, the blundering locusts
as they tried to pull back,
too late, hot air rushing oblivion,

extermination systemized in one
astonished pulse of strawstick
insect heart, the wheat saved,
and August bearable again.

I'm told that it would have worked,
they they very nearly had it—
the wife as she hauled a tin bucket,
sweet peach *Saft* sloshing the sides,

must have wiped her damp hairline
as she approached the shed where they
were building the terrible engine.
The zinging collision of wings on skin

once would have made her shriek
with the proper panic of her six, but
now she mechanically slaps and stuns,
she scoops them as they splashland

in the bucket, and flicks them wetly
to the ground. She has a case
of the heatshimmers: the field
is undulating under the iridescent

whir of locusts. All, all, feasting
on the future that should be hers.
It is their land; they work the wheat.
It is a plague, she thinks, a judgment

on riotous living, and it is well
that man answers God with a machine
that will rid the world of locusts
forever, steel cylinders chuffing.

Rhoda Janzen is a poet and teacher living in Michigan.

Singing at Orangefield Mennonite Church

by Cheryl Denise

Our four-part harmony,
and the reading of shape notes
is the closest we ever get to ecstasy.
Voices add their own harmonies
become soft and loud
but nothing else moves.
Our men can't dance.
When we sing a Negro Spiritual
from the Hymnal
they're afraid to come loose,
squashing the easy sway of bodies,
the natural dance of preschoolers.
They timidly slap their thighs
and awkwardly laugh.

The words in the old hymns,
the ones taught by grandparents
say we'll spend eternity singing.
They sound so certain.
Will the guys be standing stiff-legged in pews,
the women separate from the men,
God wildly waving his baton?

Singing at Orangefield Mennonite Church

What if a woman sways to the beat
or gets a tambourine and plays it on her hips?

I want to stay here
and be born Catholic next time,
for the dances
after midnight mass,
the ones at weddings
with loud families swinging hands,
singing on or off key,
dancing, like we were made to.

Cheryl Denise is a poet living in Philippi, West Virginia.

Overflow

by Jean Janzen

Today the young swallows
are practicing their flights
streaking in and out

in frantic patterns
from their mud nests under
the bridge. Their cries echo

over the high water of the creek,
an urgent calling from their silken
bodies, like an overflow.

Once we saw a tourist version
of "Swan Lake" danced on a stage
so small, the principals repeated

their patterns in tight circles.
And at the end the need and joy
collapsed for lack of space.

Our stories are too big
for our bodies. Our first heartbeat
is spill-over, and we are born

in a rush of water and cries.
With our whole body we lift
our first vowels to the air—

a stream, pressing
from a place we do not know.

Jean Janzen is a poet, living and writing in Fresno, California.

Cruise

by Jeff Gundy

I'm driving the curves and twists of route 6, 10:18
p.m. Drizzle, my wipers whanging back and forth,
trucks throwing big sheets of smeary water. It's a
beautiful night, a beautiful night.

The little factory's doors are wide open and they're
loading trucks at ten on a Thursday night. Down the
road the porch light blares in a stone entryway, light-
ing up everything in welcome or fear.

There's music in the raindrops but the scale's so deli-
cate that it takes better ears than mine to hear it, a
better head than mine to get the tune.

What is better than the way a voice can take a simple
string of words and tune them up, find a music that
you'd never think was there. Sweet notes from the
beat-up Martin fade slowly into the road noise.

The cruise control does this weird surging thing and I
don't know why, I just want to get home. It's good to
make the four lane highway, it's good to have some
space to move so fast when you don't know who's in
the other car and don't much trust yourself.

And the truth is the Indigo Girls are done and Emmy Lou is into "When the Trumpet Sounds," her voice clean and true and guitars floating airy and hot and angelic behind and the rain almost seems to have stopped and the pavement almost seems dry.

And what could be a light or a whole new space blossoms out between the ground and the clouds ahead, a wide orange glow and of course it's the lights of Fort Wayne and a hundred thousand of us swirling all around on the surface of the earth, nothing so special, unless it's you.

And was I just awe-struck, was I just frozen, was I just taken, was I just awakened. Was I just heading steady, steady, steady down the road.

When the rain stops the world goes clear. When the rain stops I quit worrying that these cars are filled with drunks and dopers, splashing through the dark when all the good folk are in with their feet up, glasses in their hands, watching, watching whatever's on.

When the rain stops it seems I know what I'm doing. It seems I'm ready to wrestle this ghostly measure into something real, start it off and let it move, casual, triumphant, nothing so special unless it is happening to you.

Jeff Gundy is a poet and professor living and writing in Bluffton, Ohio.

Featured Articles,
Essays, and Opinions, II

A Few Thoughts on Home and Community (and Voices from the Margins)

by Hildi Froese Tiessen

A little over a year ago Canadian journalist Avril Benoit interviewed novelist Rudy Wiebe and poet Victor Jerrett Enns for perhaps twenty minutes on national radio about a new Mennonite literary journal (called *Rhubarb*) that was just then about to be launched in Winnipeg, Manitoba. Almost all of Avril Benoit's questions to these two writers of Mennonite heritage were about the nature of the Mennonite community. An interesting concept, that one: community. A favorite topic among Mennonites. We love to talk about community. It's a concept about which we've come to feel quite proprietorial. As a teacher of multicultural Canadian literature, I've often been struck by the frequency with which many of my students, representative of a rich variety of heritage backgrounds, love to talk about community, too—their community, defined by family, friends, cultural and religious heritage, and all those other things we tend to invoke when we think in positive terms about home.

I wonder a lot about community—and what

Mennonites like us really mean when we talk about it, and whom we're referring to when we talk about our community.

What follows here is neither a manifesto nor even a list of propositions on the subject, but a small handful of questions—probably more theoretical than real, when you take a close look at them. But they are compelling nevertheless, at least for me, and I suspect some of them will resonate with questions any one of us might, from time to time, ask ourselves. And these questions have to do with community and they have to do with "home."

When I speak of home in this context, I guess I'm referring to the Mennonite community in a larger sense: a community shaped by almost half a millennium of history and tradition, a palpable religious and social ethos. It is a place of "insiders" that each one of us, at one time in our lives, experienced as unquestionably different from the world "outside": it's a site of love, instruction, and discipline.

I think about "home" a lot. That is, I wonder about the word, the concept of, home a lot. Maybe because I read and teach a lot of multicultural literature, written, for the most part, by people with a strong sense of homelessness—people trying to determine for themselves who they become when they move to a new country. "Home"is a dominant theme in the literature of our age, a time of migration, diaspora. My friend, the poet and epidemiologist David Waltner-Toews, tells me that even in science, home has become a prominent concept, especially when one speaks of such things as the health of ecosystems. It's a word that evokes the complexity and the fragility of relationships, and so it provides the scientist with a metaphor with which to invoke intricate interrelationships that determine and define health or dysfunction.

When I think of home, I hear echoes of the voices of poets like Julia Kasdorf and Di Brandt, and Sheri Hostetler, all of whom have spoken of being lost between what Brandt calls "the worldly world out there" and the Mennonite world, lost in what Hostetler calls "that crevice between worlds." "Alienating as it sometimes feels," Kasdorf says, "this non-home is my home." And I wonder, as I read the stories and poems of so many of the writers who were nurtured among the Mennonites, why so many of them feels homeless. And I wonder who else among all those people nurtured among us Mennonites—those who, unlike the writers I work with, do not speak in any context where they might be heard—who else among us feel homeless. And I wonder why there's little evidence among the Mennonites I know that we're concerned about that. I wonder how many of us wonder about all the homeless Mennonites.

I have spent many hours the past few years interviewing some twenty-five writers, all of whom were nurtured within various of the Mennonite communities of North America. Their experience of and attitudes towards the communities in which they grew up, and what they perceive as the Mennonite community at the turn of the millennium, are as diverse as are the distances they now find themselves from the places they once knew as home. They have at least this in common: they all know what it means to be Mennonite. They all remember—with varying degrees of pleasure and pain, insight and confusion, desire and aversion—the texture and tone of how family and church and a Mennonite friendship circle in childhood represented "home" to them in their formative years. Many of them—though by no means all—have left the most intimate circles of Mennonite interaction, but all uniformly identify the Mennonite community as their first home: the place in which their earliest relationships were forged and their most formative conceptions of the world were developed and shaped.

"Home," Robert Frost said in his famous poem "The Hired Man," "is the place where when you have to go there they have to take you in."

Most of these writers' family homes were more personally disruptive than I remember mine to have been. My parents, each of them the children of lay ministers within the Mennonite church, were, as one of my childhood friends observed recently, non-invasive as far as their children were concerned. We knew what they expected of us, somehow, and, for the most part, we respected those expectations. If I were to remember my parents in images, they would be compelling ones, visually and aurally: my mother lying on her stomach across her neatly-made bed just after lunch every day when I, the youngest, was alone at home with her, the only one of the five of us not yet attending school. What I remember seeing is her lying with her head resting on the soft vellum pages of the German Bible in which she had just read a brief passage, silently, before falling asleep for just a moment or two, before taking on the domestic chores of the afternoon. What I remember hearing

are the murmurs from behind my parents' closed
door every evening before they went to bed. They
never said a word about their nightly Bible reading
and prayer. Just closed the door gently, and re-
emerged some moments later. I still hear those soft,
almost melodic, murmurs when I visit them now.
My mother told me during my last visit that in the
sixty-four years of their marriage they have missed
their devotions perhaps two or three times. And
sometimes, she said, since their bodies have grown
weak with age, they find it hard to kneel for prayer.
I wouldn't have known, all those years, that they
knelt to pray. Those murmurs, of which I have never
understood a word, will probably remain the most
powerful words I have ever heard.

Many of the Mennonite writers I've spoken with
had parents who were far less subtle in their
approach to religion than were mine. Di Brandt, many
of whose early poems took the form of difficult conversations between her father and herself—arguments
she describes as "words dancing painfully across the
sharp etched lines of his God ridden book"—declared,
two years after her award-winning first collection of
poems appeared, that she'd "never have become a
writer if her father hadn't died; he owned all the
words." The struggle with parents and religion was no
less dramatic for Patrick Friesen, who grew up feeling
that his father had abandoned fatherly love for an
unrelenting obsession about the state of Patrick's, his
eldest son's, soul. Friesen's suite of "Pa Poems," published in 1983, well after his father's death in 1971,
documents the ongoing spiritual crisis his pious,
demanding father precipitated in him:

like jesus' death
pa's death split everything into before and after
and nothing was healed

Patrick Friesen's father died of cancer when Patrick
was twenty-five. "Pa," he calls him, or "father" or "old
man." His father sang, like so many Mennonites did
and do, and for Patrick, as a young man, to refuse—or
to be unable—to sing was the necessary, or involun-
tary, way he managed to maintain his distance from
the Mennonite community, which he identified with
the very core of his father's irrepressible demand that
he be "saved." Friesen's poem entitled "rehearsing for
Sunday" begins:

pa sang real well
I used to hear him at home   rehearsing for sunday
sometimes just him and ma   sometimes with
    other people

It ends like this:

pa sang real well
until his lungs went and then   the last days   his
    throat

one sunday he and I sat facing each other in the
    living room
his voice was hoarse   I hoped he would clear it
but he didn't   or couldn't   and that harsh voice
    grew into stories
of his father   and I thought he was forgiving him
    for something

> though the dates were all wrong   I wanted to
>   hallow this dying
> but I had not learned to sing

Well, I'm into the thick of it now: Mennonite writers, Mennonite community, home. I could add: voices from the margins. That's what I'd like to talk about. Writers, community, and voices from the margins. Words uttered by people who would seem to be speaking to us Mennonites, but to whom we seldom listen. Why should we? They're—most of them—self-defined outsiders, aren't they? Ah, now there's a place to begin again.

How about this? The Canadian-Swiss Mennonite writer Rosemary (Deckert) Nixon published a collection of short stories in 1991. The title story, "Mostly Country," is a poignant and engaging tale about a young boy growing up as a non-Mennonite in the Swiss Mennonite community of Wadden, Saskatchewan. Kevin McClancy is, first of all, at the tender age of twelve, in love with one of the local Mennonite girls, Beatrice Freed, but he realizes that he's unlikely ever to marry her, because he's not one of them: his father combines on Sunday; moreover, as the narrator tells us, "there's a border between Kevin's family and the Mennonites. It slips down like a window closing." When Kevin's friend Curtis Cressman's family invites Kevin to come to the local Mennonite church one Sunday morning, the author foregrounds the displaced status of this young interloper in a gently humorous scene where Curtis Cressman's mom, settled in the pews in the sanctuary with her son Curtis and his "English" friend, Kevin

McClancy, in anticipation of the first hymn, leans over to Kevin and whispers to him, "What do you sing?" "Kevin gives a little sniff of nervousness and says, 'Uh—I guess mostly country.'"

Nixon's story "Mostly Country" doesn't have a happy ending. In fact, after Kevin McClancy registers, in a variety of circumstances in the neighborhood and at school, his longing to find a legitimate place in the Mennonite community that surrounds him—a community that seems to him to be as intimate and appealing as it is ultimately inaccessible, he appears in the final scene of the story peering out the windows of his own unhappy kitchen, longing for the warm yellow gleam of the Freed's farmhouse across the way, and recalling the song the Mennonite congregation had sung that morning about "looking through the shadows for the blessed lights of home."

There's nothing unfamiliar to us Mennonites in a story like this. We know all about insiders and outsiders. But our perspective generally tends to be from the inside out, not from the outside in, the way Kevin McClancy sees things. In fact, many of us work at creating and sustaining the very boundary lines that help us distinguish who might qualify to be "in" our community and whom we might designate as "out," even though these decisions about boundaries are frequently accompanied by controversy, registered, often passionately, in the pages of our church papers.

What do we Mennonites really mean when we talk about community? I'm not referring to what we often call the covenant community which we take to operate explicitly within the structures of the church, but rather the broader Mennonite community that includes those who, for some reason or other, would seem not to desire or to qualify for church membership.

Does our community include adult children who have not yet been baptized, for example, but who are sustained among us by family and friendship ties (how old do they have to be before we begin to resent the fact that they still refer to themselves as Mennonite?)?

What about those who have drifted away from the church but remain on a spiritual search that might—or might not—eventually lead them back home?

Or the individuals raised among us who base their worldview on what they have learned among the Mennonites, but fear they will never be blessed with the gift of faith?

And those who know us intimately—and those, like Kevin McClancy, who don't—but who somehow find themselves standing on the outside looking in, longing for a sense of home that seems forever to elude them?

My questions are informed by a number of things, including a conversation that took place in my living room a year ago. A Mennonite friend was describing the memorial service he had just attended in New York City for Warren Kliewer, a mutual friend who had been one of three writers of his generation (Warren, the youngest of the three, was in his mid-sixties) honored for their outstanding contributions to Mennonite Literature at the Goshen College conference on "Mennonite/s writing in the U.S." in October, 1997. A third person in the room that evening entered into the conversation and inquired as to who this Warren Kliewer was. When I identified Kliewer as a

Mennonite writer, my friend, without hesitation, objected. No, Kliewer was not a Mennonite writer, he declared (even though Kliewer's work throughout a lifetime had been inspired and informed by his Mennonite experience). He was not a Mennonite; he was not one of us.

Warren Kliewer was intensely interested in the Mennonite community that had shaped him. His first collection of stories, published in the early sixties, was a sometimes gentle, sometimes ironic, portrayal of the Mennonite world he had known as a child growing up in Mountain Lake, Minnesota. He was enormously supportive of other writers of Mennonite heritage. What do we speak of when we Mennonites speak of community, and who sets the boundaries? What heritage do we expect Kliewer to claim if we don't allow him to name his Mennonite roots? At what point did someone decide that he belonged outside? Outside what, exactly? If he's outside, does that mean that we can readily ignore anything he might say?

As far as I know, Warren Kliewer was not an active church member when he died. But he never lost sight of who his people were, of where he came from. The last project he completed before his death was a volume of personal essays about the Mennonite culture in which he was raised. In what sense do our concepts of inside and outside, center and margin, deprive him of a lived past—a community, a home— that he once claimed as his own? What troubles me about my friend's brief, dismissive words is the absence in them of any expression of loss at the fact that Kliewer must be an outsider now. Implicit in his words, instead, was an expression of indignation that

someone like Warren Kliewer should have presumed
to identify himself with us.

We can hear many voices of loss and lament in the
work of writers who claim a Mennonite heritage. It's
not unusual to hear, in their stories and poems, about
some of the marginal souls whom we once called our
own, but who seem to have, temporarily at least, lost
the way. Should we think of them simply as lost?
Consider Di Brandt's "at Basil's," a poem about
"Menno's sons," who "meet every Wednesday/evening
at Basil's for beer" and "pretend they've gone worldly"—about Jake, whose "mother worries about him."
And Pete, "who will cry someday/Pete will for another
chance." Brandt's poem ends like this:

> & where
> will Menno's promises be then & where
> was God when all these young men
> felt their souls crumble to dust &
> where is he now when all i can see
> in the mirror is the vines & tendrils
> of something wild growing in their
> brains & where's my long lost brother
> Mike who might have inherited the
> earth with me Menno where's Mike

I'm simply asking questions, and most of the questions—because of my active interest in the creative
work of writers of Mennonite heritage—involve the
marginalized artists and writers among us. An artist
friend of mine, whose step-father was once one of
the most prominent Mennonite churchmen in
Canada, was perfunctorily dropped from the church

membership list decades ago, because, as a poor art student, he had fallen behind in his dues. How do I respond when, a tender man in his eighties, he asks me tentatively, poignantly, if I think he's a Mennonite?

Recently I taught a course in Canadian Multicultural Literature. We read the literature of the Mennonites alongside the work of other Canadian writers of Native, Japanese, Chinese, South Asian, Italian, African-Canadian, and Jewish heritage. My wonderfully engaging students included a Pakistani Moslem, a Bengali Hindu, a Portuguese Catholic, a Japanese Protestant, a Russian-Mennonite Mennonite, a Swiss-Mennonite Presbyterian. Now there's an interesting one. Maybe I should refer to her as a Canadian Presbyterian, even though she speaks of her Swiss-Mennonite heritage just as freely and passion- ately as the other students speak of the communities that have shaped them. I was struck, a few years ago, when I taught a number of Jewish and Mennonite sto- ries side by side, by how tenaciously members of the Jewish community seem to hang on to their own, even when individuals make dramatic gestures to escape the confines of the world outside their commu- nity. I was struck, in stark contrast, by how quickly the Mennonites seem to want to release the marginal, to let them go.

I know full well that many people leave home with no intention of ever coming back. And I know that we can't deny them that option. But, to quote a line out of context from Michael Ondaatje's latest volume of poems, I can't help wondering, sometimes, "who abandoned who"?

WHAT MENNONITES ARE THINKING, 2000

The Winnipeg Mennonite poet Sarah Klassen once observed that no one leaves home because she intends to be homeless.

I like to imagine that this matter doesn't have any real relevance in our time. But I fear it isn't so. If it isn't so, we're faced with the challenge of sorting out how we can, at once, *sustain* a community that is distinctive enough to have real meaning—and that implies some boundary-maintenance, I know—and, at the same time, *be* a living, welcoming community to the individual whom we know so well because he or she was once at home with us.

Hildi Froese Tiessen is a teacher, writer, and editor in Kitchener, Ontario.

Peace and Unity

by Levi Miller

But I say to you, Do not resist an evildoer. But if anyone
strikes you on the right cheek, turn the other also.

—*Matthew 5:39, NRSV*

During the 1980s, I helped plan a half-dozen peace
events called Presbyterian-Mennonite Shalom
Conferences with Jack Lolla, who headed up the
Pittsburgh Presbytery's peacemaking task force. Lolla,
also a pastor, would occasionally remind me that as
he listened to the Mennonite speakers, he was struck
by how much they sounded like Presbyterians.

As nearly as I could tell, he meant that a small
group of pacifists were leading the denomination with
strong liberationist and leftist political sentiments
while the rank-and-file church members paid little
attention to them. If Lolla had listened to the
Mennonite church members themselves, he would
have discovered that many were also Christian pacifists. However, even some of the Mennonite leaders
had become selective pacifists.

The most poignant moment for me came when
we had a discussion between LeRoy Friesen, then
of the Associated Mennonite Biblical Seminary, and
Richard Shaul, who presented the Reformed view

on liberation theology. In a pointed discussion, the only difference that Friesen could articulate for Anabaptists was that they believed in a greater degree of community.

Poor Friesen would not renounce violence because he had defined peace and violence broadly. Having just returned form Central America, he could not ask the guerrillas to put down their arms in what he thought was a just struggle. We did not ask him whether he would ask the government to put down its arms. Given his political commitments, I suspect that he would have assented to this at least.

I mention this incident to note another reason why I pulled out of the liturgical left in the 1980s. I no longer considered this movement a reliable carrier of biblical pacifism, even though it often spoke of peace and justice. It seemed to me that the price of staying with this movement was too high. For the Quakers, this movement had meant the eventual abdication of pacifism among the rank-and-file members, even as it had among the leaders.

Among the Quakers were members such as Richard Nixon, commander in chief of the American forces in the Vietnam conflict. On the other hand, some American Friends Service Committee leaders openly supported the Vietnamese Liberation Army.

It seemed to me that in God's economy there must be room for a denomination of consistent biblical pacifists or nonresistants, even if such a position is compromised. John H. Yoder convinced us in *Nevertheless* that all positions are compromised. So consistent biblical pacifism is not purity nor is it even the most responsible.

But it is what Jesus taught and lived, and I have come to define peace as a church and biblical belief of pacifism in a narrower way out of a pastoral concern. Pacifism and nonresistance is a church teaching almost all Mennonites and Amish agree upon, and it provides a kind of unified, albeit flawed, voice.

I realize that some Christians define peace in broad strokes that include every movement from radically redefining gender roles and supporting welfare rights to promoting homosexual marriage. Here you can make up your own list of just peace causes, but I doubt that most of them will gain a wide church consensus.

That brings me back to my friend Jack Lolla's statement about the Mennonites becoming Presbyterians. The price for groups to espouse a wide range of causes that do not have a church consensus in the name of peace is that we tend to privatize peace. We finally discredit peace so that we do not pay much attention to it, at least in any communal way. In regard to pacifism, this is to become like the Presbyterians, Baptists, and or even the individualistic Quakers.

Whatever the merits of the many causes that currently are being projected under the banner of peace and justice, I leave you to decide. However, there may be some unifying value in defining peace, at least among the Mennonites, as pacifism, even if that is not the only definition. During a time of family, church, and community fragmentation, a modest unity may be of some virtue.

Levi Miller, Scottdale, Pennsylvania, is a writer and editor.

Humility Is Valuing Others

by Ardie S. Goering

The pursuit of humility is an elusive goal. Once you think you've got it, you probably don't.

It's equally hard to write about. To begin with, how do you define humility?

Like the dictionary definition, a lack of pride or arrogance is how most Mennonites would describe it. Sounds simple.

But attaining humility has always been more difficult.

As a girl growing up in the Mennonite church of the 1970s, I watched some men denounce women for their lack of humility in striving for positions of leadership and responsibility. In that case, humility was so good it was for women only.

Today, humility is often a badge of honor for Mennonite leaders (both men and women) as they declare they did not seek out their high level positions, because they're not ambitious. They only applied for a job or accepted a position when encouraged by others in a community discernment process.

Indeed, we as Mennonites seem to take pride, ironically, in our concept of servant leadership.

But this is the easy part. Criticizing people on the subject of humility is not difficult.

What is much harder is to speak of humility in a meaningful way. And I believe there is value in the concept of humility when it speaks to equality and mutuality. For Mennonites, humility is closely linked to community, and deservedly so.

What I suggest is that we change the definition. Instead of humility being an absence of our own significance, I see humility as the belief in the importance of people besides ourselves.

Think of it as one part respect, one part empathy. To be humble is to assume others are more like us than they are different from us.

For Mennonites, this slight twist carries large ramifications, for the very definition of ourselves is to be separate, and thus different, than the rest of the world.

I'm not advocating eliminating authentic distinctiveness in a broad sweep. In fact, Mennonites can tie themselves into knots trying to decide if articulating our "differences" keeps us humble or makes us too proud. (For more details, talk to anyone working in marketing for Mennonite institutions.)

What I'm talking about is an underlying assumption of how we view ourselves in relationship to others.

Seeing humility as less about meekness and more about empathy would change how we relate to each other within the Mennonite church as well. If we believe that the deeply held convictions of others are as important as our own, we would handle conflict better.

That is not to say the outcomes of our organizational disputes and theological disagreements would necessarily be different. But we would emerge as different people. Less grumpy. Less wounded.

I find that respecting others is one of the most difficult tasks I attempt from day to day. But to me it is a calling. It is what Christ asked us to do: love our neighbors as we love ourselves.

Ardie S. Goering lives in Albuquerque, New Mexico.

Toward a Culture
of Global Understanding
by Pakisa K. Tshimika

We as Mennonite Brethren (MB) around the world
consider ourselves to be members of one family of
faith despite being from many different nations,
tribes, and people groups. We become one family of
faith when we profess Christ as our personal Savior,
in spite of different ways of contextualizing our
shared doctrine.

While visiting India in November 1998, an older
woman we met on the road to a local church asked
me if Elsie Ann and Werner Kroeker were my parents. I am much closer in skin tone to the Southern
Indians than I am to the Kroekers, but for some reason she thought of me as belonging to the Kroekers'
family. Did she see something that we, as members of
the MB family of faith, do not usually see?

The Current Meaning of "Belonging"
Currently, most expressions of our global belonging
are related to material aid, financial assistance, mission outreach, and crisis management. Mennonite
Brethren from around the world have sent prayers,
funds, and people in the wake of crises such as the

Japan earthquake, conflict in India, Angola, and the Democratic Republic of Congo, and flooding in Latin America.

A new way of expressing our global belonging was introduced in 1997, when the Esengo music group from Congo brought joy to those who heard them in North America, India, and Japan, and brought the Democratic Republic of Congo into the households of their hosts.

These experiences are expressions of our belief in rejoicing with those who rejoice and mourning with those who are mourning. Structurally, the development of the International Committee of Mennonite Brethren (ICOMB) in recent years is a way of building conference to conference relationship rather than always using intermediaries from the North to reach other conferences either from the North or the South.

The Ingredients of Friendship

African people believe that a true friend is seen in time of suffering. But single-sided assistance is not a sign of a true friendship either. What are the key ingredients of a culture of belonging?

1. Covenant Relationship: The case of Ruth and Naomi is a good example: two people and two cultures meeting with an engagement in which each other's people and culture are accepted. Can such a relationship be developed between our respective conferences?

2. Mutual Respect: Lack of understanding about each other's cultures or languages should not be used as a major obstacle for developing a sense of belonging. I have yet to discover two people meeting, not knowing each other's language, who go away from each other without a minimum level of communication.

Financial and material goods cannot be appreciated when perceived as being cold gifts given out of guilt. What counts is the spirit with which the gift is given. People from the South can also learn to provide for those from the North. The South has more than it would like to admit, even in terms of finances.

3. Mutual Accountability: We need to develop a system of checks and balances for each other in all areas of our lives, which can only develop when one is accepted fully as a member in a given community.

I dream of a day when international students are accepted in churches as full members rather than people who are passing through, and when *all* our missionaries will be ready to be full members of church fellowships in their countries of service.

4. People Rather Than Structures: Institutional and structural relationships are very important—but only as they facilitate relationships between people and communities of faith. As I write this article, Elmer Martens is teaching at a school here in Kinshasa. He was not sent by any institution, but came out of a personal belief in being part of a larger family of faith. During the same time period, a group of eight people from European and Canadian congregations are visiting the Congo Mennonite churches to assess ways of building people-to-people relationships, with the French language as the glue that brings people together. Many other kinds of glue could be explored to connect different people from our different cultures.

5. Learning To Be Rather Than Always Doing: At a wedding or wake ceremony in the Democratic Republic of Congo, people share space and feelings without having to express anything verbally. Just sharing the "joy or pain space" is all that might be needed. As with anything else, this can be learned with discipline and practice.

From Ideals to Practice

So what are some practical things we could do to move toward this culture of belonging?

People to people covenanting: Common interest, such as professional background, can be the glue that brings together people from different cultures.

Institutional covenanting: Twinning our respective training institutions can be a wonderful tool for developing a true sense of belonging and learning to help each other in other areas of our lives.

International study conferences: I can see a day when our different conferences get together to tackle common issues while keeping in mind each conference's distinctiveness. For example, issues related to leadership development are becoming crucial in all our conferences.

Common projects: Short-term missions programs could become even more meaningful if members from two or three conferences could be brought together to work in one of our conferences.

Many of these concepts are not new. What is needed is for us to apply what we believe in our daily lives. With a little effort, we could get there.

Pakisa Tshimika is Africa program director for Mennonite Brethren Missions Services (MBMS) International and currently lives in Fresno, California.

Mennonites and Music

by Isaac R. Horst

Sometimes it seems I have a mean streak in me. Whenever I come across anything written about Mennonites, I pull it apart at the seams to see how accurate or inaccurate it is. If I find something with which I agree, I pounce on it eagerly.

Sometimes such articles come from the most unlikely sources. A local police officer recently brought me a manuscript with the heading: "Mennonites and Music— Microsoft Internet Explorer." I must admit that my knowledge of the Internet is only a little less than the officer's knowledge of Mennonites—I hope.

I offer my responses to a series of quotations from this manuscript:

> Mennonite kids grow up making music an important part of their lives. It leads to a maturity of sound, and the ability to carry parts, and enjoy it. It's such a natural part of their environment that they are simply capable of doing things other people have to learn.

I agree. I have often been asked when I learned to sing a certain song. Often this precedes my memory.

Hundreds of songs I learned over seventy years ago from my dad as he sang while milking.

> Although Mennonites regard singing as integral to church life, an affinity was not immediately apparent at the beginning of the Anabaptist movement in the sixteenth century.

I doubt that. First, Paul and Silas prayed and sang praises unto God (Acts 16:25). The Anabaptists were disciples of Paul, so to speak. Why should they not sing as well? Second, the Anabaptists composed hymns in prison, so they must have had an early affinity for music. Third, in writings taken from the time of the Anabaptists, it was stated that they sang at their meetings. In fact, the *Ausbund* was already in use among the Anabaptists in 1564.

> Brought to North America in the early eighteenth century, this hymnal (the *Ausbund*) is still used by the Amish in the U.S., and the Amish and Old Order Mennonites in Canada.

Try again. The Amish, yes; but the Old Order Mennonites, no! The early Mennonite settlers in Ontario brought the *Unpartheyisches Gesangbuch* (Impartial hymnbook, 1804), the Lancaster Conference hymnal, with them from Pennsylvania. In 1836, a pocket-sized hymnbook, the *Gemeinschaftliche Liedersammlung* (Common hymn collection), was compiled and printed in Canada. This has become the exclusive hymnbook among the Ontario Old Order Mennonites.

> The Old Order Mennonites, a conservative group in southern Ontario, only permit unaccompanied unison singing.

Yes, at church services. At other informal singings there is unaccompanied four-part singing from English hymnbooks.

> There is concern today that the Mennonite emphasis on quality four-part singing may be dying out.

Not among the Old Order Mennonites, whether in Ontario, Pennsylvania, Virginia, or elsewhere. Perhaps it should not be called "quality" singing, but at least it continues to be a combination of worship service and pleasure, enjoyed by young and old.

> Music has long been important to Mennonite faith and life.

Amen. So shall it be.

"So you have an 'affinity for music'?"
I imagine that is what one could call it. I wouldn't like to say that I have the best voice, but I have always enjoyed singing. I was a song leader in church, as well as at singings. So were two of my brothers, my father, and my grandfather. I have the latter's hymnbook in my possession, which he used when a song leader in 1892.

"Did Benjamin Eby compile the *Gemeinschaftliche* hymnbook that was first printed in 1836?"
This is difficult to say. It is commonly supposed that he did, since he had an interest in the printery. Many of the hymns originated in Lutheran or Reformed hymnals. Whenever the composer's identity is not given with a hymn, it was likely composed by Mennonites.

"Are these hymnals used only in Ontario, by the Old Order?"

They are also used by the Old Order Mennonites in Elkhart County, Indiana.

"Are there still singing schools in operation among the Old Order Mennonites?"

Yes, although it is not necessarily practiced on a regular basis. There is always enough interest in singing schools to warrant their existence. Yet sometimes there is a lack of teachers. Our young people have singings every Sunday evening. There is always good singing at weddings, family gatherings, and frequently at nursing homes and with shut-ins.

Isaac R. Horst is an Old Order Mennonite writer from Ontario.

Closed
on Sundays

by Arthur Bert

"No, we won't be open tomorrow—it's Sunday. No, I haven't changed my mind about that."

This little dialogue or variations of it became a matter of routine for me after I made the decision that my restaurant would no longer be open on Sunday. When one has served a local community seven days a week for 18 years, the patterns of the "regulars" become pretty well established. And these patterns don't go down without a struggle.

Sunday has always been the busiest day of the week for us—the most traffic, the biggest sales. We were busy from the time we set up our breakfast buffet at 7 a.m. until we cleared out the last after-church dessert group after 9 p.m.

Toughest Day of the Week

Sunday was also the most difficult day of the week—the day when the end of your shift just couldn't come soon enough. Part of that was due to the heavy customer flow. But there were other factors. It was the day that required the largest number of staff to maintain the operation, but also the day that the most people wanted to be off. It was the day that I typically got the most last-minute calls from staff members who were "sick." For unknown reasons even the ice machine was the most troublesome on Sundays, as if it too needed a rest!

And our customers were noticeably more demanding and less pleasant on Sundays! I won't go into my theories on this phenomenon, but in discussing it with others in the retail/service field I have found that I am not alone in that observation.

It finally became perfectly clear to me that this is not what Sunday is supposed to be about. On Monday morning, July 6, 1998, I informed my customers and staff of my decision to close on Sundays and it went into effect immediately.

I should say here that this was a move I had considered two years earlier for all the same reasons. At that time I carefully studied my sales records and statistics—that's what prudent business people do—and came away telling myself there was no way I could close on Sunday. This time I intentionally refused to study those charts; I knew what they would say. Instead I looked at my scheduling sheets and focused on the fact that it took 35-40 people to staff my restaurant on a Sunday. I don't kid myself that all those people will be in church, but I do know that it represents three dozen people who now are able to be in church or to spend the day with their families or friends. I knew this was the right thing for me to do.

A Price to Pay

I knew there would be a price to pay for this decision. I never assumed that God would in some way multiply my business the rest of the week so I wouldn't miss the Sunday sales. And he has not. I knew that our profit at the end of the year would reflect this rash decision. And it did. I'm still convinced it was the right thing for me as an individual Christian in business to do.

The reactions to this decision have been varied, sometimes affirming and sometimes frustrating. Response from my customers can be sorted into three groups.

The supporters represent the smallest group. I've enjoyed hugs, handshakes, and cards of appreciation from fellow Christians and business people who appreciate my reckless move. I've had similar affirmation from nonchurch people for "back to the family" kinds of reasons. I like this group a lot!

The next two groups are about equal in numbers. The more pleasant of the two wants to know why, and upon hearing my explanation they respond with something like, "We understand, but we will miss you." I've had some exciting and spontaneous faith discussions with individuals in this group, something that is typically not easy for me to do. That has been strengthening.

The last group is still angry with me! They too want to know why, but no answer will satisfy. It just doesn't make sense. I'm sad that this group includes a lot of churchgoers, some from my own congregation. A couple of them still hammer me when they encounter me in the narthex after our morning service. Besides the weekend travelers, we had always been a favorite place to eat before or after Sunday services. For this group I've spoiled all that. One gentleman pointed out that with church services spread all over the weekend from Saturday night through Sunday, everyone can get to church if they want to, and still put in a fair day's work.

Staff Reaction Was Mixed

How about my staff? The response there has also been mixed. I had a couple who were displeased because Sunday was the one day they could work since their spouses were home to take care of the kids. But the positive reactions are far more numerous. I have been surprised in the last months at how frequently a new job applicant will include the fact that we are closed on Sunday as a reason she or he is making application at our shop.

Roger (not his real name) was for me the most exciting result. Roger is 18 and always worked Sundays. I don't believe Roger came from any kind of church home and working on Sunday was no big deal to him. But the first Sunday we were closed, and every Sunday after that for several months, Roger was at my church with school friends in our youth department. I think this was God's way of telling me that if for only one person, this decision had been the right one.

Then there is another group—my own family! What a release to know that I don't have to go in to work, that no one else is at work, that I can attend church uninterrupted and spend the day with my family doing things we like to do. My wife, Donna, feels this every bit as keenly as I do.

Strictly speaking, I'm not sure what this has to do with ethics in business. I am pointedly not on a cru-

sade to say that it is sinful to do business on Sunday.
But for me as an individual Christian, to have continued "business as usual" seven days a week would
have been turning a deaf ear to God's leading in my
life. Closing on Sundays was the right thing to do.

Oh yes. What about the ice machine?
Unfortunately now it breaks down on Saturdays.

*Arthur Bert is a businessman from Grantham,
Pennsylvania. Since writing this article, Art has sold the
restaurant and the new owners have chosen to open again
on Sundays.*

What Families Should Value

by John D. Roth

In 1992, in the midst of a heated election-year campaign, U.S. Vice President Dan Quayle committed the
worst *faux pas* of his error-prone political career. In a
speech to journalists and media critics, Quayle publi-
cally challenged the way in which a TV sitcom called
Murphy Brown had casually dismissed the sanctity of
marriage when the main character—an unmarried,
career-oriented woman—decided to have a baby.

Predictably perhaps, Quayle's criticism of Murphy
Brown's "lifestyle choice"—that is, her easy separation
of sexual intercourse and parenthood from marriage—
aroused a chorus of derisive hoots and indignant
howls. But underneath all the jokes and outrage, one
thing became very clear: issues of marriage and
morality in our public culture are potentially explo-
sive landmines. They reveal hidden fault lines of conflict in our culture, and they spark disagreements that
go to the core of our deepest convictions and assumptions.

Must of the tempestuous public debate over family
values that ensued in the years following the *Murphy
Brown* speech has focused on the meaning of a series
of fundamental changes in the structure of the North
American family that have unfolded over the past

three or four decades. In 1960, for example, there were 35 divorced persons in the United States for every 1,000 married persons. Today there are closer to 140 for every 1,000, an increase of 400 percent. During the same period of time, the cohabitation rate—the percentage of couples living together outside of marriage—has increased by 1000 percent.

A parallel revolution has taken place in the separation of the institution of marriage from sexual relations and parental responsibilities. Today some 60 percent of teenage girls have experienced first sexual intercourse by the age of 18 (up from 35 percent in 1970), and they are sexually active, on average, for 7-8 years before marriage. The figures suggest that young men are even more sexually active at an even earlier age.

At the same time, sociologists have also tracked the rapid growth in the number of father-absent households, a sharp rise in households where both parents hold full-time jobs, and a very troubling correlation between single-parent households and drug use, dropout rates, emotional instability, and suicide among children (even when adjusted for other variables).

Seen together, these trends all suggest that the idealized traditional or nuclear family of the past can no longer be assumed as a statistical norm.

The public debate over family values during the past decade has focused less on the accuracy of these figures than on their significance and interpretation. In simplified terms, spokespersons for the religious conservatives have insisted that the rising tide of premarital sex, divorce, domestic violence, and child abuse reflect nothing less than a moral breakdown in American culture.

Only if local communities can re-instill moral values in our children—through a varied blend of educational programs, religious instruction, personal encouragement, and punitive sanctions—can these realities be reversed.

Liberal activists, on the other hand, are likely to dismiss this analysis as nostalgic at best and misguided or mean-spirited at worst. Rising divorce rates and new sexual liberties, they argue, are actually positive trends indicating greater gender equality for women and more personal freedom for the individual.

Moreover, if children have suffered negative consequences from these changes in family structure, then the fault lies not with individual parents, but with an unjust economic system that forces adults into low paying jobs without provision for adequate daycare, and continues to be heavily biased against women in terms of pay and promotion.

Communities such as the Mennonites have not been insulated from all this, either from the broader transformation in family structures or the intensity of debate surrounding the meaning of these changes. Though the statistics of family breakdown among Mennonites are clearly not as bleak as the national averages, it is also becoming clear that our idealized image of the agrarian Mennonite family—gathered in domestic harmony around the kitchen table for family worship and a hearty meal—no longer conforms to the reality of most Mennonite households.

Spiraling costs of health care and housing (to say nothing of the tuition at private high schools and colleges) have made it difficult, if not impossible, for families to maintain a household on one income alone. Families that have opted for university education and a career track know that the logic of modern capitalism often demands being mobile and transportable.

Uprooted and then replanted as the laws of supply and demand dictate, Mennonites in the professions are almost certainly less connected to their extended families of grandparents, uncles, aunts, and cousins. Their roots in local communities will also very likely be shallower than those of their parents.

Nor have our congregations been exempt from the deep confusion about sexuality and sexual expression that characterizes the broader culture. Although we have given significant energy to conversations about homosexuality in recent years, we invested nowhere nearly a comparable amount of attention in our sermons and after-church conversations to the realities of premarital sexuality, extra-marital sexuality, abortion, or cohabitation.

Yet in ways that we can scarcely recognize, our assumptions about romantic love and sexuality have been profoundly shaped by a culture of mass media that easily confuses our humanity with our bodies and our deep and natural craving for intimacy with sexual desire.

Paradoxically, at precisely the time when issues regarding marriage, sexuality, and parenting are fraying the fiber of our community, we are finding it increasingly awkward to speak about them openly in our congregations. Though we may have opinions about families *in general,* our high value on personal privacy makes it extremely difficult for the church to speak prophetically to specific matters within the congregation without appearing to meddle or to condemn.

In the absence of a clear framework for conversation and debate within the church over issues related to marriage, singleness, divorce, parenting, and sexuality, numerous families have found practical counsel on these issues in sources outside the denomination, such as James Dobson's *Focus on the Family,* Promise Keepers rallies, and dozens of publications by well-known evangelical authors.

To be sure, our congregations have largely been spared the polemical white-hot character of the public debate over family values, but the growing reality of divorce, teenage sex, single-parent households, abortion, and cohabitation has left congregations confused and divided in their responses.

At the risk of oversimplifying an extremely complex and multifaceted set of issues, I would like to propose three suggestions to consider as we engage issues related to the family. I offer these less as solutions for the issues at hand than as a framework for the necessary conversation and discernment that needs to take place if we are to hear God's voice amidst our current cultural confusion.

1. Redeem the language of commitment. Many Christians—and perhaps especially many Mennonites—have understood commitments in church or marriage to be a joyless matter of gritting their teeth and holding the course as a matter of human willpower and fortitude. The Anabaptist understanding of commitment, by contrast, begins with an invitation and a decision: the invitation is to a journey. The decision is to embark on that journey together in the recognition that we are united by the love of Christ, sustained by God's daily gift of grace, and supported by the presence and encouragement of our fellow travelers.

Christian commitments, be they in baptism, marriage, or parenting, do have genuine consequences: they quite consciously narrow our freedom and limit our choices. And yet—paradoxically, miraculously, wonderfully—we discover that it is precisely these commitments that give focus to our choices and a foundation for emotional growth and spiritual maturity.

In the context of the debate over family values, the language of commitment can easily slip into nostalgia or a heavy-handed moralism that is driven by guilt and obligation. But the genuinely good news of commitment in the Christian tradition is that the "yoke is easy and the burden is light." Made and sustained in community, commitments that endure the storms and stresses of change are a source of true joy.

2. Engage the debate over family values with conviction and compassion. Often lost in the contemporary debate over the complex questions of marriage and sexuality—even among Christians—is a sense of proportion between conviction and compassion. Christian discernment always begins with a sense of shared commitment to Christ and a willingness to engage the conversation with the goal of hearing God's word afresh.

In the conversation over issues related to the family, it should not surprise us that we are not all of one mind. Indeed, that is precisely why discernment is necessary. But as that debate unfolds, our congregations are called to the challenging task of tempering the clarity of deeply held convictions with the humility born out of Christian compassion.

At the heart of compassion, of course, is the idea of "co-passion," or shared passion—a willingness to enter genuinely into the thoughts and emotions of another person with a kind, gentle, and generous spirit. Not pity, but empathy is compassion's driving force: a readiness to suspend for a moment our own view of the world in order to listen carefully to the insights and experiences of someone else.

Compassion in our churches and in our marriages qualifies the language of rights and justice and suggests instead that we ask ourselves daily what it would mean to love each other as God loves us. We should pray for the gift of looking at everyone we encounter through the eyes of God.

Compassion does not assume that we relinquish our convictions or let go of the high standard of commitment. Indeed, it is precisely the clarity of our commitments that frees us, as compassionate families and churches, to absorb some of the world's pain, to bring healing where there is brokenness, and to open our doors and our lives to people beyond the ties of blood and marriage and ethnicity who are in need of good news.

But compassion, in the Christian context, does remind us of our own vulnerability and the ways in which all of us are sustained and embraced by God's free gift of grace. Commitment joined with compassion is a rare combination, but in our hard-edged world that is precisely why it is so urgently needed.

3. Think structurally, act locally. Finally, as we discern issues related to marriage and sexuality, let us become better aware of the deeper structural forces at work in our society without retreating from the challenge to act in small, concrete, and tangible ways.

Clearly, many of the problems in our society surrounding the family are deeply rooted in economic structures that make it difficult for many households to feed their children and have sufficient time and energy and resources left over to nurture meaningful relationships. Many family problems are rooted in patterns of addiction and abuse that cannot be quickly or easily resolved. But even as we recognize these larger structural realities, I hope that we will also not shrink back from working for change in our own local congregations and communities.

What might this mean concretely? I think compassionate families and churches will inevitably be porous in their boundaries—clear in their commitments, yet willing to resist the powerful impulses to privacy and self-absorption. I know, for example, of a local couple, moving toward retirement, who have consciously decided to rent their basement apartment to single moms with the idea that they can also serve as friends and mentors—a sounding board, a broader perspective, a point of contact with stable relationships that the people now living under their roof may have never experienced before.

I know of several older couples in my church who have become, in effect, surrogate grandparents for children in their neighborhoods, absorbing some of the reckless energy of a four-year-old on behalf of a harried, stressed-out parent, and providing a bright light of structure, attention, and unconditional love for children whose lives are otherwise filled with lots of uncertainty.

Our churches should be places where people broken by the pain of divorce can find healing, unity, and hope again. Families in our churches should be at the forefront of opening their homes to foster children— one of the most vulnerable and abused groups in North America today.

In the end, none of these specific suggestions—or even the larger strategies for engaging the issues— offers tidy solutions to the vexingly difficult questions that regularly present themselves in our congregations and communities. And yet in a culture deeply divided by the debate over family values, our churches can offer a creative alternative. Though we will likely not solve all the issues related to marriage and divorce, singleness and sexuality, parenting and grandparenting, it is possible that our commitments to each other can become a source of deep joy.

Our compassion-filled convictions are the foundation of Christian discernment, and our quiet deeds of kindness a gift of community to those who are alienated. Our efforts at addressing these issues are bold expressions of God's love and God's transforming grace to a hurting world.

John D. Roth, Goshen, Indiana, is a history professor and editor.

A Benedictine Mennonite: Prefer Nothing Whatever to Christ

by Arthur Paul Boers

As part of my spiritual discipline, I regularly study a spiritual classic that is heavily inspired by the Sermon on the Mount. It teaches about prayer, worship, nonresistance, community, not swearing oaths, loving enemies, mutual aid, Matthew 18's Rule of Christ, and the importance of faithful works.

This is no Anabaptist document (although I believe it inspired Anabaptists). The Rule of St. Benedict was written by an abbot in the sixth century as a guide to running monasteries. It became the prevailing guide for most monasteries in the West, second only to the Bible.

Many who are not monastics find that the theology and counsel of this spiritual treasure—in between advice on diets, bedtimes, kitchen work—has much to teach all Christians.

I have been going to an Anglican Benedictine monastery, St. Gregory's Abbey, since 1981. At times, especially on peaceful retreats, I fantasize about joining a monastery. But God calls me to be a Mennonite minister, husband, and father. When I remember that, my regular rhythm of retreats helps me to be more faithful in those commitments.

Longing to deepen that rhythm, I began several years ago to relate more intentionally with St. Gregory's. As a "confrater" (brother), I made a promise to live out Benedictine values, to love of God and neighbor, to prayer, humility, silence, creation, and life in Christ. Yet I wanted something more. I tested with the Abbot the possibility of being an oblate.

"Oblate" means "offering" and here implies offering one's life to God. Oblates live outside the monastery but are accountable to a monastery for how they live out their spiritual commitments.

Intriguingly, while monasteries have increasing difficulty attracting new monks, the number of oblates is growing. Kathleen Norris (a Presbyterian) did more than anyone to celebrate what it means to be an oblate with her book, *The Cloister Walk.*

The Abbot was clear that my oblation would mean strengthening my commitment to the church I serve and to my family. It would mean living by the Benedictine motto "ora et labora" (pray and work). This calls for a practical spirituality that balances work with prayer and worship (both corporate and individual).

Being Benedictine means:

- Being involved with the church and encouraging Christian community.
- Being committed to continual self-improvement and renewal (spiritually, intellectually, culturally, through prayer, retreats, and study).
- Growing in ministry to others, especially by learning contentment, patience, generosity, and hospitality.

- Growing in virtues, with special attention to wisdom, prudence, justice, fortitude, and moderation.
- Being peacemakers. A Benedictine watchword is "pax" (peace). Benedict saw nonresistance as a primary step of growth in the Christian life. Joan Chittister, a nun, says that nonviolence is the center of the monastic life.
- Practicing accountability and seeking guidance in one's Christian life.

As part of my testing of whether I was called to be an oblate, I submitted my personal rule (or discipline) for spiritual life and reported regularly on how my commitment was going.

I discovered that promising before others to stay faithful encouraged me when I was tempted not to pray. And when I do pray, I know I am upheld by the prayers of brother monks (just as I pray for them). Never have I been offered such support by other Christians.

After a year and a half as an "aspirant," I became an Oblate Novice. This was a further time of discernment by both the monastery and me. I received a monastic name, "Brother Barnabas." After a year and a half, at a worship service in the monastery with my family present, I did my oblate profession. This is a life-long commitment.

Being an oblate deepened all the other important commitments I have made: baptism, marriage, family, ordination. For many years I explored different forms of intentional Christian community, but either I or the group did not endure. Now I am part of a community that is over 1,500 years old.

I am not alone. I am in contact with other
Mennonites who are Benedictine oblates. Some people wonder whether being a Benedictine Mennonite is
a contradiction. But Anabaptism has much in common with monasticism. Many Anabaptist leaders
received spiritual formation as monks.

Spiritual Cousins

Anabaptists and monastics are at least spiritual
cousins. We see their reliance on similar scripture passages, especially the Sermon on the Mount, Matthew
18, and Acts descriptions of common life.
Monasticism, like Anabaptism, is rooted in protest
against compromise in the culture and the church.

Anabaptist, like the original monastics, showed sus-
picion toward clergy. Monasticism was originally a
movement of lay Christians, and clergy were not
encouraged to apply!

Schleitheim, the first Anabaptist confession, reiter-
ates many themes of the Rule of Benedict. (Hardly
surprising, as one of its primary authors, Michael
Sattler, was formerly a Benedictine official.)
Anabaptists were accused of being "new monks."
They encouraged all believers to live up to the
Sermon on the Mount's high "standards of perfection"
which were previously considered the responsibility
only of monastics.

As well as affirming my Anabaptism, through my
oblation I made deeper connections with the wider
church. Benedictinism is ecumenical. Benedictines are
in a good position for fostering Christian unity
because their foundation and inspiration go back
beyond the schism between the eastern and western

church, and the controversies which split western Christendom in the sixteenth century.

Benedict reminds us that God's "divine presence is everywhere." That is one reason for all his practical advice (which resonates well with both my Dutch heritage and my chosen Anabaptism). Norvene Vest, an oblate, notes that Benedict "truly believes that our sanctification is realized in our daily choices and habits." Benedict taught us, as did Anabaptists later, to translate God's "holy teachings" into action.

All of my Benedictine commitments are summarized in my desire to "seek God." The monastery helps me and is, in Benedict's words, a "school of the Lord's service," a place that teaches me, inspires me, and calls me to be a better Christian.

Ever since I was a child, I believed that if Christianity is true then it must be the most important aspect of one's life. Thus I continually remind myself, in Benedict's words, to "prefer nothing whatever to Christ." My oblation as a Benedictine Mennonite compels me to be more faithful to this challenge. "Ora et Labora."

Arthur Paul Boers, Waterloo, Ontario, is a writer and Mennonite pastor.

Micah,
My Twin

by Robert J. Baker

Being honest can be pretty expensive.

Recently it cost me $1,100. But I wrote the check cheerfully and handed it to the person to whom I had owed it for the past 15 years. That person had never mentioned it to me; in fact, I don't think that person even thought I owed it. But I knew I did.

I was reminded of that past debt, the need to make restitution, as I was reading Judges 17. That's another thing: Reading the Bible can be dangerous. To me it is amazing how practical the Bible can be, how it can embarrass one and remind one of past or present sins. The number relationship between Micah's sin and mine is remarkable. He stole 1,100 sheckels from his mother and repaid it, while it cost me $1,100 to make things right with my wife and repay a debt I had weaseled out of 15 years ago.

Making restitution is not new with me. Fifty years ago I straightened out two cases God reminded me of, cases that went back to when I was a teenager. I squared both away. One was for sneaking into a football game at Goshen High School; another was for swiping an old rusty, iron pipe from behind a place of

business and selling it for junk. I sent money through
the mail to both the school and the place of business
to clear my conscience.

The biggie, the $1,100 restitution? You would like
to hear about that one? Don't blame you.

About 15 years ago, my wife, Anna Mae, was heavily involved as the state treasurer for the Woman's
Christian Temperance Union (WCTU) of Indiana.
Early in her work she saw how a paper copier would
be of great help to the project she had undertaken.
She approached me about purchasing one from our
joint checking account. It would cost close to $1,000. I
did my own copying at the library for ten cents a
sheet. "Sorry, Anna Mae, it doesn't sound like a good
investment to me."

Another tactic of the good wife. She had, in addition to our joint checking account, a small one of her
own that came from an inheritance and a small gratu-
ity from the WCTU for her treasurer's work. What if
she purchased a Canon PC-20 copier, lowering her
personal checking account $1,000.

It did not take me long to see the advantage, to take
advantage, of having a copier at my instant disposal. I
needed manuscript copies, copies of readings, and
handouts for Sunday school class. Naturally, Anna Mae
made her copier available. I jokingly offered to pay her
ten cents per copy, but, of course, she sweetly refused.

Over the years, I used the copier more and more,
often thinking of how great a blessing it was, a great
gas and time saver, and a help to others in our family
and church friends.

Moreover, with increasing frequency over the 15
years, especially as I stood there using the copier, my

conscience assailed me. While the faithful PC-20
rolled out my copies, it seemed to hum, to strum out
a little tune, directed personally at me:

> Bob Baker, Bob Baker,
> Skinflint supreme:
> Isn't it time,
> Your sin to redeem?

> You owe your good wife
> For this great machine:
> Cough up a thousand,
> You skinflint supreme.

So, on January 5, 2000, I handed Anna Mae a
check for $1,100. I said with shame, "I want to get
this off my conscience. The copier cost should have
come out of our joint account. The extra $100 is for
interest. Put this in your personal account."

Anna Mae, surprised, smiled, accepted, and
thanked me.

Today, when I use our copier, I flinch at the past
and smile at the present. Making restitution can be
embarrassing, but it is also satisfying and releasing.
Plus the copier no longer shames me with its skinflint
tune.

Robert J. Baker is a writer living in Bristol, Indiana.

Living on the Iceberg: "The Artist as Critic and Witness" 36 Years Later

by Rudy Wiebe

For three weeks during the summer of 1999 I was part of a Geological Survey of Canada camp on the northeastern coast of Ellesmere Island, in one of the many areas of our giant country where no human beings have lived for at least a thousand years. From the gravel beaches of the Nares Strait, which at that point narrowly separates Canada from Greenland, I watched the winter sea ice gradually shatter into pans and drift south; often its flatness was studded by icebergs broken away from some immense glacier even farther north, that sailed imperceptibly by like white craggy islands lost forever to the ocean blazing blue in the niveous summer sun. But there was one iceberg, not discernibly larger than the rest and despite all the ice grinding past, which remained motionless in the middle of the channel; obviously, it was grounded. After some days I began to feel I wanted to stand there, on it. It was not until several months after I had returned to my home in Edmonton that my imagination penetrated what, beyond the cold facticity of ice, I had been looking at, and felt.

Much of the fiction I have written in the last four decades rests on facticity—or perhaps I had better say *hinges* ("rests" implies far too much fixedness—too grounded, if you please), much of the fiction I write hinges on *facticity*: data such as exact dates, precise places quite accurately described, the actual acts that living people have (insofar as they can still be established) literally, historically, done. In fact (!), I have often found far more imaginative stimulus in such historical, geographical data than in any fictional structure I might invent—though I do love inventiveness. My thinking often goes: why expend energy in concocting a world and people (as speculative fiction does, for example) when we actually live in such a marvelously evocative one already, one more dense with mystery and secrets and contradictions than anything most of us most of the time could possibly make up?

So, let me offer you a further, personal, fact (not a factoid): on the day I turned 28, October 4, 1962, I received in Winnipeg from my publisher McClelland and Stewart in Toronto, copies of my first novel, *Peace Shall Destroy Many*. Further copies appeared in Canadian bookstores at the same time, and after that many people asked me two questions:

1) "Why did you write a novel?"
2) "Is it true?"

That is one of the things I liked about the literary scholar Bill Smyth of Elora, Ontario: he never asked me those questions. Of course, Dr. Smyth was an intelligent and highly skilled reader from whom you might not expect such queries, but I can assure you that numerous literary scholars have asked me exactly those questions, albeit using somewhat longer words such as "autobiographical" or "historiographic meta-fictions."

The fact is, Bill Smyth never asked me, personally, any question at all, and the first I heard of him was in a typically cryptic note of two sentences which John Howard Yoder wrote me from Notre Dame University on June 11, 1995. The first sentence (the second, and last, referred to a completely different matter) John wrote was: "Dear Rudy: Just met one T. W. Smyth who seems to have a good grasp of your work." Among other things, that is what I greatly admire about the scholar in whose honor this lectureship is established: it seems he read the novels with great intensity, and whatever they told him, that he dealt with; he did not contact me—as he easily might have—and expect me to give reasons for actions per-petrated perhaps thirty years ago which are often as inexplicable to me now as anything I might have imagined then. Indeed, if I answer at all now, I have to make it up—as I sometimes do, especially in quick media interviews.

Smyth studied the text, as it stands, or as it falls—no matter—the novel text is what matters, not what the writer can elaborate about it half-a-lifetime after the fact. He did what I have at times advised scholars to do: "If you want to, write about what is published, but leave me personally out of it; just pretend I'm dead."

Well, time inevitably, and certainly, teaches us our mortality. But in 1962 I was too young to think that way. Besides, a Mennonite novelist was such an oddity, especially to Mennonites themselves, that speaking personally was demanded, and though I resolutely kept silent for six months after publication, I did write a piece about writing my first novel for the weekly newspaper *The Canadian Mennonite* (April 11, 1963), though I prefaced my short comments with a careful:

> Any work of art worth the name . . . bears within itself its reason for existence and its own justification . . If (*Peace Shall Destroy Many*) does not say it [that is, explain *why* it exists], (then) why burden a dead matter with the appendage of an explanation?

Five months later, however, I was a professor of English at Goshen College, Indiana, an institution sponsored by the Mennonite Church, and so, more than ever, I was expected to speak professionally, or as it were, "professingly," about what I wrote; I tried to do that, in an arm's-length, third person kind of way, in an invited lecture first given in November, 1963 at Tabor College, Kansas (a college sponsored by a different branch of Mennonite church), entitled "The Christian as Novelist."

In the following year this talk metamorphosed itself variously and was finally published in 1965 under the more encompassing title of "The Artist as a Critic and a Witness" (*Christian Living*, Scottdale, Pa., March, 1965; an earlier, and lengthier, incarnation appeared somewhat later in print, in *The Journal of Church and Society*, Fresno, California, v. 1, n. 2, Fall, 1965). To judge from his footnotes, Dr. Smyth used the *Christian Living* form of this essay as a certain basis in reading my novels, and, when considering this lecture, I thought it might be interesting to look at the essay again after all these decades.

If I may quote myself from an unpublished lecture called "Words to the End of the World" (1982):

> In his essay, "The Wind at Djemila," Albert Camus writes:
>
> A man lives with a few familiar ideas, two or three at the most, and here and there, in contact with the world and men, they are polished, shaped, changed. It takes years for a man to evolve an idea he can call his own, one he can speak of with authority.
>
> I take the term "a few familiar ideas" to refer to large concepts, the great bones and spinal cord that hold an individual's human shape erect in the factual and ideological confusion of contemporary life.

So now, if Camus is right, can I in 1999, beginning with ideas first expressed in 1963, can I see any imaginative evolvement of "a few familiar ideas" in the hundreds of thousands of fictional words I have since written?

(As a predictive aside: if no discernible imaginative change has taken place in my thinking and writing since 1963, then we are all wasting our time, me writing, you reading.)

The piece "The Artist as a Critic and a Witness" tries to explicate three fundamental principles about art:

1) that the work itself, not the artist as a person or a personality, is the crucial matter in artistic creation;

2) that there is no one, single "meaning" to a complex artistic work. "Its meaning depends upon the interaction between the work and beholder";

3) that there is an inherent moral quality in all art. "Literature is never amoral; it is either moral or immoral. Bad art is inevitably immoral."

It seems to me that in 1963 I had a much clearer concept of both morality and meaning in art than I have now; certainly a much more dogmatic one. I went on to speak specifically about the novel (the art form I am still struggling with), and asserted that the novelist was not a teacher of anything because the medium (that is, the art form itself) did not allow it, and that in order for the novelist to be a critic of and a witness to society, he must *allow the novel to be a novel*, that is, not try to make it a propagandizing or sermonic instrument but rather let it speak:

1) through the metaphor of story;

2) by showing life as it truly is. That meant, showing us man (I meant all human beings, of course) both as he is and as he may be. "The artist must have the guts to look at everything man can do, in his best moments as well as his worst. He cannot allow himself to be stared down by life."

This is a hasty summary of what I said in 1963, and it still rings basically true. What seems clear now is that, after publishing one novel, I had learned at least one irreducible fact.

The controversy *Peace Shall Destroy Many* created in the Mennonite community taught me once and for all that, to a very large extent, *every reader reads their own novel.* If you can imagine the writer as an organ-master playing a concert on the pipe-organ consciousness of the reader, then not even the greatest of masters— Tolstoi or Faulkner or Dickens, or take your pick—ever plays exactly the same concert twice: every pipe-organ-reader is simply too drastically different to sound the same.

But, however prescient these principles in that 1963 talk were, I did not understand their implications for trying to live a writer's life. However separated writer and fictional text may be, the writer's personality is nevertheless absolutely crucial to the text: every text begins (as creative writing instructors always underline) with "what the writer knows," *but* that is simply the beginning. What I understand from over forty years of writing fiction is that the best texts go on into what the writer does not, indeed cannot, know when beginning to write. To speak personally, the fiction must move into worlds that perhaps I don't like, that I wouldn't ever want to explore, perhaps could not even have imagined existed until fiction itself forced them into visibility. In other words, "Write what you know" is barely a doorstep into the house of fiction— better we should say "mansion of fiction" or "skyscraper," because certainly fiction at its most magnificent is always a building complex and immense beyond any of our known conceptions, and that includes the writer.

Oddly enough, it was the book which I wrote together with Yvonne Jackson, *Stolen Life: the Journey of a Cree Woman* (1998), which forced me to realize this most clearly. The book is called nonfiction because it tells the facts Yvonne remembers of her literal life, and also the facts of my searching it out with her, an overwhelming and wrenching life which, truly, I would not, could not, have imagined on my own. And oddly, in a similar way, I realized that the fiction I have tried to write all my adult life is also

that: though I always began with "what I knew," or at
least thought I knew, as each particular fiction developed, I always at some point found myself trying to
write what for me was, in the first place, unknown
and therefore, through ignorance, essentially unimag-
inable. The act of making fiction made the knowledge
for the imagining unavoidable.

In that sense, writing *Peace Shall Destroy Many* gave
me small experience for writing any subsequent fiction. Following the concept of "write what you know,"
I wrote the last chapter of that novel first; then,
knowing the end, I backed up just far enough until I
had a beginning from which I could get the whole
story in to explain the ending I had already made.
Simple, eh? That—and inexperience, of course—was
why I could write it so fast: I began in July, 1959 and
by March, 1960 it was finished. At one point I re-
wrote a complete draft in 2½ months.

Well, may the Creator be praised, writing novels is
not a stopwatch competition with Donovan Bailey. It
is not speed but nerve that counts, the courage of
your imagination in exploring the black, mysterious,
mostly opaque room of the house of fiction that opens
before you, a room, you gradually realize, which cannot and will never exist in any human imagination
unless you and *you alone go in there* and explore it.

The other implication of the writer principles I
could not quite comprehend in 1963 was the one
about not letting life stare you down. Again, trying to
put Yvonne's life into words proved to me, in my soul
as in my digestion, how grotesquely difficult that can
be. You will understand if I mention one of the most
unbearable human events of this century: how do you

write about the holocaust? The ancient Jewish tradition that speaking about evil may in itself evoke that very evil, so great is the power of language—well, what if you write about it? Not only hear the words, but hold them in black and white before your eyes, make an indelible record which can be looked at and *contemplated* again and again? Should one actually remember, look into the very face of such absolute evil? Is writing about it not dignifying it? The "better" you write, is it not possible you will so much the more awaken, stir, that very spirit of inexpressible evil within yourself, and within your reader? Therefore, must you—as so many survivors have found it necessary—must everyone remain silent?

Thousands of European refugees came to Canada after the war, and around 1950 in the prairie town of my teens I remember that, among many others, three Mennonite refugee sisters arrived with some seven or eight children between them, but no husbands. The oldest boys were my age, their fathers had been destroyed by the war, and their mothers as I saw them were beautiful women. They came to Canada sponsored by our church, and there was a time when I heard one male church member say to another about those three: "I wonder what they did to make it through the war."

I do not know, now, whether it was an older or a younger man speaking, or if perhaps he said, "I wonder what they had to do to make it through the war." But no matter, his meaning was in his tone; that tone makes those words indelible still, a half century later.

I once asked my friend Harry Loewen if his mother had ever talked about what happened to her, personally, on their trek in 1943 from the Ukraine with the retreating German armies, of being overrun by the Red Army, of their years in hiding and the eventual refugee camps. He told me essentially what he wrote in a book he edited called *Road to Freedom* (to be published in September, 2000):

> "Mennonite women were willing and able to describe vividly many aspects of the terror they experienced, except for their sexual victimization. I know my mother knew much about this horrific aspect of the war, but she never spoke about it even when I asked her directly to tell me."

So, nothing remains except to say, with Hamlet, "The rest is silence"?

But—human beings are animals that talk; for me, language is what makes us as god-like as we can conceive of God to be; in *Genesis* Elohim creates our entire world by his spoken Word. For human beings to remain wordless in the face of the greatest evil that humanity can perpetrate upon itself is to deny humanity its greatest gift: the very image of God in us. As a writer, a human being who all his life has tried to make things with words, I *must* dare to explore my greatest terror, even as it may prove to be my greatest ignorance. I may well make a grotesque mess of it— but I must try, or indeed, as Jesus himself told us, the very stones will cry out against me.

When I left Ellesmere Island on July 17, 1999, all the pack-ice of the Nares Strait had streamed south, but the solitary iceberg remained in its spot, grounded. I had tried to persuade our helicopter pilot to fly me there; I had never, I told him, touched an iceberg. But he refused.

"Any weight on it, it could shift, roll, and you're sliding hell-and-gone for ice water."

"So hover, I'll stand with one leg on a pontoon."

He laughed; like every pilot I've met, he knew himself to be in absolute control of his particular mechanical world, and he did not bother answering me. But late one afternoon, after the helicopter had been repaired for a malfunction and he was testing it with the mechanic aboard, he roared way low over the strait and landed on the iceberg; when they returned, he had a jug of water collected from its surface pools: perfect, clear water, totally empty of taste in its niveous purity. I found it hard to forgive him.

Could one live on an iceberg the way a writer lives on fiction?

Purely; obsessively; trying to speak the hitherto unspeakable, to inscribe the hitherto unfaceable until both become the writer's and reader's unknowable but nevertheless determining mystery, as the genetic codes in our every cell determine our ancestry even as they focus our imagination? The ineffable joy of being a writer even as the iceberg of fiction breaks loose at last from its stolid grounding in sea-bottom mud and moves out between landmasses into the immense waters that girdle the earth, even as it sails on into its slow, inevitable, and human, dissolution.

*Rudy Wiebe, Edmonton, Alberta, is the author of many works of fiction and nonfiction. He received the Governor General's Award for two of his novels—*The Temptations of Big Bear *(1973) and* A Discovery of Strangers *(1994).*

A Sermon

Who Is
the Greatest
in the Kingdom?

by David Ewert

One of the passages given to me for our Bible
Study Series, was Matthew 18:1-5. It's a rather embarrassing passage. That the Evangelists felt led to report
such embarrassing events, as the one described in this
text, speaks volumes for the trustworthiness of the
Gospels.

Although none of the Twelve is mentioned by
name, the disciples, we are told, came to Jesus and
asked: Who is the greatest in the kingdom of heaven?
How shameful, we say, how puerile! Of course, we
are far too sophisticated to ask this question so brash-
ly, so blatantly. But, if we are completely honest with
ourselves, perhaps that question is a mirror in which
all of us can see ourselves. And so, we are dealing
with a rather uncomfortable question: Who is the
greatest in the kingdom?

The Context of the Question
   1. The Temporal Context. "In that hour." The
word "hour" is not to be understood in its literal sense

of 60 minutes. It is used rather in the sense of "shortly after," or simply, "at that time."

Jesus and his disciples had just returned from Caesarea Philippi, where Peter had confessed his Master as "the Messiah, the Son of the living God." From that time on, Jesus becomes explicit about his suffering and death. He is on his way to Jerusalem, where he will be utterly put to shame; he will die with other criminals on a cross.

According to the parallel in Mark 9, it was while Jesus was teaching his disciples about his coming betrayal, his humiliation, his death, that a dispute broke out among his disciples over who was greatest among them. Matthew doesn't mention this dispute; perhaps he found that event too embarrassing. He simply reports the question: Who is the greatest in the kingdom?

If ever a question was ill-timed, it was this one. In the shadow of the cross, when Christ would humble himself and be obedient unto death, the disciples were arguing over who was the greatest among them.

2. The Geographical Context. Jesus and his followers had come down from the Mount of Transfiguration and had returned to Capernaum (Mt. 17:24), the city which served as the geographical center of Jesus' ministry, although he will always be called "Jesus of Nazareth," not "Jesus of Capernaum."

Precisely where in Capernaum they were lodging is not stated, but since Peter had a house in this city, and since they had gathered there on an earlier occasion when Jesus healed Peter's mother-in-law, some Bible readers suggest that they may have been in Peter's and Andrew's house.

3. The Literary Context. Matthew has divided his Gospel into five major sections, in which narrative and discourse regularly alternate. The discourses all conclude with the formula "when Jesus had finished saying these things."

Our text is part of the fourth of the five discourses in Matthew. It has often been suggested that Matthew had the five books of the Pentateuch in mind when he structured his Gospel in this rather interesting manner. Was the Pentateuch, with its laws for the old people of God, the backdrop for the ethical norm, according to which the new people of God were to live? There is, of course, no correlation between the contents of the five books of Moses and the five divisions of Matthew's Gospel.

Some scholars have seen parallels between the *Manual of Discipline,* found at Qumran, and Matthew 18. In the Qumran community, rank was very important. For example in IQS ii. 19-25 we have a paragraph that begins this way: "First the priests shall enter . . . according to their spiritual quality, . . . after them the Levites, . . . and thirdly, the whole people . . . that every single Israelite may know his standing place, i.e. his rank, in God's community . . ."

It should not be thought, however, that Matthew drew upon the *Manual of Discipline* as a source. Moreover, the emphasis in Matthew 18 runs counter to this emphasis on rank.

In our chapter, Matthew brings together a number of sayings of Jesus that appear to have been spoken at different times. With these few comments on the temporal, geographical, and textual context, we turn next to considering what may have prompted the disciples to put their question to Jesus.

The Prompting of the Question

Biblical scholars are not entirely agreed on what may have given rise to this rather selfish question: Who is the greatest in the kingdom of heaven?

1. One suggestion is that the disciples were a bit upset about the overwhelming promise our Lord had just recently given to Peter. After Peter had made his great confession about Christ's messiahship, Jesus explained that flesh and blood had not revealed this to him, but rather Christ's Father in heaven. And then followed the promise: "You are Peter, and on this rock I will build my church and the ages of Hades will not prevail against it"—a saying that is usually toned down in its force in Protestant circles because of anti-Catholic sentiments.

2. Another suggestion is that the question about who is the greatest in the kingdom was prompted by what had happened on the Mount of Transfiguration, an event that had just taken place. Peter, James, and John, the famous apostolic trio, had been singled out once again and had been with Jesus when he was transfigured. And again, Peter had been the speaker, (although Mark says Peter didn't really know what he was talking about). The other disciples had been left behind and had failed to cure the demon-possessed boy.

3. Some scholars feel that the discussion on the payment of the temple tax, which is reported immediately prior to our text, again focused on Peter. Jesus asks him, "What do you think, Simon? From whom do the kings of the earth take toll and tribute?"

Whatever else may have prompted it, this is a question that doesn't really need too much to incite it. Jealousy and envy are what Peter calls "works of the flesh," expressions of our sinful nature, and although we may not verbalize the question—who is the greatest in the kingdom?—it tends to lie very close to the surface in all of us. We need to temper our condemnation of the disciples for asking this rather childish question.

The Perverseness of the Question

By asking this question, the disciples indicate clearly that they had not yet grasped the fundamental message of Jesus, that of the kingdom of heaven. They were still thinking in traditional Jewish terms. When the Messiah would come, he would restore the kingdom to Israel; he would clear the land of evildoers; with the help of the angels he would push the Romans into the Mediterranean. The Messiah would inherit David's throne; he would be a king or a mighty Warrior (as the Song of Solomon portrays his message).

To be sure, he would be a king, but as Jesus explained when he stood before Pilate: "My kingdom is not of this world. If it were, then my followers would fight." To realize the messianic age, the disciples seemed to believe that the princely, kingly line was central. But they had overlooked the fact, that the Messiah was also to be a suffering Servant.

The kingdom which Jesus had come to establish was not a political kingdom, where rank plays an important role. The question—who is the greatest in the kingdom of heaven—is quite perverse, for it shows that those asking it had not yet grasped the message of Jesus.

The expression "kingdom of the heavens," which Matthew uses regularly, is, of course, the "kingdom of God." "Heaven" was one of a number of surrogate terms for the word "God," whose name was so holy that persons tended to use it rather infrequently, and to use substitutes, such as "the power," "the highest," or simply "the heavens."

And the word kingdom (*basileia*) means kingly rule, the reign of the king, and has nothing to do with land or territory. Jesus had come to establish the reign of God. God, of course, does not reign in a vacuum. He reigns over people who acknowledge him as King, over the members of his church, the new people of God.

The disciples ask, who is the greatest in the kingdom of heaven? This question showed that they did not yet understand what God's kingdom was all about. Even after the resurrection of Jesus, they are still caught asking, "Will you at this time restore the kingdom to Israel?" They were hoping, no doubt, that they would belong to the King's inner circle, his cabinet. In the verses just previous to our text, Jesus had spoken of them as "sons of the kingdom" as compared to foreigners, and they now wanted to know about their place in his kingdom. After all, monarchy presupposes hierarchy.

But the kingdom that Jesus brought was not like the kingdoms of the world. In the kingdom of heaven greatness is not measured by rank or position.

Kingdom theology was at the very center of Anabaptist thought in the 16th century. The early Anabaptists lived in the tension between the kingdom of God, on the one hand, and the kingdom of this world (or the kingdom of darkness), on the other. This was quite different from Luther's two-kingdom theology. To belong to Christ's kingdom, they held, meant to live according to different ethical standards than those which prevailed in the kingdoms of this world.

And this is the tension in which we, as heirs of the 16th century Anabaptists, live—to be in this world, but not of it, as Jesus said.

The Response to the Question

Jesus had a twofold response to this perverse question. First, he answered them by a symbolic act, and then he gave his followers a severe word of warning.

Jesus took a child (the word could refer either to a boy or a girl) and put it among them. Whose child it was is not known, but if they were in Peter's and Andrew's house in Capernaum, it may have been Peter's. After all, he was married.

In fact, there is an ancient tale, no doubt apocryphal, in which we are told that this child grew up to become the bishop of Antioch—Ignatius—a man who left us seven valuable letters and who was taken to Rome where he died a martyr's death. This story may have arisen due to the fact that Ignatius came to be called "Theophoros"—carried by God—and because Jesus had carried this child, the name Theophoros was given to it. It's a lovely story, but probably has no basis in fact.

We have many examples in the Old Testament, as well as in the Gospels, of symbolic acts, of action parables. Jesus responds to the question of his disciples, a question which must have pained him, by one such act— taking a child in his arms and putting it among them. He follows this up with a severe warning.

"Truly I tell you, unless you change and become like children, you will never enter the kingdom of heaven. Whoever humbles himself like this child is the greatest in the kingdom of heaven."

There has been an endless debate over precisely what Jesus meant by becoming like children. Some interpreters suggest that little children are humble. It's only as they grow up in a competitive world, that they begin to struggle for first place. For those of us who have brought up children, that interpretation doesn't have too much weight; humility is not the most outstanding characteristic of children, at least not ours! Others, who see in the little child a symbol of humility, say that a child does not feel humble, but, because of its small stature, is "humble." The word *paidion*, little child, is a diminutive, they say.

Another suggestion is that Jesus wanted to teach his disciples dependence on God. A child, to begin with at least, is totally dependent on those who care for it. If that's the meaning, then Jesus wants to remind his disciples that they must learn to say "Abba" and to recognize their complete dependence on God the Father.

Another suggestion is that children are trustful. They believe what their parents tell them, at least when they're little.

There are biblical scholars who take a different approach to this question. A child, they say, was not greatly valued in the ancient world. Joachim Jeremias points out that children are sometimes listed with the deaf and dumb and the weak-minded. Children were to be "looked after," but not "looked up" to. They were subject to their elders and were taught to respect them.

It is, in that case, the status of the child that is in focus, rather than any characteristic quality of children, such as humility, innocence, or trustfulness. Jesus, of course, valued children very highly.

If that is the correct reading, then true greatness is seen in being little. To humble oneself like a little child, of course, does not call for phony, false modesty, but the acceptance of a lowly position, as modeled by our Lord who "humbled himself and made himself of no reputation."

To turn and become like children calls for a radical reorientation from the fierce desire to climb the social ladder to a willingness to be insignificant. Jesus goes so far as to say, that unless his followers are willing to go the path of humility, they cannot enter the kingdom of heaven.

There is some ambiguity about the call of Jesus to "turn around." Is the verb *strepho* to be understood in the sense of "conversion," of "repentance?" *Strepho* could be a translation of the semitic *shubh*, which means to turn around, to return to the covenant, to repent.

Others suggest that *strepho*, to turn around, is used here in a more general sense of "change," as the New Revised Standard Version of the Bible translates it: Unless you change and become like children you will never enter the kingdom of heaven. Notice the double negative in Jesus' warning: "Never, no never" can you enter the kingdom, unless you change, unless you repent, unless you are converted. The disciples were asking the question, who is the greatest in God's kingdom? Jesus replies, unless you change your attitude, you won't even get into the kingdom.

But, however we may understand the word "turn around," the question the disciples asked showed that they were going in the wrong direction; they were moving *away* from, not *toward,* the kingdom. For members of God's kingdom, the fulfillment of selfish ambitions, the enjoyment of personal prestige, the exaltation of the self, is not the chief purpose of life.

Jesus calls for a reversal of society's values. The word "child" in this chapter shifts from its literal meaning to a designation of the followers of Jesus. Notice the term in verse 6: "the little ones who believe in me," and again in verses 10 and 14.

Jesus, in fact, calls his disciples "children" (John 21:5). Much later the apostle John addresses his readers in this way: "I am writing to you, little children, because your sins are forgiven on account of his name" (I John 2:12). And again, "I write to you, children, because you know the Father" (verse 13).

Conclusion

We might fairly ask, is there then no place for structures in the kingdom of God? What shall CEOs, and principals, and chairpersons, and elders do to be like children?

Perhaps we can find the answer in Jesus himself. He spoke with great authority; he was fully conscious of his divine calling, but he modeled humility for us by serving others.

The Son of Man, he said, had not come to be served, but to serve and to give his life as a ransom for many. Where God's people manifest a servant attitude, they can fill high or low positions. They can hold leadership positions, but, as servants, they do not strive to leave their names in the halls of fame, but to help others.

And what might this passage have to do with the Anabaptist emphasis on peace? The apostle James asks the question, "Where do conflicts and disputes among God's people come from?" And his answer is, "Do they not come from the cravings that are at war within you?" (James 4:1)

Insofar as these sinful cravings to be number one are also overcome by the Spirit of God working in our lives, we will be able to live at peace with one another. But where envy, jealousy, and selfish strivings rule our lives, there is always great potential for conflict. May God help us to live in peace.

David Ewert, Abbotsford, British Columbia, is a retired Bible teacher.

Humor

Menno Simons Shares the Podium with Myron Augsburger and Tony Campolo at the Mennonite General Assembly;

can't remember which
one is supposed to
speak first; is
embarrassed by
the small
number of books
he's written;
wonders if his
accent will be
understood;
thinks that
maybe he should
have sat this
one out alone in
a seminar room,
or watching three-
on-three in the gym;
checks his fly
to make sure
the zipper is
closed; hopes
that Tony forgets
the punch line of
his jokes, because
he knows, for sure
that he, Menno, doesn't
have any good ones;
wonders why
Myron hasn't
retired to
cooking for the
kids at Camp
Laurelville or
Hebron, or
maybe working as
a model for Esther;
can't believe he
ever agreed to
be on the same
program with these
two effervescent
overachievers;
wishes that he could
sit down to read his
ten minute speech;
feels exhausted from
waking up repeatedly
last night, pursued
in nightmares, by
bounty hunters

by Leonard Nolt

Menno Simons Sighs and Leans Back in His Seat

smiling
as the lights
come on in the
Gronigen
Cinema after a
double feature.
"That was great,"
Menno said to
himself, swallowing
the final kernels
of popcorn,
"my favorite
movies, a
comedy and a
western."
Bounty hunters
seeking
Anabaptists
rarely bugged

unforgiving
movie fans,
so Menno
frequently
sought a few
hours of peace
and safety
at the cinema.
And what more
does any
Anabaptist need,
Menno thinks,
besides a
good laugh
and a
fast horse.

by Leonard Nolt

Leonard Nolt is a photographer and writer who lives in Boise, Idaho.

Mennonites and Love

A dramatic monologue

by Merle Good

I'm not so sure that I have much to say about—
ah—about Mennonites and—ah, you know—
Mennonites and love.

I can't say as I'm much of an expert, you see, on
romance and such like. I see these young people
these days, even some of my own grandchildren, and
I ask myself, what do I know. Not much, I can tell
you, not much.

So much I don't understand, really. Like what is the
point of a—well, I better not go into that. A private
matter, really. My sister Eunice always said, live and
let live, or something like that—but it always left me
confused. Seemed to work for her though. Well, sort
of.

I was taught that to be—how should I say—well,
you probably wouldn't understand if I said it. Oh,
you'd know the words, but the sentiments might
shock you. I say shock, but not the way I'm shocked.
The reverse. You'd be shocked to hear how—what
word should I use—how reserved we were when we
were young. Why, you didn't touch a young woman
unless you were getting married—at least I didn't.

Except something like "Walk-a-Mile" or something like that. Even at the taffy pulls you didn't touch the girl's hands, unless by accident of course—Henry Gingrich was good at that *[a tiny but restrained giggle]*—he and Lester Martin were always up to something *[tiny giggle]*—but on the whole I would say that we boys simply didn't touch girls—at least I didn't.

But nowadays, I see these kids with their arms all twisted around each other and they kiss over anything—I mean, not just when they've been away for awhile, but if one of them makes a lame joke, they all kiss each other—like what for? Twisted arms and kiss-kiss-kiss. And then they say they're not even dating—oh sorry, no one says that anymore—they're not "in a relationship," I think that's how they say it. I've seen them rolling down the hill together, falling all over each other, they ride each other piggyback, they even go swimming together with no adults around. I try to smile—as though I understand what's happening—but I'm plum confused, I am.

Do young people know about love anymore? Sometimes it seems like they're at a smorgasbord all day long, week after week, and they don't know what it's like to be even a little bit hungry—they have no appreciation for the desire of food, if you follow me. Oh well, I promised myself I wouldn't say anything. So I'm not going to. *[pause]*

I never was a kisser. Never quite got the point of it, really. Sorta odd, when you think about it. Hugs I can understand. We all need warmth and—well—ah—closeness, I guess. You can see it in children, they like to be held. That makes sense. And Verna and me—we hugged some over the years, I guess.

Never in front of others mind you. It would cheapen
it, I always thought. Although in the years there
before she passed away, Verna would put her arm
around me more than before. Maybe she needed
hugs more than I realized. [*pause, voice mellow*]
Maybe I wasn't as warm as I should have been.

She loved me, that I never doubted. I don't understand my one granddaughter when she talks about
love being a thing that comes and goes. Verna wasn't
like that. She was constant, if you know what I
mean—constant. [*smiles*] The first I saw her was at
the hayride over at the Beiler place. They went up
through the back woods and Henry and Lester were
whooping it up, pushing everyone back and forth in
the loose hay as the tractor went around a corner in
the dark woods—and I lost my balance and ended up
with my face in the hay—and everyone's having a
good time, laughing—some were singing gospel
songs—and as we came back into the moonlight I
looked up from the hay and saw Verna looking right
at me—oh, she had such lively eyes—always did,
right to the end—and she reaches out her hand and
said in a matter-of-fact but friendly way—"Here, let
me help you," and she helped me to sit up straight
again. [*pause, fighting tears*] Here, let me help you,
she said. And that's what she did all her life. I don't
think I thanked her enough. I loved her with all my
heart, but did I say it enough?

Anyhow, I guess we had the last laugh on Henry,
for all his energy and tricks. We all pushed back on
the wagon as we came through the creek and Lester
lifted the end board and yelping Henry went sailing
into the cold water that night. [*laughs*] We had good

times. And come to think of it, that may have been the first time I held Verna in my arms, what with everyone pushing and sliding on that loose hay. Only for a jiffy, mind you. Nothing intentional. Not a hugging thing or anything like that.

Well, anyhow, Henry married Barbara and their second son Lamar married our oldest daughter Alice—and it's Lamar and Alice's son Zachary who's coming to see me tomorrow night with his friend Sarah. I like my grandson Zachary a lot—always have. And Sarah I've only seen once. They hang on each other a lot, if you know what I mean. And she has rings everywhere—all over her fingers and ears—and one in her nose even. Raised some questions in my mind, I'll say that much. Like how does she manage—oh, forget it. It's none of my business, really.

Lamar thinks they may be getting married. Beats me. I've given up trying to pick up on signals these days. Nothing's the same. Got some pie and ice cream on hand. Hope that hasn't changed. I guess they want my blessing, so to speak. Who am I to bless anyone? I sure hope they don't ask me any questions. [*suddenly alarmed*] What could they ask—young people these days know everything. Besides, I'm not sure I know the proper terms for—oh, I'm sure someone's counseling them. But what if they asked me about—you know—kissing and stuff. What would I say? It's O.K., I guess, in its proper place. Oh, they won't ask. Now I'm all in a sweat and I'll have myself beside myself before Zachary arrives with his jewellried-up girl. What would I answer them? Or even love—if they say something silly about love—what do I do?

WHAT MENNONITES ARE THINKING, 2000

Settle down, man. What can be more embarrassing than falling into the loose hay at Verna's feet— and that worked out all right, didn't it? Just serve the pie and ice cream and shut up. They'll have plenty to say. After all, they're modern Mennonite young people. They know all about love. Nothing to learn there, I guess. [*eyes alarmed*] But what if Zachary's Sarah tries to kiss me, like they do everyone? What do I do? And that nose-ring of hers—I guess it doesn't scratch or anything. Seems a mite unpleasant. What if it unhooks and falls down into my shirt with all that—well, you know—with all that stuff on it. [*makes a face at the thought of the unpleasantness*] Whew! Yikes! [*deep breath*] Oh, well, she probably won't try to kiss me. Look at me—expecting to be kissed! Ain't that a leap. [*pause*] Maybe I could rub something on my skin that doesn't smell so great—to discourage her. Like Vicks.

Well, I told you I didn't know much. Wish me the best.

Merle Good of Lancaster, Pennsylvania, is a writer, dramatist, publisher, and a co-editor of this volume.

Short Fiction, II

Dickie Derksen

by David Elias

Dickie Derksen had no business being fat. None of his brothers and sisters were fat. In fact, all nine of them looked like they might be just a crust of bread or two away from starvation. They were as thin and pale-looking as any clan of children in the valley. Dickie, on the other hand, was built something like a well-fed dwarf, except that he was a foot taller and fifty pounds heavier. As for his disposition, he was more like an elf, jolly in his own simple way, in spite of the fact that his might have been the last house in the valley to receive a visit from Santa.

His place was all by itself out in the country, where only two kinds of people ever lived: those that were too rich to live in the village, and those that were too poor. Rich people had a fancy place with a garage attached to the house instead of a barn, and windows out front big enough to see right into the living room where people sat looking back out at you.

Poor people had a place thrown together from scrap lumber or buildings dragged out of the village before they got torn down, a place where a few scrawny hogs and chickens scrounged around in the dirt and kids played outside all day, hungry and half-naked. Where there was always smoke coming out of the chimney, even on the hottest days of summer, for cooking, and the light came yellow through the windows at night from a lantern instead of a light bulb. Dickie Derksen lived in a place like that. A place where there was never enough to eat. Dickie Derksen was poor.

But that didn't stop him from wearing a grin bigger than any of us could manage most of the time, especially if it was his turn to go up on the big swing. Standing in line for the big swing was what Dickie Derksen did every recess. Just stood there and waited as patiently as he could to go up on the big swing. When it finally came around to his turn, he'd wrap his thick fingers around the rope on either side and pull himself up on the board, then kick his stubby legs out to try and get up some speed.

He never got anywhere until someone pushed him, usually my sister Trudy, but she could never get him as high as he wanted to go. The only one who could do that was Sarah. She was as strong as most of the boys, not to mention a foot or two taller than any of them, and the combination of those two things allowed her to get him up to where the soles of his shoes were flat up against the sky, his thick body blocking out the sun.

That was the way he liked it. It was the only time we ever heard him make a sound—a little squeal—just at the top, before he fell back out of the air.

So when school started up that fall Dickie didn't mind it that the new teacher might treat him badly, the way Mr. Friesen had two years before, so long as he got to go out for recess and wait in line for the big swing. Last year's teacher, Mr. Giesbrecht, had more or less ignored him, in the same way that he ignored all of us, so long as we didn't disturb him. Being ignored suited Dickie fine. He was used to it.

We should have known from the first time we saw Miss Thiessen, the new teacher, step up to the front of the room, that things had taken a turn for the worse. Instead of explaining to us how she was going to run things, or handing out books for us to write our names in like any other teacher would have, she stood at her desk, hands cupped in front of her like a bird's nest, and talked for a solid hour about sin. About how we were all sinful in the eyes of God and didn't even have to do a thing at all for it to be a sin, but just think about doing it. How all children were full of "unclean thoughts," as she put it in that thin voice of hers, and could only be cleansed through confession. Right there we should have guessed what we were in for.

You could just sense that in behind all that talk about purity and righteousness there was a mean streak, and it only took until the second week of school to find out just how mean. We were all making our way to our desks after recess when Betty Unger, who was always teasing the boys, turned around and made a face at Bill. He said something, and when she pushed him, he fell against the window shelf.

The window shelf was where Miss Thiessen kept her plants. She took more time for those plants than she ever did for any of us. You would have thought they were prize-winning roses instead of spindly look-ing things with more stalk than leaf. The one that Bill knocked over reminded me of a weed my mother might have pulled out of her garden.

"Now look what you've done," said Miss Thiessen. "That plant came all the way from the Holy Land."

"I didn't mean it," said Bill. "Honest."

The pot was cracked open and some of the dirt had been knocked off the roots, but it looked fine otherwise, and only needed to be put back into a new pot. The whole thing wouldn't have taken more than a minute to clean up, but Miss Thiessen just stood there looking down at the floor as if someone was dying at her feet. Then a different kind of look came across her face. A look I'd never seen on any face before, man or woman. A hard look.

"You deliberately knocked that plant off the window sill," she said.

"I'll clean it up, Miss Thiessen," said Trudy. She was down on her knees, scraping dirt into the pot. Miss Thiessen yanked her up by her dress and the pot fell against Trudy's brace, then back onto the floor.

"Nonsense. You will go to your desk and sit down. All of you."

She waited until we were all seated and went up to her desk. Then she opened a drawer and pulled out the strap. She walked around to the front and stood there with the strap across the palm of her hand. Then she called Bill up.

It wasn't anything new for him to get the first strapping of the year. Something about Bill just seemed to bring out the worst in teachers. And even though it seemed unfair that he should be getting it just for knocking over a plant—even if it did come all the way from the Holy Land—in a way we were glad to be getting it over with.

It wasn't like we were worried about him. Nobody could take a strapping better than Bill. He never pulled his hand away when the strap came down, like the rest of us did sometimes when the sting got too much and we just couldn't take anymore. Watching Bill take a strapping gave the rest of us courage, somehow, so that when our turn came it would be just that much easier, knowing he'd got through it all right.

When Bill got up to the front, Miss Thiessen said, "Hold out your right hand." Bill put his hand out. "All the way out." She grabbed it and yanked like she was going to pull it right out of his shoulder. Then she turned it palm down. Nobody expected that. Getting strapped palm down was guaranteed to hurt more than just about anybody could stand. It would turn your hand black and blue, and stiffen it up like a piece of cardboard, so you couldn't use it for a couple of days. A strapping palm down could put the fear into anybody. Even Bill.

Miss Thiessen took a step back and raised her skinny body right up on the tips of her toes, like she was going to leave her feet. Then she gave a little grunt. An ugly little grunt. A grunt that sounded all wrong, somehow. Then the strap came down on Bill's knuckles harder than any of us could believe. I could tell after the first lick that he was in trouble. Not even big Mr. Friesen with his thick forearms and cheesy breath had ever put that look on Bill's face.

Miss Thiessen gave him four more and he got through them okay, but then she stepped back and said, "Other hand," and yanked it out the same way she had the first one. We all looked at each other. She was going to give him five more on the other hand.

She lifted herself up with that grunt and brought the strap down on Bill's left hand.

Sarah held her two large hands over her flat stomach, like she was going to be sick, and Trudy, fists clenched, let out a little wince every time the leather came down on Bill's knuckles. But the worst was when I looked over at Dickie. He usually just sat there grinning when somebody was up getting the strap, like it was all a big joke. Nobody ever got mad at him for that. He didn't understand about getting the strap the way the rest of us did.

But Dickie wasn't grinning this time. He'd turned himself sideways in his desk, and was rocking back and forth, one fist in his mouth and the other one pounding against his thigh. Every time the strap came down he sucked a big gulp of air in through his knuckles. That scared me, seeing Dickie like that. Scared me as much as anything. That's when I knew for sure Bill was really getting hurt.

When it was over Bill went back to his desk and sat down quickly with his hands folded up under his arms. He leaned forward and put his head down over his chest and kept it there, not looking at anyone. Normally he would've turned and slipped me a wink to say he was okay, but all he did was lean further over his desk and hug himself tight like he might be shivering from cold. I thought I heard something come up in his throat, but I wasn't sure until I saw him blink hard and a tear splashed down on his desk. After that I looked away.

Miss Thiessen slipped the strap back into one of the drawers and sat down behind her desk like nothing had happened, except that she was shiny along her neck and across her forehead, and her eyes looked harder than ever.

It seemed to me that she took something away from us that morning—not just from Bill, but from Dickie, and Trudy, and me, and everyone in that room—something that didn't belong to her. Something she had no business taking. I had a pretty good idea it wasn't something we could just take back, either.

Bill didn't come to school the next day, but the day after that he was back and seemed to be okay, except that he was quieter than usual. Everybody just left him alone. At recess we went out to the field and played ball the same as always, and Bill came out with us, except he didn't bat and played outfield instead of pitching.

We were all careful after that about doing anything to make Miss Thiessen mad, and thought maybe the worst was behind us until one day she stepped out onto the landing in the middle of recess and called Dickie in. He was in his usual place, waiting in line to go up on the big swing. I was worried he wouldn't go. Dickie didn't like giving up his place in line. He could be stubborn that way. If he made up his mind to do something he could turn so hard and solid you just had to leave him alone.

The fact was he could have turned anyone of us— Miss Thiessen included—into a cripple with a blow of his fist. He could reach down and pull out a sapling from behind the backstop with one hand that three of us had spent the better part of the recess trying to wrestle out of the ground.

We were all relieved when he went inside with her, but we couldn't figure out what she wanted

with him. It wasn't like she was in there talking to
him, unless it was her doing all the talking, since
nobody had ever heard more than a few grunts and
groans come out of Dickie's mouth. Nobody was
exactly sure what the problem with his tongue was,
except that it didn't work. Somebody heard a story
that it had attached itself to the roof of his mouth
when he was a little baby and stayed there because
there was no money for a doctor to get it off.
Another story we heard said that he'd gotten so hungry once, when he was only a little more than a
baby, that he'd chewed off most of his own tongue
and eaten it like it was meat.

It was true that Dickie would eat almost anything:
apple cores, orange peels, pork gristle, watermelon
rinds—any scrap of food you offered him. But it was
hard to believe somebody—even somebody like
Dickie—could eat their own tongue.

Miss Thiessen kept him in the whole recess, so he
never did get his turn, and when the rest of us got
back in he was already in his desk, just sitting there
not looking at anybody.

After that she started calling the rest of us in, too,
one at a time. Some people came out looking like
they'd been through a strapping, except that their
hands weren't swollen or red, or like they'd been
caught out in a terrible windstorm. It got to where we
didn't even feel like playing anymore, knowing somebody was in there with her.

"You like Dickie, don't you," she said, when it was
my turn. She was in behind her desk and I was in a
chair beside it.

"Everybody likes Dickie."

"And Dickie likes everybody."

"Sure."

"Especially girls."

"I guess."

"He likes girls especially, doesn't he?"

"He likes everybody."

"Your sister Trudy is probably the closest thing Dickie has to a friend, wouldn't you say? Her, and maybe Sarah?"

"Maybe."

"They're always pushing him up on the swing."

"That's his favorite thing to do. Go up on the big swing."

"What about when he touches them?"

"Touches who?"

"The girls. Touches them where he shouldn't."

"Who? Dickie? He wouldn't do that. He's not like that."

"You understand, don't you, that by protecting him you're as guilty as he is."

"But he wouldn't do a thing like that. Not Dickie. Honest, Miss Thiessen. He isn't like that. He just wants to go up on the swing, that's all. That's all he cares about."

"And if he was doing something he shouldn't? You'd want to help him if you could, wouldn't you?"

"Help him how?"

"Help him to confess, of course."

"But he didn't do anything."

She kept it up like that for a long time before she let me go and called everyone in from recess. After that I knew why the others looked the way they did when she got through with them.

All week long she called people in, one after the other, and kept them in longer and longer, until folks driving by must have wondered what kind of teacher would let her students play for the better part of a morning when they should be inside working. They must have wondered just what kind of education their children were getting in that school. But they never wondered hard enough to come in and find out what was going on. If they had, maybe things wouldn't have happened the way they did.

One morning, just before recess, Miss Thiessen got up and said, "Dickie is no longer to play at the swings with the girls. He is to go out to the ball diamond with the boys and stay there. Does everyone understand?" We all knew exactly what she meant. "Good. Class dismissed."

Some of us got Dickie to come out to the field with us, but it wasn't easy. We sat him down behind the backstop and tried to distract him when we weren't out in the field or batting, but he just kept rocking back and forth and looking over to where the girls were swinging. I could pick out Miss Thiessen watching through the window, just standing there with her arms folded looking out at us.

We managed well enough the first few days, but then one morning we were walking by the big swing and somebody threw a half-eaten apple on the ground. Dickie spotted that apple and went for it like he would any other scrap of food. He got down on his hands and knees to pick it up, and when he saw that it was full of dirt, grabbed Susie Peter's skirt to rub the sand off. She brushed his hand away and told him to cut it out and then everybody looked up and there was Miss Thiessen on the steps watching the whole thing.

She rang the bell right away and we all headed in. When we got to our seats she went to the drawer and pulled out the strap. She came around the front of her desk and held it across the palm of her hand.

"Dickie," she said. "Come up here."

When I looked over at Dickie he was grinning and looking around at everybody in the same way he always did when the strap came out. "Dickie thinks it's funny, boys and girls. You see what you've done." She was getting that hard look. "I hope you realize," she said, "all of you, that you've brought this on him, as much as he has on himself. Come up here, Dickie."

Dickie looked around the room, still grinning, then shook his head slowly from side to side. Miss Thiessen walked up next to him and snapped the strap down across the top of his desk. "You will come up to the front of the room," she said, "and receive your punishment."

Bill got up out of his desk. "Dickie didn't mean anything, Miss Thiessen. He was just getting sand off. That's all."

"I know what you're up to, all of you," said Miss Thiessen. "I won't allow it to go on any longer. It's time to put a stop to this." She looked back down at Dickie. "Now," she said, "you will come up to the front to receive your punishment."

Dickie didn't move. The grin was gone from his face and there was that expression he got sometimes when you knew it was best just to leave him alone. "You will do as I say," she said, and brought the strap down across his broad back. It took a minute for the pain to register, but then his face crunched up, and his fists along with it. "Get up." Miss Thiessen brought the strap down on his back again, harder this time. Dickie let out a yelp that was different than anything we'd heard before.

"Stop it. Stop it." Trudy was yelling now and Sarah was up from her desk. She stepped in between Dickie and Miss Thiessen and when the strap came up for another blow she made a grab for it. Miss Thiessen yanked it away from her. "How dare you," she said, and lashed her across the face with it. Sarah staggered back against some desks.

Miss Thiessen looked around the room. "You're against me. All of you," then turned back to Dickie. "I'll teach you to keep your fat filthy hands to yourself." She got up on her toes and gave that grunt none of us ever wanted to hear again and brought the strap down on Dickie's back. It made a sound like a branch snapping. Dickie jumped up and shot a fist out at the pain. It caught Miss Thiessen hard on the side of the head and sent her backward across a row of desks. She slouched onto the floor and lay very still.

Sarah bent down over her and put one hand against her cheek. We were all on our feet by that time, and gathered around, just staring down at Miss Thiessen. Nobody knew what to do. "Get help," said Trudy finally, looking up at Bill.

"Who?"

"Anyone. It doesn't matter."

I watched him run out of the school, and when I turned back there was Dickie, stooping over to pick up the strap where it had fallen out of Miss Thiessen's hand. He walked slowly and deliberately over to the desk, pulled open the drawer, and lowered the strap in gently.

Trudy took Dickie by the hand and led him out the door and sat him down on the steps of the school. I followed her out.

"You take him home," she said. "It's too far for me to walk. So you have to do it."

"But why?"

"Because you have to. You have to take him right now."

None of us had ever been out to his place, but I walked with him all the way out there, just because my little sister told me to, and when we got there, the two of us stood in the middle of his yard, surrounded by squawking chickens and the sound of a baby bawling in the house. You could tell Dickie had already forgotten about what happened back at the school and was looking over at me like he finally had a visitor for the first time and didn't know what to do with him.

I thought about getting him into the house, but he didn't seem interested in that. Then an idea came across his face and he took me by the hand and led me in the direction of the barn. I stopped at the doorway and he went in ahead of me, disappearing into the musky dimness. I stood in the entrance, waiting for my eyes to get used to the dark. I guessed he was rooting around for some newborn kittens or puppies to show me.

Then I made him out, standing over a barrel at the far end of the barn. He beckoned, and I went and stood across from him. Daylight seeped in through the cracks in the weathered boards. The smell of dust and stale manure filled my nostrils. Dickie had lifted the lid off and now he leaned far over it until his head disappeared inside. When he came back up he brought out a shiny fist covered in thick dark liquid. He put the fist to his mouth and sucked up some of the dark liquid between his teeth, then swallowed loudly. He held it, dripping tarry goo, out to me.

"Lasses," he said. The word tumbled out, warped and wobbly, and hung there for a moment, between the two of us—the syllables glued one to the other, in the same way that Dickie's tongue was glued to the roof of his mouth.

I stepped up and took some of the liquid off his fist with my finger. I brought it up to my mouth and licked a little off with the tip of my tongue. It stuck in my throat when I tried to swallow, while Dickie lifted up more of the awful stuff and grinned over at me with black teeth. It was running down the sides of his mouth now, and dripping off the end of his chin.

I realized that he was telling me, in his own way, the secret of how he'd managed to get so fat when all of his brothers and sisters were so thin. It wasn't just the scraps of food he picked up here and there. All this time he'd been filling himself up with blackstrap molasses. Molasses that was meant for the livestock.

I knew there was a good chance he'd be expelled from school, and that if he ever said another word, it wouldn't be where there was a teacher around to hear it. Miss Thiessen might be dead, or she might wake up and tell everyone how Dickie Derksen had tried to kill her. Either way I knew that school was over for him. He wouldn't be spending any more time waiting in line for the big swing.

But I also knew that no matter what happened, they couldn't stop us from bringing him back there someday, me and Sarah and Trudy, to let him have a good long turn on the big swing. We'd get him up on the seat, and then, after he was good and comfortable, push him up just as high as he needed to go.

David Elias teaches and writes in Winnipeg, Manitoba.

Gone

by Kate Good

It's a bad day when there are three people dead already, it isn't even 3:30 yet, and I'm still without my first cup of coffee.

> Nancy Martin, 68, of 1200 Bluebonnnet Lane, Engelville, died Tuesday morning at Hampshire Hospital of natural causes.
>
> A homemaker, Mrs. Martin ran a small roadside produce stand on Bluebonnet Lane.
>
> She was a member of Engelville Mennonite Church.
>
> Born in Hamburg, she was the daughter of the late Lloyd and Maggie Engel.
>
> She is survived by a daughter Beth A., married to Donald Bollinger, with whom she resided, and three granddaughters.

Done. Making it through a phone call with Mr. Rosenbloom of Rosenbloom's Funeral Home with a person's life intact can be a bit tricky. His strong Dutchified accent tends to blur the difference between, say, "f" and "s." We've worked together on the phone for the last few months and can now complete an entire obit through an elaborate code that allows us both to understand what is being said. The result leaves me shouting into the newsroom like a radio operator, "A as in apple, S as in Sam," and on and on. Oh, and did I mention Mr. Rosenbloom's hard of hearing?

Writing obituaries is an exact science. Each paragraph on page B-2 in the newspaper follows a precise formula. There's no room for creativity, and, believe me, I've tried. Alter anything standard and your loyal readers will revolt, sending you hate mail and calling your editor.

Obituaries remain one of the most popular sections of the daily newspaper. I guess people read them with the same interest that draws them to the birth announcements or engagements. They are as much a memento of accomplishments and failures as yearbooks or photo albums.

Me, I only began to turn to B-2 when I got this assignment. I look to see if, in layout, any of my people's lives have been arbitrarily disrupted by an editor. I'm possessive of them, I guess. Perhaps, in a sentimental way, my interest runs deeper than protecting my own writing. If you want to sound a bit corny, you could say that I provide the record of a person's life, the last reassurance of their existence.

But make no mistake about it, there's no glamour in writing obits. It may take some skill, but it's not something you get into on purpose. I have yet to meet the child who dreams of writing obits. Most of us end up doing this by accident. I blame my acquisition of this job on my editor, Sam, who, after observing my "remarkably tidy desk," decided I would be great at condensing other people's lives into three or four graphs.

I dream of being a writer. It's what I've wanted since I first discovered those strange squiggles called letters. When I realized they formed words which became stories, I was ecstatic. My first word was fox. Once I got started I couldn't stop.

Growing up, I developed something of what my grandmother calls an "overactive imagination," which led to commands like, "Sarah, stop dawdling and finish picking the beans." By the time I was eight I was searching for a way to put those daydreams to work. Becoming a writer seemed a good bet. The next year for Christmas I asked for a typewriter and a subscription to *The New York Times.* Surprisingly, neither materialized, although my grandmother let me read her *Hampshire Daily News* whenever I wanted.

After my initial burst of ambition, I struggled with my next step. My family's not real literary; of course, books are fine as long as they don't get in the way of work.

I didn't know where to begin. I kept a journal. I worked at poetry. Still nothing much really developed. I spent lots of time writing in my head or dreaming about writing, but little of it got put on paper.

I graduated from high school with a big, spiral-bound notebook full of half-stories but nothing of much substance. I began to realize that somewhere between reading in my room or daydreaming while picking beans, I had missed accumulating some real living of my own.

So one day, the summer after high school ended, I put some of my writing into a shopping bag, pulled on my nicest dress, told Mom "I'm going to town to see about a job," and caught the bus to Hampshire City before she could say a word.

I showed up at the *Hampshire Daily News* slightly disheveled and sweaty (my nicest dress is polyester) and announced in my best reporter's voice, "I'm here about a job."

The secretary, Mabel Esch, bless her heart, somehow managed not to laugh and handed me an application. She told me to have a seat and fill it out. And so I sat on a sticky, molded plastic chair under the gold letters which spell out *Daily News* and wrote down my qualifying experience. It took two minutes.

To this day I don't know what possessed Sam Johnson to hire that sweaty, eager girl who sat in front of his desk. Then I thought it was because he saw some kind of potential in me, but now I'm pretty sure all he saw was my wonder and my ability to place a comma correctly almost every time. He spotted the makings of a fastidious copy editor who would do overtime without protest.

When I got home, Mom already knew about the job. Mabel Esch's family and mine go way back. So I knew as soon as I left the waiting room Mabel would telephone my Aunt Mary Beth, Mabel's best friend, and then it would only be a matter of time until my mother heard.

> Jacob Miller, 89, of 16 Adamstown Rd, Easton, died Tuesday morning at home after a long illness.
> A master furniture maker, Mr. Miller sold his work through many local craft stores.

He was a member of the Old Order
Amish Church.

He was married to Annie Stoltzfus Miller.

Born in Easton, he was the son of the late
Abner and Anna Miller.

Surviving in addition to his wife are three
daughters, Mary, married to Allan Fisher of
Hampshire Township, Susan, married to
Andrew Carpenter of Marytown, Rachel,
married to Keith Neff of Hampshire
Township; two sons, Michael, married to
Anna Miller of Easton, and John Miller of
Easton; 30 grandchildren and 70 great-
grandchildren.

He was preceded in death by five brothers and two sisters.

The *Hampshire Daily News* is the morning paper for
Hampshire County. There is also an evening paper
called the *Hampshire Sun*. We are the less politically
conservative of the two, and consequently we have
the slightly smaller readership. We console ourselves
with the knowledge that evening papers are dropping
in readership across the country, and so it's only a
matter of time until the *Sun* begins to fade. This is a
point Sam emphasizes whenever we are scooped by
the *Sun*.

Interestingly, one of the wealthiest families in the
county, the Colsons, own both papers. The Colsons
are rich and they're also stingy. In a fit of thriftiness
they decided at some point to save money and space
and put both papers' staff in the same offices. The
Sun arrives every morning at seven and works all day

until three, when *Daily News* reporters kick them out of their desks. We all keep our files locked, and there are two different access codes for the computers.

Today began like most others. I arrived at the office in time to intercept Mary Alice, the *Sun* obit editor, as she flew to the door. Mary Alice is a bit, well, as my grandmother would say, she's a sandwich short of a picnic. You see, I depend on Mary Alice for obit information she's taken earlier in the day so I can rewrite the obits for the next morning's paper. She is a flighty filer and often mislays faxes in the trash can rather than placing them easily in the clearly marked files I've provided.

She tossed me a handful of faxes and notes and scuttled towards the door before I could say much. I perched on my chair and contemplated several thoughts I wouldn't mind telling Mary Alice sometime when she pauses long enough to focus.

I started to consider a cup of coffee (a close cousin to tar) when the phone began to ring endlessly. Three deaths later I focused my eyes enough to realize the newsroom was full and loud. I looked up to see Anthony Jackson, the assistant editor, heading across the room towards his desk which butts up against mine.

When Anthony and I both sit at our desks and face forward we look each other full in the face. Several months of sitting that close to Anthony has been quite an education. I think most people thought we would struggle to get along or even avoid each other all together. I must admit we present an odd combination. I, a simply dressed girl with light brown hair and what must be innocent eyes, seem to contrast deeply with Anthony, a middle-aged, dignified man who worked the cop beat for years. But surface evaluations rarely last long or count for much.

Anthony provides a nonstop dose of entertainment, amusement, wisdom, counseling, and knowledge to my otherwise calm and stable life. He knows more about nothing than anyone else I know. He can state the facts on almost any sports event, presidential debate, or local political matter. And, he's the first person I've met who believes in aliens.

During the past several weeks, we've been running a series of articles about Einstein and his theories. As Anthony worked at laying out one of the pieces one afternoon, he began to mutter under his breath. Bored, I made the mistake of asking him what he was rambling on about.

"Einstein's a chimpanzee," he said.

Somewhat surprised to hear him criticize the character of the eminent scientist, I asked him what he was talking about.

"Einstein's a chimpanzee to them," he said impatiently.

"Who's 'them?'" I asked. Then, just as he began to answer, I remembered what other staff said about Anthony's views. "Oh, please," I continued, cutting him off, "please tell me you're not talking about the people on other planets."

He looked at me and grinned.

"But how do you know they exist?" I asked. "I've never seen them."

"We're chimpanzees to them, Sarah," he repeated as if speaking to a small child. I stared at him, trying to figure out how to argue with his logic. The phone rang again and Sam yelled across the room, "Obit on line five."

> John Martin, 25, of Hampshire County,
> died Monday morning in Columbus, Ohio,
> of injuries sustained in a car accident.
> A carpenter, Mr. Martin worked for
> Steven's Kitchen Design of Columbus.
> He was also a student at the University
> of Ohio.
> He attended South Street United
> Methodist Church.

The funeral director paused. "I don't really know anything about survivors," he said. "The friends who took care of the funeral didn't know much about family. They just knew he was from Hampshire. They had a picture of him, though, which I dropped off earlier today. Maybe his family will recognize him."

If I close my eyes I can picture Johnny Martin like he's standing in front of me. Even now, my heart still picks up a little, my breath pauses, when I hear his name.

I see him sitting in the back rows at church with the older boys or sometimes over at our house visiting my older brother Reuben. It was Johnny I thought about now and then late at night lying in bed unable to sleep.

My interest in Johnny eventually faded, mostly because he started to date Anne Weaver. Still, when I ran into him occasionally, for a moment my heart would lurch and I would think about lost possibilities and misguided dreams.

And then he left. I noticed gradually, first absent-mindedly realizing his slouching figure wasn't among the men at the back of the church anymore. Then he didn't visit for what must have been months.

Finally I asked Mom about it one night after supper.

"Where's Johnny Martin?" I asked as nonchalantly as possible. "He's not been around for a while."

She paused with her hands submerged to the wrists in dishwater.

"He's gone," she said, finally looking up. "His mom said he left."

I didn't know what to say then. What do you say about someone who leaves all that is real to you and joins something foreign, outside the borders of your geography.

I shuffled the papers on my desk, looking for the envelope with the picture of John Martin. I found it in the trash can somewhat crumpled. The photo I pulled out revealed the same wise brown eyes and the same lovely wavy hair I remembered. It took me a moment to believe it was him. I began to think about his family, and suddenly I felt tired.

What could I do? If you asked me what responsibility my job entails I would tell you about the restrictive construction of the obituary formula. Perhaps I would tell about the sadness I feel when I write the words "self-inflicted gunshot wound" or about mourning the early deaths of unusual people. When I think of families, I try to spell their loved one's name correctly and emphasize the positive. That's all I know to do.

I come across a lot of people I know at this job, their lives neatly conformed to the obituary formula—

name, age, of address, died, when, where, of what. Then job and accomplishments. I always hope this extends beyond the one that announced "scored a hole-in-one at the public golf course in 1980," but you learn not to be picky.

Next come hobbies, affiliations, and/or member-ships. Finally, a list of family members. The *Daily News* doesn't include nieces, nephews, grandchildren, great-grandchildren, or dogs by name, though many a battle's been fought over this point.

Anyway, all I know to do each day is to do my job well. That means writing one last story about some-one in such a way that the people left behind feel a little more at peace, but without stretching the truth too far.

I knew what I needed to do. I picked up a pen and notebook, told Anthony where I was going, and head-ed out of the newsroom. The newspaper building is large, about half a city block, but we reporters and editors tend to spend most of our time, apart from the bathrooms and cafeteria, in the newsroom and the morgue.

Not too long ago someone decided that the word *morgue* was morbid and offensive to someone some-where, so they erected a fake brass plaque and renamed the room "The Library." But, as is always the case here, nothing changed. You'd be hard pressed to find anyone in the building who can give you direc-tions to The Library, but they can easily show you the morgue.

The morgue is a medium-sized room containing thousands of newspaper clippings, a few random ref-erence books, some out-of-town papers, and two librarians who spend their evenings gossiping and dissecting sections of the paper into clips they then file. Running along the back of the morgue is a wall of boxes containing archived clippings, alphabetized by subject or a subject's last name. The left side holds clips A through M; the right side N-Z.

The *Daily News* has a computerized data system, but when time allows, I like to do my research in the morgue. There's something about holding the yellowing pieces of paper in my hand. Somehow it makes my writing a bit more manageable.

I moved to the left and began to trace my eyes over the boxes, looking for the M's. I figured there would be plenty of Martins and I was right. Two boxes full, with about half a box devoted to several different John Martins.

I riffled through the different folders separating each individual's clip. My eyes caught several familiar faces—my old Sunday School teacher, our milkman. Finally, I found a miniature version of Johnny smiling above the crease of a folded clip.

I pulled out the two envelopes holding Johnny and moved over to one of the wooden tables at the front of the room. I sat down, opened my notebook, and began to lay out pieces of Johnny's life in front of me.

That's him in the front row of the Maple Road Mennonite Church softball team. Next is a slip of paper which reads, "A boy was born to Aaron and Susie Martin Sunday night at Hampshire General Hospital." The date on the clip is June 15, 1975. There's a picture of him running track, of him singing in the school's choir. Somehow he stands out in a group of high school graduates.

I assemble the pictures so they lay chronologically,
birth through the summer following graduation.
There's still a lot of table space left empty after that. I
look at it for a long time. I want to say something
clever about what that expanse of wood says to me,
maybe some kind of symbolism, but really it just
makes me sad. Tired and sad.

I pick up each picture and stare at his face, pulling
the clipping tight to my eyes, but the closer I get, the
less of him I can see until he is nothing but black,
gray, and white dots patterned together. The harder I
look, the less I can see.

Suddenly I remember a father I'd spoken with earlier in the week. He called in the obit for his son who
died in a farming accident. Funeral directors normally
phone in the obits, but every once in a while a family
member or a friend wants to instead. I sat at my desk
and helped him through the formula, telling him what
I needed to know at each step.

"What was his middle name?" I asked.

"Robert," he answered.

"How old was he?"

"Twelve."

We went on like this for a while, question, then
answer, like we forgot what we were really talking
about. I thought it was going to be okay, considering the
situation, until I asked about his hobbies. I was hoping to
round out the obit with a bit more personal information.

"He loved horses," his father said. "He never got
one; we didn't really have the room, but he hoped."

I didn't say anything for a minute.

"He wanted to run a horse farm when he grew up,"
the father said. "You have to include that."

Tim Robert Andrews, 12, of 146 White
Swan Lane, Adamsville, died unexpectedly
Friday afternoon. The Hampshire County
coroner has not yet ruled on the cause of
death.

Born in Adamsville, he was the son of
Arnold and Mary Andrews.

He was a sixth grade student at
Adamsville Elementary where he played
soccer and baseball.

He loved horses and dreamed of owning
a horse farm.

Surviving besides his parents are two sisters, Susan and Elizabeth, both at home; his
maternal grandparents; his paternal grandparents; four uncles; three aunts; and several cousins.

Looking down at Johnny on the table, I know there
isn't enough I can do. There never will be. I can only
do what I do. I pick up my pen and begin to assemble
the order of his life. There is the correct spelling of
his parents' names. That's right, he went to
Hampshire Mennonite Church. Slowly, I begin to do
my job.

The next day, the *Daily News* ran the following obituary.

John Martin, 25, of Columbus, Ohio, died
Monday morning at Columbus General
Hospital of injuries sustained in a car accident.

A carpenter, Mr. Martin worked for
Steven's Kitchen Design of Columbus.

He was a graduate of New Morning
Mennonite High School in East Hampshire
and a student at the University of Ohio.

He attended South Street United
Methodist Church of Columbus and was a
member at Hampshire Mennonite Church.

He enjoyed baseball, literature, and making furniture.

Born in Hampshire Township, he was the
son of Aaron and Susie Martin.

Surviving, in addition to his parents, are
two brothers, Peter Martin and Jacob
Martin, both at home; one sister Nancy,
wife of John King of New Easton; two
nieces and a nephew.

Kate Good lives in Washington, D.C.

Poetry, II

Coat of
a Visiting Nurse
by Julia Kasdorf

I put on Mom's coat the way we put on
the clothes of the dead, out of duty
or thrift or because I could not refuse.
Machine wash, she urged, permanent press,
this zip-out lining will take you
into November most years.

Walking alone in it, I think of the way
we remember those who've gone on,
frozen in one frame of their lives,
slightly heroic: she drives a tiny VW
on an unmarked country road toward
a trailer where a man is dying,
his wife worn out by his yellowing form
on the couch. His cancer, neatly charted
on Mom's clipboard. A stern jaw,
sturdy shoes, and this practical coat
are her only defenses against death
or a flat tire in wet weather.

As sleek city ladies stride past me
on the street, this stiff oatmeal coat,
which she grew too stout
to button and had to pass on,
feels conspicuous, indestructible
as so much I stand to inherit.

*Julia Kasdorf is a poet, living and teaching in State
College, Pennsylvania.*

God and Farmers

by Cheryl Denise

I'm not sure
but I think God likes farmers best,
people that work outside in blue jeans.

I don't get it
why they're so poor
unless God wants them
to have the very best of heaven.

I bet He doesn't watch us much
in offices,
over spread sheets and lawyer briefs,
He gets bored.

Mom said when the bridge on 92 went out,
the one the horse and buggies use,
the Council proposed a hundred thousand dollar plan
to be completed in six months.
The Old Orders decided to do it themselves,
in a week it was done
for five hundred.

Farmers know how God made the earth.
When something dies they make something else live.
Their bodies last longer.
They don't need gyms, Spandex, magazine diets.

Farmers get that noontime famished feeling
not the dull rumblings after inside work.
They know where food comes from;
they pray better.

It's easy to forget God in offices.
I can't see God calling someone to be a financial plan-
     ner.
Even jobs we think of as good
get all screwed up.

Nursing seems noble, working with old people
but sometimes I think
if I just let the residents go outside more,
bring in golden Labs and chickadees,
stop giving out pills,
God and the old folks would hold hands more.

It's easy to like lobster in the city,
to go to Pittsburgh to see the ballet,
to have nice homes in pretty neighborhoods
to keep the kids safe,
but I don't know that God wants our money
if we're rich.

WHAT MENNONITES ARE THINKING, 2000

I think in heaven
God will tell the farmers jokes
the rest of us won't understand.
I think they'll still farm
because they want to
but if a crop goes bad
God will order them pizza and beer.
At noon when the angels harp
and the rest of us sing,
God and the farmers will be playing games
making the corn and wheat sway.

Cheryl Denise is a poet living in Philippi, West Virginia.

Ice

by Jean Janzen

1

My mother dies in upheaval,
emaciated. Hollow eyes,

mouth like stone.
She is an empty house.

No kindling
for the iron-cold stove.

No one rattling
the pots in the morning.

2

Her voice is a needle, calling.
A stitch this time tears nine,
and the cold wind howls.
Her feet on the treadle faster now;
pins in her mouth.
I am too slow. She can't see me coming.

WHAT MENNONITES ARE THINKING, 2000

3

Her hot flat-iron sizzled
a Gothic arch through
the thick porch window ice

so I could watch
the rink at recess—
the kids circling, falling.

My breath kept the glass
in a blurred thaw, and I saw
what I would become—one of them.

Now she looks through,
she without breath, her lips frozen,
her hands still at last.

I can't see in.
I want her hot again, working
through the icy layers

so my eyes can see hers,
clear blue with recognition.

*Jean Janzen is a poet, living and writing in Fresno,
California.*

Thinking of Certain Mennonite Women

by Julia Kasdorf

When I think I can't bear to trace
one more sorrow back to its source,

I think of Lois those summer evenings,
when, supper dishes done, she'd climb

a windmill and cling beneath its great blades,
drawing water from under her father's fields.

She'd stay there until the sun went down
on barn roof, garden, and the one paved road

pointing toward town. When I am afraid
to set out once more alone, I see Julie

pumping her legs so hard she believes
she will fly off the swing set and land

gently on the lawn. I see her let go,
braids streaking behind, then see her knees

WHAT MENNONITES ARE THINKING, 2000

shredded on gravel, stuck to stockings
each time she kneels to pray at a pew.

When I can't tell my own desire
from the wishes of others, I remember

my mom, too young to know or care better,
flinging her jumper, blouse, socks, and slip

into the wind, dancing for flower beds
until her mother discovers. When I wonder

how I should live this only one life,
I think of how they tell these stories:

honestly, without explanation,
to whomever will listen.

*Julia Kasdorf is a poet, living and teaching in State
College, Pennsylvania.*

A Longer Essay

A Traditioned
Theology of Mission

by Wilbert R. Shenk

Introduction

Nearly all theology of mission produced in the past fifty years may be characterized as generic. That is to say, theology of mission has not been related to a particular theological tradition. This may be regarded as a positive development inasmuch as theologians of mission have devoted their efforts to laying a foundation for missionary obedience by the whole church. But this is an anomaly when placed in the context of theology generally. Numerous theologies treating a range of pastoral topics, evangelism, ethics, and systematic theology have been produced by and for particular theological traditions. Why is it not appropriate to work out a theology of mission on foundational themes of a theological tradition?

In fact, we may put the challenge more forcefully: The validity of any theology can be established only by its proven effectiveness in assisting the church in fulfilling its missionary obligation in the world. And this requirement can only be met when a particular church puts its theological convictions to the test in missionary practice. A theology of mission is essential if the church is to formulate its theological position with this missionary purpose as its aim.

With this goal in mind, I propose to survey and summarize the themes that have emerged from the theological reflection on missionary engagement by Mennonites in the period since 1970. This is the traditioned theology of mission I am presenting.

To set this work in its proper context, we must first clarify the definitions of "Anabaptist" and "Mennonite." These terms are often used imprecisely and loosely. I contend that the reality with which we have to deal today is Mennonite rather than Anabaptist, and that we should not confuse the two, especially when we are discussing theology of mission.

In the second section I examine the various sources of a Mennonite theology of mission. This will show that this emerging theology of mission is heavily dependent on modern sources. Nonetheless, these recent efforts have intentionally combined insights from biblical studies, Anabaptist studies, Mennonite history, and the contemporary theology of mission in articulating a theology of mission to serve the Mennonite tradition. These theological labors have come after more than a century of missionary work, both at home and abroad, and more than fifty years after the launching of the movement to "recover" the Anabaptist vision.

We begin, therefore, with a clarification of the terms that figure importantly in our study: "Anabaptist" and "Mennonite." Historical Anabaptism is not synonymous with contemporary Mennonitism. Anabaptism can be defined in terms of at least six dimensions.

"Anabaptism"

1. Anabaptism is a *historical* phenomenon. Anabaptism is a specific religious reform movement of the sixteenth century. It represents one stream that flowed within the wider Reformation. Anabaptism is that part of the Reformation variously called the Radical or Left Wing because of its thoroughgoing criticism of established views, values, and institutions, both Roman Catholic and Protestant.

2. Anabaptism is a *theological* stance. In common with other Christian traditions, Anabaptists affirmed the foundational doctrines of the Christian faith. In addition, they called for a more rigorous application of the teachings of Jesus by their emphasis on discipleship as *Nachfolge*, the church as a voluntary community (rather than being linked to the state), and the way of love in human relations.

3. We may define Anabaptism *ecclesiastically*. Anabaptists had broken away from Roman Catholicism but were also out of step with the main Reformers. The Anabaptists stressed that the goal of reform was to restore the New Testament church. They saw themselves as representing a "third way" that was neither Protestant nor Roman Catholic.

4. *Ethics* was of crucial importance. The Anabaptist conception of ethics placed the movement at odds with other Christian traditions. They believed the life and teachings of Jesus to be normative for Christian discipleship. Followers of Jesus were to renounce the use of violence. Certain vocations were incompatible with Christian discipleship. Ethics informed vocation.

5. Anabaptism was marked by a strong *missionary consciousness*. For the Anabaptists it was crucial that

the church maintain a missionary stance vis-à-vis the world, the realm where spiritual and human reality did not consciously submit to the reign of Jesus Christ. Indeed, this was considered to be the normal self-understanding of the church. The faithful church expected to live in tension with the world, and the absence of such tension was a sign of apostasy.

6. "Anabaptist" and "Anabaptism" also have a *contemporary* usage. In recent years the term has increasingly entered into the vocabulary of those groups that trace some lineal descent from the sixteenth-century Anabaptists and that wish to identify themselves as a part of this stream. Sometimes it is used to encompass the wider Mennonite/Brethren in Christ constituency. At other times it is a designation for certain contemporary renewal movements that consider themselves neo-Anabaptist. On other occasions it is a convenient trans-denominational label applied without regard to theological identity. When a term is used in such an elastic and imprecise fashion it is no longer functional.

"Mennonitism"

We now turn to a contrasting set of definitions of "Mennonite" or "Mennonitism." For purposes of comparison we will use the categories we applied to Anabaptism.

1. Speaking *historically* and *sociologically*, Mennonitism, as it evolved in the seventeenth century, was what survived the persecution of the Anabaptists in the sixteenth century. The price of survival was to come to terms with the larger society, that is, the world. In other words, survival was contin-

gent on accommodation to the demands and reality of society at large. Except in the Netherlands, Mennonitism adopted as its primary strategy withdrawal from society in exchange for the possibility of pursuing its own agenda.

Internally, Mennonitism fortified itself for survival through ethnic cohesiveness and a system of group controls characteristic of any socioethnic group. Societies of this sort generally guard against innovation and change. The outsider who enters such a society will be required to undergo cultural circumcision and conform to the group.

Innovation was threatening, yet it did come as the result of interaction with the larger society and with other churches. Typically, some trusted individual who was able to stand on the margin of Mennonitism and interact with outside groups became the channel for mediating innovation within the Mennonite community. This led to various changes—economic, geographical (i.e., migration), theological, and spiritual. Significantly, the Anabaptist legacy did not serve as the basis for renewal and change. Instead the early confessions of faith and *The Martyrs Mirror* were used to warn against innovations out of fear of compromise. Not until the twentieth century, as a result of the "recovery" movement, did it come to be expected that the heirs of the Anabaptists might find in sixteenth-century experience resources for the renewal of the church in the twentieth.

2. The *theological* identity of Mennonitism is essentially that of conservative Protestant orthodoxy, albeit noncreedal in formulation, with a bias toward biblicism and a mistrust of systematic and formal theolo-

gies. Particularly from the nineteenth century on, as Mennonites began to mingle more widely with other Christians and accommodated to the dominant culture, they have taken their cues in theology and piety largely from the evangelical mainstream.

3. In terms of *ecclesiastical* relations, Mennonites, in contrast to Anabaptists, identify strongly with Protestantism in its severe critique of Roman Catholic sacerdotalism and sacramentalism, yet share with Catholicism its strong sense of the church and its discipline. A major source of Mennonite distinctiveness has been ethnic cohesion and cultural identity, as well as lay ministry, nonliturgical worship, and congregational polity.

4. The Mennonite understanding of *ethics* is based on discipleship with a strong concern for simplicity in lifestyle, honesty and peace, the maintenance of group integrity, and minimal participation in and responsibility for the larger society. Until recently Mennonite ethics were shaped significantly by Mennonites' strategic withdrawal from the wider society.

5. The fifth distinctive is Mennonite ambivalence toward *mission*. In contrast to Anabaptists who understood their raison d'être to be mission, Mennonites have been preoccupied with conservation. The mindset and ethos of historical Mennonitism has been nonmissionary. The Anabaptists were dynamically missionary. By comparison the ethos of modern Mennonites is conventional Protestant. Protestants (whose origins lay in the reformation of church structures and doctrines) and Roman Catholics face no such contradiction. Christendom was nonmissionary in outlook, and both Protestants and Roman Catholics

worked to keep the Christendom framework intact.
For Catholics and Protestants alike mission became
the vocation of missionary orders and voluntary
groups rather than the concern of the church qua
church. Mennonite missions have been oriented more
to duty and obedience by the select few than to spontaneous witness of the whole church.

The thrust of the foregoing analysis is that at critical
points there is fundamental discontinuity between historical Anabaptism and its lineal descendent,
Mennonitism. This is particularly true with regard to a
theology of mission, as the next section seeks to show.

Contributors to a Theology of Mission for Mennonites

A number of important background influences have
contributed to the development of a Mennonite theology of mission.

Nineteenth-Century Spiritual Awakening

One of the significant influences is the spiritual
quickening of Mennonites in the nineteenth century.
This quickening owes a great deal to the Pietist movement, especially in Germany and Russia, and to recur-
ring waves of revival in North America. One of the
early mission promoters among American Mennonites
was Samuel Haury.[1] Haury received missionary training
at the Rhenish Missionary Training School at Barmen,
1871–75, an influential Pietist institution, and then
offered himself for missionary service on his return
from Germany. The General Conference Mennonite
Church appointed him to work among the Arapaho in
1880.

Mennonites were also influenced deeply by the revival message and methods that were rapidly introduced across the western world in the nineteenth century. At the same time Mennonites began to feel the impulses set in motion by the wider Protestant missionary movement. The modern missionary movement dates from the beginning of the nineteenth century and grew in strength throughout this period. The movement itself was both a product of and a stimulus to renewal. With its appeal to the biblical injunction to "Go into all the world" at a time when new means of transportation were making the whole world more accessible, this powerful initiative drew Mennonites along.

In summary, the nineteenth century proved to be a crucial period for Mennonites.[2] During this time several centuries of cultural isolation began to break down. Mennonites increasingly were exposed to the wider Christian church. At the end of this century the basic institutional framework for future church life was established, including mission agencies, publishing houses, educational institutions at the secondary and higher levels, and conference structures. All of this was accompanied by an accelerated acculturation to North American society, particularly in the twentieth century.

One Hundred Fifty Years of Missionary Experience

The century and a half of missionary experience that Mennonites have had since the nineteenth century awakening has shaped the sending church in ways never anticipated. This experience has irreversibly altered Mennonite horizons. This impact has occurred on both domestic and foreign fronts. Domestically, this has meant a new engagement with the urban world as well as with other ethnic groups. Although the bulk of Mennonite congregations remain in rural areas, they have been deeply influenced by urbanization and industrialization. By definition mission involves crossing cultural and political boundaries. The experience of encountering diverse cultures around the world has internationalized the Mennonite horizon, especially since World War 2.

Three learnings can be gleaned from these years of cross-cultural experience. First, from a *historical* perspective, we have gained a new appreciation of the fact that all cultures and institutions are relative. No culture may be regarded as the standard by which to judge other cultures. Second, we have learned that every *theological* expression is time-bound, each one shaped by a particular context or tradition. Consequently, each theological statement must be understood as partial and incomplete. Third, from a *sociological* point of view, we have discovered the importance of context. Along with others who participated in the modern missionary movement, Mennonites have moved from a concern for indigenization to a concern for contextualization. It is increasingly clear that the proper posture for the missionary is not that of answer-giver but fellow-learner.

Modern Missionary Movement

Mennonites have also learned much from the modern missionary movement. Mennonites have been ecumenical borrowers. Participation in this missionary movement has itself become the occasion for increased contact with and cooperation in various ventures. In some instances Mennonites have sought out these associations to meet their own needs for fellowship and camaraderie. More significantly, during the first century of Mennonite missions, from 1870–1970, they relied almost wholly on the ideology and missiology of the missionary mainstream. Mennonites were not writing theologies of mission or manuals on missionary methods during the greater part of this century.[3] This meant that Mennonite missionaries largely accepted the guidelines set by the Protestant mission movement in matters of methodology and rationale.

Indeed, Mennonites owe a great debt for what they have appropriated from the wider movement. They have depended to a great extent on the literature produced by missionary councils and agencies. Perhaps most important of all was the impact made by the Student Volunteer Movement on college-age Mennonite youth in the first decades of the twentieth century.

A Vision

Since the mid-1940s the Mennonite imagination has been stirred by a vision, the Anabaptist vision as first articulated by Harold S. Bender in 1944. As the movement to recover the Anabaptist vision gained momentum, it was increasingly evident that Anabaptism posed a challenge—perhaps "threat" would be more accurate—to historical Mennonitism in regard to mission. The work of Mennonite missions has produced a double effect. The formation of new Mennonite bodies in various parts of the world has resulted in the spread of Mennonites throughout the world, but this raised unsettling questions about the content of their identity. What remains unclear is the extent to which that identity can be clarified and shaped by Anabaptist perspectives.

At the end of the twentieth century Mennonitism was suffering an identity crisis. At least three streams of influence have contributed to this sense of crisis. The first is the so-called ethnic Mennonites who continue to have a confused identity in relation to the wider culture. They are increasingly accommodated to that culture but not without a guilty conscience. The second stream consists of other ethnic groups that have been joining this Mennonite reality over the past decades. Gradually they have discovered they cannot fully integrate into traditional Mennonite culture. They are attempting to appropriate those elements of a theological and ecclesiological vision of Christian discipleship that attracted them in the first place. But this same gospel-inspired vision has also spurred them to reclaim their own cultural and historical past. The third group that is participating in this crisis are the new Mennonites in Asia, Africa, and Latin America. They too are asking who they are theologically, historically, and culturally. Recovery of the Anabaptist vision may well rest with people outside North America and Europe less inhibited by social location and institutional security.

Renewal

Another contributor to a theology of mission for Mennonites is found in the movements of biblical theology and Holy Spirit renewal, including the so-called charismatic movement, which has affected many of those directly associated with Mennonite missions over the past generation.

Need for a Theological Foundation

Finally, the felt need for an articulated theological foundation for Mennonite mission propels us forward. The various theologies of mission available from mainstream Protestants, evangelical Protestants, Roman Catholics, Orthodox, and Pentecostals all contribute valuable insights. But none of these can speak out of the historical Mennonite experience. People directly involved in mission recognize the gap between theological vision and ideal, on the one hand, and what happens in practice in the field. This disjunction is underscored by the fact that there are now two and three generations of Mennonites in some churches in Asia, Africa, and Latin America who themselves look and feel more like evangelicals or Protestants than Mennonites. What is the significance, then, of Mennonite identity at all? It is evident that Mennonite missionaries frequently placed low value on their Mennonite heritage as they went about their work, and that they had little clarity about what it might mean missiologically. Thus the outcome is not surprising. And yet Mennonites in the nonwestern churches are asking for help in understanding Mennonite identity in order to be able to decide whether they want to grow in that direction or remain what they are.

The need for a clear theological identity takes on even greater urgency when we recognize that the Mennonite churches in the nonwestern world all live as minorities, and frequently in hostile environments. They want to be prepared to stand in the times of testing that continue to be their lot, and at a time when western Mennonitism is more clearly identifying with the mainstream of the western social, economic, and political realities.

Therefore, the challenge to articulate a foundation for a theology of mission for Mennonites is an important opportunity to clarify Mennonite identity—to move beyond maintenance and self-preservation to mission. The quest for recovery of the Anabaptist vision, which never realized its promise in the historical heartland of Europe and North America, lies in this direction. It will not be found in building more museums, holding more folk festivals, visiting more historical sites, and tracing more family genealogies. To recapture the Anabaptist vision we must above all else embrace a missionary consciousness.

Toward a Mennonite Theology of Mission

As demonstrated above, a theology of mission in the Mennonite tradition will be the product of a variety of influences. Such a theology of mission will seek to draw on the core theological ideas that have been passed down from the Anabaptists of the sixteenth century and that have shaped the Mennonite movement, but it is the task of theology to refocus the whole in light of the *missio Dei.* A Mennonite theology of mission must reflect the drive for a holistic theology that holds in tension proclamation and demonstration of the gospel, evangelization and reconciliation, preaching peace and making peace, advocating for justice and working for justice. Anything less than this will lead to a reduction of the gospel to a fragment of the whole.

Introduction

In 1984 an attempt at a comprehensive bibliography of Mennonite missions was published in *Mission Focus*.[4] This bibliography carried some 865 items, beginning with the pioneer Dutch Mennonite missionary to Indonesia, Pieter Jansz, writing in 1859 on the problems of Dutch colonial policy. This bibliography excluded articles that appeared in the official denominational organs, plus the long list of items in the *Bibliography of J. D. Graber's Printed Writings with Index,* compiled by Steven D. Reschley and Barbara Nelson and published separately in 1980. Graber was the most prolific Mennonite writer on mission themes prior to 1965. Of the items included in this "Bibliography of Mennonite Missions," less than five percent, or approximately forty, have been classified as dealing with the theology of mission.

For purposes of this study we shall exclude the J. D. Graber writings. He saw his role to be that of educating his constituency by drawing on the best missiological insights coming from the wider missionary movement, rather than of attempting to work out an explicitly Mennonite approach to these questions.[5] By the same token, we will also exclude the considerable body of writings by G. W. Peters, the Mennonite Brethren professor of missions at Dallas Theological Seminary who self-consciously wrote as an evangelical for evangelicals.[6]

Although the mission theme did not figure prominently in the early phases of the "recovery of Anabaptism" movement, already in 1946 Franklin H. Littell made the case for interpreting sixteenth-century Anabaptism as essentially a missionary movement.[7]

He developed this thesis fully in *The Anabaptist View of the Church: An Introduction to Sectarian Protestantism*.[8] This was followed by two doctoral dissertations in German and one in English: Wolfgang Schäufele, *Das missionarische Bewußtsein und Wirken der Täufer* (1966);[9] Georg Gottfried Gerner, *Der Gebrauch der Heiligen Schrift in der oberdeutschen Täuferbewegung* (1973);[10] and Ray C. Gingerich, *The Mission Impulse of Early Swiss and South German–Austrian Anabaptism* (1980).[11] The last in particular focused the importance of missionary consciousness for Anabaptist identity. Each of these studies reinforced the historical picture of sixteenth-century Anabaptism as a movement seeking to live out the Great Commission in its day as the apostolic vanguard. But throughout the period 1945–1970 no one undertook to work out a theology of mission for today from an explicitly Anabaptist/Mennonite perspective.

In 1967 Mennonite Brethren scholars produced a Festschrift, *The Church in Mission*,[12] in honor of long-time missions and educational leader J. B. Toews. This volume contained a section on "Historical Recovery of Mission," which included chapters on sixteenth-century Anabaptists and the Pietists of the seventeenth century.

Hans Kasdorf's thorough study of Mennonite Brethren mission thought for the period 1885–1984 yields several observations and conclusions that are applicable to Mennonites more generally. The Mennonite Brethren have largely depended on others for the mission language they have used. And this borrowed language has, in turn, reshaped them in the direction of "American Evangelicalism and Fundamentalism—more than Mennonitism."[13] Kasdorf summarizes the development of a theology of mission among Mennonite Brethren in several stages: implicit holistic theology; salvationist theology emphasizing the love of God and the cross of Christ; kingdom theology—incarnation as model, church as instrument of kingdom, spiritual gifts bestowed for ministry by the whole people, all members are called to be servants of the King; a trinitarian theology. These stages, of course, overlap and intertwine, but in each stage a particular theme was dominant. Kasdorf concludes that a theology of mission is always in process of development. What is needed is an overarching vision of the direction in which this development ought to take us.[14]

With the decade of the 1970s we began to see self-conscious efforts to develop a theology of mission within the Mennonite tradition. A flurry of articles appeared around 1975, and several collections of essays have appeared since that time. In 1983 Donald R. Jacobs published *A Pilgrimage in Mission,* with the avowed purpose

> to study what part modern missions have played in increasing and decreasing these tensions within the brotherhood; to propose a way of understanding missions whose foundation is scriptural; and to reflect on some of the lessons God has taught us Anabaptist Mennonites who have been preserved and nurtured for over 450 years by God.... It is only in participating with God in his mission that the Anabaptist people and, for that matter, any denomination, find fulfillment. So this study is not only a study of the church's mission but of the church itself.... For Mennonites, hopefully this book can help update

our understanding of how we can maintain both a vision for a 'pure church' and a vision for a 'missionary church.'[15]

It remains to be noted that the most significant theological influence during the period 1955–1980 was that of John Howard Yoder. His seminal work, *The Politics of Jesus*, was published in 1972 and, together with his many other writings, was deeply formative for subsequent missiological developments.[16] Yoder both clarified the continuing missionary significance of the believers church vision and criticized the lack of integrity in Mennonite church life.[17]

Basic Sources Used

The method adopted here has been to select certain texts, largely published in the journal *Mission Focus* during the years 1973–1980, that have contributed to the development of a missiology growing out of the Anabaptist/Mennonite theological vision. These include pieces by David A. Shank, "The Shape of Mission Strategy,"[18] "Anabaptists and Mission,"[19] "Towards an Understanding of Christian Conversion,"[20] and "The Shape of Mission";[21] Wilbert R. Shenk, "The Dynamics of Mission";[22] Robert L. Ramseyer, "The Anabaptist Vision and Our World Mission (I)";[23] Takashi Yamada, "The Anabaptist Vision and Our World Mission (II)";[24] Marlin E. Miller, "The Gospel of Peace";[25] John Driver, "Mission—From a Believers Church Perspective";[26] Mennonite Board of Missions, "A Theology of Mission in Outline";[27] and Hans Kasdorf, "Toward a Mennonite Brethren Theology of Mission."[28] Although not incorporated in this study, two volumes have been published more recently that bring together subsequent work: *Anabaptism and Mission*[29] and *The Transfiguration of Mission*,[30] both edited by Wilbert R. Shenk. Finally, a compendium of papers originating from a consultation sponsored by the Council of International Ministries, titled *A Relevant Anabaptist Missiology for the 1990s*,[31] will repay careful study.

Defining Themes

Ten main themes run through these writings; these themes will be examined in turn.

1. *Mission originates in God's mission to redeem the world.* The specific missions in which we engage are responses to the *missio Dei*. This statement is the fruit of a long development in missiological thought. From the beginning of the modern mission movement the basis of mission was established by identifying the motive. Over time various motives have been advocated.[32] What we observe is that the motivation for mission has been fluid. Historical perspective and context have been of critical significance in shaping understandings of mission in particular eras. The sociopolitical forces have had great influence on the motives for mission in successive periods. It is clear that we cannot rely on motives for mission to provide us with a sure basis for Christian mission.

A new concept emerged after 1950. Gerald H. Anderson studied representative writers for the period 1928–1958 and demonstrated the continuing profusion of ideas concerning the basis of mission. Anderson identified six different positions, including culture-centered (A. G. Baker), human-centered (Vernon White), church-centered (Roman Catholic),

Bible-centered (Harold Lindsell), kingdom-centered (E. Stanley Jones), Christ-centered (John A. Mackay). Nevertheless, Anderson discerned an emerging trend toward a theocentric/trinitarian basis for mission. In the early 1950s the concept of *missio Dei* was introduced and has gained wide acceptance.[33]

Mennonites played no direct role in these debates about the starting point and motives for mission, but their engagement in missionary work since 1850 exposed them to the range of missiological issues. They have readily embraced the emerging theocentric position. The biblical theology movement also exerted a salutary influence with its emphasis on Jesus Christ as Savior and Lord, the foundation for mission and ethics.

If we read the Scriptures from the standpoint of God's missionary intention, at least three points stand out. First, the basis of that salvific plan is *agape* (John 3:16–17; Rom. 5:8; 1 John 4:7–21). It is God who takes the initiative in seeking out humankind. God does this not because men and women deserve to be delivered from the power of sin but because that is in the nature of *agape*. Second, God's ultimate purpose is "to unite all things in Christ," that is, to liberate men and women from the power of death, their mortal enemy. This salvation redounds "to the praise of his glorious grace" (Eph. 1; Col. 1:15–29; Rom. 8:20–23; Rev. 4:11–5:14, 7:9–12; Ezek. 36:16–32; Isa. 43:1–44:8). Third, the Bible shows God acting in a threefold manner. We meet God first of all as loving creator of the world and humankind. Next we encounter God as redeemer, the one who patiently and in grace continues to seek out a people who respond to God's love. Finally, the Bible discloses God

as the consummator, the one who guarantees the outcome of history and leads in the triumph of good over
evil. God is shown to be a missionary God: the one
who initiates, comes to the world seeking and wooing,
calling and restoring. By contrast, all human efforts to
work out salvation are futile.

2. *Mission is essentially a messianic movement led by
the Suffering Servant in the power of the Spirit.* God's missionary intention for the world is entrusted to the
Messiah, the one called Suffering Servant. A major
theme in Old Testament prophecy is that the people of
God will finally find rest, that is, salvation, when the
Messiah comes. This prophecy concerning the Messiah
reaches a high point in Isaiah. The prophet Isaiah
envisaged the day when God would do a new thing in
human affairs through the Messiah. The Old Testament
contains three strands. One strand has to do with the
Messiah, "the anointed one," the just and righteous
king who will reign in the future. The second strand is
Daniel's prophecy concerning the Son of Man. The
third strand is Isaiah's vision of the Suffering Servant.

Jesus fuses these three strands by embodying all
three within himself. The coming of Jesus inaugurates
a movement. Peter's sermon at Pentecost reaches its
climax with the recognition of Jesus as the Messiah
(Greek: Christ) when he asserts: "Let all the house of
Israel therefore know assuredly that God has made
him both Lord and Christ, this Jesus whom you cruci-
fied" (Acts 2:36). From the New Testament record it is
evident that Jesus was deeply conscious of his call to
carry out God's plan from the moment of his baptism
by John the Baptist. Jesus' public ministry is a working out of that obedience. Jesus became the Suffering

Servant of God by whom the world was reconciled to God. Jesus was aware that as Son of Man he was elected to inaugurate God's new order. This is evident in the way Jesus initiates his ministry. He begins with this announcement: "Repent, for the kingdom of heaven is at hand" (Matt. 4:17; cf. Matt. 4:23, Mark 1:14, Luke 4:18-21).

Early in his public ministry eyewitnesses sensed the extraordinary character of Jesus. Matthew notes: "And when Jesus finished these things the crowds were astonished at his teaching, for he taught them as one who had authority, and not as their scribes" (7:28-29). Instinctively the disciples interpreted this special character through conceptual categories from Judaism such as "eschatological prophet" or "political Messiah-king." But such categories did not correspond to Jesus' self-consciousness. Only gradually, and after much struggle and confusion, did the disciples eventually break through to new insight.

Following the death, resurrection, and ascension of the Lord, the community of disciples was gripped by the conviction that God had entrusted the whole outcome of history to the One, the Suffering Servant whom they now acclaimed Lord and Christ. The presence of the Holy Spirit further attested to the messiahship of Jesus. Integral to messianic expectations was the promise that the Spirit of God would be fully present in the Messiah. The life and witness of Jesus gave convincing evidence that he was truly Spirit-anointed. Ultimately, he would claim that "all power is given to me," thus linking himself with God in the power of the Spirit.

We should recall that this christological development in early Christianity occurred in the context of missionary engagement. The surrounding cultures and religions regularly and vigorously challenged the Christian witness. Caesar presented himself as *kyrios* and Christians had to stand against this idolatry or be co-opted by it. Thus, the early Christian witnesses were cast in a role of confrontation with opposing forces of various kinds—religious, traditional, political, and social.

Mission may also be viewed as messianic movement from the sociohistorical angle. In the 1960s two notable works appeared: *A Theology of Hope* (1967) by Jürgen Moltmann, and *A Rumor of Angels* (1969) by Peter Berger.[34] As a theologian, Moltmann drew attention to the importance of hope for understanding human experience. This eschatological dynamic propels history forward. Sociologist Berger's book serves as a complement to Moltmann's. Berger's purpose was to challenge the conventional wisdom regarding secularization. He identified five "signals of transcendence" which attest to the enduring reality of religion even in so-called secularized societies. One of these signals is the universal and irrepressible human need for hope.

In *The Sociology of Hope*, Henri Desroche studies messianism and millenarianism sociologically and historically.[35] He documents the pervasive role this dynamic has played in human experience. Desroche analyzes the messianic/millennial dynamic as it moves through a succession of three stages: from oppression to resistance to liberation. Drawing on the insights of Desroche and theologian John H. Yoder, David Shank summarizes the processes and stages in the outworking of the messianic dynamic.[36]

a. In the midst of oppression, domination, and injustice, someone appears as God's instrument for bringing about a new humanity—interpreted as new creation, new kingdom, new order—visualized as a holistic reality encompassing religious, social, economic, and political aspects of life.

b. Those who break with the old order to follow this messianic leader form a new community that becomes a critique of the old order and a foreshadowing of the new when it is achieved fully.

c. When the promised ideal new humanity fails to appear, the initial impetus wanes and the movement undergoes a fission, one part veering in a religious direction and the other taking on political forms. The breakup thus diffuses and denatures the original holistic thrust. Each wing becomes in itself a movement that reinterprets the original holistic intent, but from a reductionist perspective. (Veering toward the religious means abandoning the political, and vice versa. Yet the vision of the messianic kingdom holds the whole together.) This reductionist stage may continue for a long time.

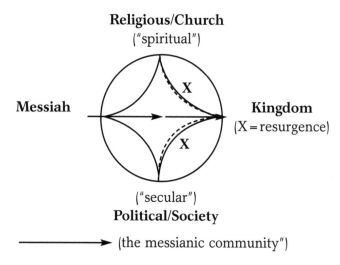

d. But with the passage of time and the emergence
of new conditions and demands, the inadequacies of
the present order become apparent. This ferment and
growing dissatisfaction form the seedbed for a messianic resurgence. A new leader arises who interprets
once again the possibility of a holistic new order. This
resurgence moves toward the messianic core message
and draws on the vision and dynamic.

e. Desroche suggests that early Christianity understood itself as a millennial/messianic movement.[37]
With the rise of Augustinian theology in the fourth
and fifth centuries, millenarian consciousness waned.
The church had now moved from being in the position of an oppressed minority to being in a dominant
role in society. Desroche concludes, "Thus messianism
is a plan for a Kingdom conceived in the lands of
Exile."[38] The bane of the people of God has been that
they frequently forget that they have been liberated
from exile and allow themselves to be seduced by the
old enslaving order once again.

*3. The missionary's task is to announce and witness to
the Messiah's reign.* As we examine the witness of the
early church, we note that it had two focal points. On
the one hand, the first Christians understood that they
were to continue the works characteristic of the kingdom that Jesus had inaugurated but which were yet
incomplete. In giving the Great Commission, Jesus
establishes the structure for this ongoing ministry
through the community.

The goal of mission then is the fulfillment of the
Messiah's reign. This goal becomes the touchstone for
determining and evaluating missionary action. What
is authentic will be faithful to this messianic vision,

and what is false and contradictory will be opposed to the messianic goal. As missionary experience shows, our obedience is always less than perfect and consistent. Therefore we need constantly to keep before us a standard by which to guide and correct our undertakings.

The history of missions demonstrates that as the Scriptures are released into new churches—although imperfectly and unfaithfully transmitted—the originality and power of the message can break through again and the messianic core will stimulate fresh movements. Ultimately, every attempt to channel, control, and institutionalize the messianic dynamic is doomed. Humanly speaking, we can only respond to and follow after the Messiah; we cannot put ourselves in charge and determine the exact course the movement must take.

4. *The Messiah's message is the gospel of peace.*[39] The New Testament writers employ a variety of terms to describe the gospel: good news of the kingdom; gospel of God/gospel of Jesus Christ; gospel of salvation; and gospel of peace (Acts 10:36; Eph. 2:13–22). All of these terms refer to the same reality. In Jesus the Messiah, God has made possible our redemption from sin. This results in a new relationship with God (at-one-ment) and with other men and women. As members of this reconciled community we are called to live out the messianic peace and actively invite others to accept the offer of God's shalom. The messianic order is characterized by the commitment to peace. Jesus Christ consistently rejected the use of violence in effecting God's reign through him in the world. This is paradigmatic for the messianic community.

5. *Mission strategy grows out of the nature of this messianic movement.* Some of the most tragic chapters in the history of the Christian movement have been written when zealous people have resorted to methods and strategies that fundamentally contradicted the messiahship of Jesus. Whenever violence and subterfuge have been the hallmarks of witness, the results have been counterproductive. We must always strive for integrity between the messianic community's life and its witness. This is the ultimate test of regeneration and new birth into the life of the messianic kingdom. To put the matter positively, in the Sermon on the Mount, Jesus described his community as light and salt. This means that the essential values of the new order are to characterize the life of the community.

Vicarious sacrificial suffering is also integral to missionary witness.[40] Against the backdrop of his own public ministry, death, and resurrection, Jesus addresses the disciples: "As the Father has sent me, even so I send you" (John 20:21). Thus, the Messiah's example and model is made normative for the community. Jesus modeled servanthood, and transformed lordship into servanthood (Mark 10:45; Isa. 53:10–12). This statement is not first a doctrine of the atonement but rather a description of a missionary lifestyle (cf. Phil. 2:5–11). According to the Apostle Paul, voluntary renunciation of our own program in favor of the Messiah's is at the heart of missionary obedience (cf. 1 Cor. 1:17–2:5).

6. *The goal of mission is the establishment of the new order under the Messiah's rule.* That is, mission is the means by which God is establishing the reign of God

in the world. In the first place, this means that mission leads to the formation of concrete communities living out the new order which Jesus inaugurated. In other words, the messianic movement must be rooted in specific times, places, and among particular peoples. But there is also the universal/cosmic thrust. The Apostle Paul asserts that it is God's intention to unite all things in Jesus Christ. We must hold together the particular and the universal. Typically, the particular becomes the path to the universal.

Reflecting on the mission task, we make several observations. First, the world belongs to Christ by right of creation and redemption. But in this age, the world remains in the grip of the evil one. Second, God sent Jesus to liberate the whole of creation from the power of evil. Third, the basic dynamic in history is this conflict between Christ and anti-Christ, between the forces of good and evil. Fourth, the missionary witness is addressed into that conflict where the battle rages. We do not understand Christ or our salvation apart from meeting Christ at work in the world redeeming the world. Finally, the outcome of this struggle has already been decided. Jesus Christ can already be acclaimed victor, and those who place their faith in Jesus and live in fellowship with him are assured of a share in that victory.

7. *The church is both the first fruit of this messianic movement in the world and the primary carrier and instrument of messianic purpose.* As such, the very nature of the church is missionary. The church's vocation is prefigured in the calling of the people of God beginning with Abraham in Genesis 12:1–3: "By you all the families of the earth shall bless themselves."

The phrasing of this promise emphasizes several things. First, it is universal in scope: "all the families of the earth." Second, it emphasizes the instrumentality or vocation of the people of God rather than according them a privileged status. Third, it strongly suggests a servant relationship. The people of God are available; through you the peoples "shall bless themselves." God acts through the community. Isaiah describes the vocation of the people as that of being a "light to the nations" (42:6–7). God also views the church as collaborator. In the words of the Apostle Paul, "that through the church the manifold wisdom of God might now be made known to the principalities and powers" (Eph. 3:10). And the church is the means through which God's power is being displayed before the world (3:20–21).

The Bible describes no other means by which God is reaching out to the world than through the people of God.[41] Through this people the witness becomes concrete and incarnate. This people actualizes God's love.

8. *Mission is an act of radical obedience and discipleship.* The sixteenth-century Anabaptists were noted for their frequent reference to the Great Commission.[42] They correctly sensed this commission to be definitive. For the Great Commission provides a permanent structure for the church in its relationship to the world. God loves the world and Jesus Christ died for the world, thus making possible the forgiveness of sin and opening up a new future. This is at the heart of the apostolic proclamation which Jesus commissions his disciples to carry to all parts of the world (Matt. 28:16–20, Mark 16:15–18, Luke 24:46–49, John 20:19–23, Acts 1:6–8).

Being converted to Jesus Christ begins with the fundamental decision to *turn* Christ-ward, but it includes embracing the mission of Jesus to the world. The disciples are in the world but not of the world; and the disciples are sent into the world as the apostolic vanguard for the salvation of the world. Whenever the church turns its back on this commission, it loses its identity and authority, and surrenders its integrity.

This missionary witness is, of course, perceived by the world as judgment on it. The Gospel according to John puts the matter pointedly: "This is the judgment that the light has come into the world, and men loved darkness rather than light because their deeds were evil" (John 3:19; cf. 12:30–32). To be faithful in witness requires that we maintain a clear perspective on the radical nature of the missionary call and the crucial role mission plays in the outcome of history.

9. *Mission requires deep penetration into the world— for the world, against the world.* Missionary obedience involves penetration into all areas of life, for all of life is to be brought under the lordship of Jesus Christ. The gospel is as comprehensive as the new order that it announces. The power and persuasiveness of the gospel is precisely that it alone offers an adequate alternative to the old order that is in the grip of the forces of death and destruction. This of course demands a deep respect for and understanding of culture, social and economic structures, and political reality, in order that we may truly communicate good news in those precincts. The vision of the new order suggests the scope of the task—the breadth, depth, and priorities that arise out of the gospel.

The Incarnation is basic to all missionary approaches. God chose Incarnation, complete identification, as the means by which to reach the world through the Messiah. What God did in the Incarnation of Jesus the Messiah was, of course, unique and cannot be repeated. But Jesus challenged his disciples to follow him into the world as he had been in the world, identifying with humankind in order to witness to God's new order of salvation. The Incarnation judges all missionary methods by calling into question those that reduce the gospel to fit the missionary's categories or that truncate the gospel in order to squeeze it into our preconceived notions, methods, and strategies.

10. *The present age is the missionary age, the age of the Holy Spirit, the time between Pentecost and Parousia.* Pentecost marks the inauguration of this age; Parousia will signal its ending. The Holy Spirit mediated to the church the power of the resurrection and confirmed to the church that Jesus Christ was indeed the ascended and exalted Lord. The Holy Spirit released into the body the power and grace of Jesus the Messiah. The work of the Spirit is to extend the Messiah's reign. Jesus Christ has never relinquished his claim to the whole of creation. Yet parts of that creation are living in rebellion and the Messiah's sovereignty is not acknowledged everywhere. But the sovereignty of the Messiah will indeed be made manifest when "his enemies become his footstool" (the Old Testament phrase most quoted in the New). The state, for example, is God-ordained to maintain order in human society, but the state does not in fact submit to Jesus Christ as sovereign. Even the church frequently fails to honor Christ's rule fully.

Nonetheless, through the community of the Spirit, Christ's authority and saving presence is being extended in the world. The formation of the people of God in every part of the world is basic to the realization of God's plan, for this people are the vanguard of the new age.

This present time is marked by the tension of the "already/not yet." This is the age in which the Messiah's people live in anticipation of the consummation of their salvation. They live amid the continual struggle between Christ and antichrist. Although they are confident that victory is assured, the battle is not yet over. This is the age of ongoing struggle between Christ and Satan, between the old and the new orders. This is the age of the martyr and of redemptive suffering. But this is also the age when, through the fulfillment of the Great Commission, Christ's plan to redeem the world will be completed. Then Jesus the Messiah will be acclaimed as King of kings and Lord of lords (1 Tim. 6:13-15; Rev. 19:13-16).

Part of this chapter is reprinted with permission, with changes, from Calvin E. Shenk, ed., *A Relevant Anabaptist Missiology for the 1990s* (Elkhart, Ind.: Council of International Ministries, 1990).

1 Samuel S. Haury, *Letters Concerning the Spread of the Gospel in the Heathen World Presented to All Mennonites in North America*, trans. Marie Regier Janzen and Hilda Voth (Scottdale, Pa.: Herald Press, 1981); originally published as *Briefe über die Ausbreitung des Evangeliums in der Heidenwelt* (Halstead, Kans., 1877).

2 For brief overviews, see Theron F. Schlabach, *Gospel Versus Gospel: Mission and the Mennonite Church* (Scottdale, Pa.: Herald Press, 1980), chap. 1; and James C. Juhnke, "Prologue," in *A People of Mission: A History of General Conference Mennonite Overseas Missions* (Newton, Kans.: Faith and Life Press, 1979), 1-14.

3 Cf. "Bibliography of Mennonite Missions," *Mission Focus* 12 (December 1984). This comprehensive bibliography of writings by Mennonites on missions up to 1984 reveals no significant consideration of mission theology or the biblical basis of missions prior to 1940.

4 "Bibliography of Mennonite Missions," *Mission Focus* 12 (December 1984).

5 An exception to this generalization is his contribution to the H. S. Bender Festschrift. See J. D. Graber, "Anabaptism Expressed in Missions and Social Service," in *The Recovery of the Anabaptist Vision*, ed. Guy F. Hershberger (Scottdale, Pa.: Herald Press, 1957), 152–66.

6 See J. B. Toews, "George W. Peters: A Measure of the Man," in *Reflection and Projection: Missiology at the Threshold of 2001*, ed. Hans Kasdorf and Klaus W. Müller (Bad Liebenzell: Verlag der Liebenzeller Mission, 1988), 26: "He did not see the Mennonite Brethren Churches as only a segment of the larger Mennonite-Anabaptist but a distinct entity with a theology of its own which was neither particularly Mennonite nor Anabaptist. He saw the future of the Mennonite Brethren Church in the mainstream of Evangelical Christianity of America. The concern for world mission as the passion of his life at times seemed to overshadow his deep commitment to a basic Anabaptist understanding of theology." This Festschrift in honor of G. W. Peters (1908–1988) includes a bibliography of his writings.

7 In conversation David A. Shank has reported being present when Littell first presented his paper in 1946 with Harold S. Bender in the audience. Bender acknowledged that in formulating his "Anabaptist vision" statement three years earlier he had overlooked the centrality of mission to the Anabaptist movement. In Bender's *These Are My People: The Nature of the Church and Its Discipleship According to the New Testament* (Scottdale, Pa.: Herald Press, 1962), chapter 5, he attempts, rather obliquely, to include mission in his discussion of ministry.

8 Franklin Hamlin Littell, *The Anabaptist View of the Church: An Introduction to Sectarian Protestantism* ([Hartford?]: American Society of Church History, 1952). Republished as *The Origins of Sectarian Protestantism: A Study of the Anabaptist View of the Church* (New York: Macmillan, 1964).

9 Wolfgang Schäufele, *Das missionarische Bewußtsein und Wirken der Täufer* (Neukirchen-Vluyn: Neukirchener Verlag, 1966).

10 Georg Gottfried Gerner, *Der Gebrauch der Heiligen Schrift in der oberdeutschen Täuferbewegung* (Thesis, University of Heidelberg, 1973).

11 Ray C. Gingerich, *The Mission Impulse of Early Swiss and South German–Austrian Anabaptists* (Ph.D. diss., Vanderbilt University, 1980).

12 A. J. Klassen, ed., *The Church in Mission* (Hillsboro, Kans.: Mennonite Brethren Publishing House, 1967).

13 Hans Kasdorf, *A Century of Mennonite Brethren Mission Thinking, 1885–1984* (Th.D. thesis, University of South Africa, 1986), 332–33.

14 Hans Kasdorf, "Toward a Mennonite Brethren Theology of Mission," *Mission Focus* 16 (March 1988): 1–6.

15 Donald R. Jacobs, *Pilgrimage in Mission* (Scottdale, Pa.: Herald Press, 1983), 14, 19.

16 John Howard Yoder, *The Politics of Jesus* (Grand Rapids: Eerdmans, 1972).

17 See Yoder's various contributions to *Concern: A Pamphlet Series for Questions of Christian Renewal,* nos. 1–18 (1954–1971).

18 David A. Shank, "The Shape of Mission Strategy," *Mission Focus* 1, no. 3 (January 1973): 1–7; reprinted in *Mission Focus: Current Issues,* ed. Wilbert R. Shenk (Scottdale, Pa.: Herald Press, 1980), 118–28.

19 David A. Shank, "Anabaptists and Mission," in *Anabaptism and Mission,* ed. Wilbert R. Shenk (Scottdale, Pa.: Herald Press, 1984), 202–28.

20 David A. Shank, "Towards an Understanding of Christian Conversion," *Mission Focus* 5, no. 2 (November 1976): 1–7.

21 David A. Shank, "The Shape of Mission," *Mission Focus* 8 (December 1980): 69–74.

22 Wilbert R. Shenk, "The Dynamics of Mission," *Mission Focus* 1, no. 2 (November 1972): 1–3.

23 Robert L. Ramseyer, "The Anabaptist Vision and Our World Mission (I)," *Mission Focus* 4, no. 4 (March 1976): 1–6. Reprinted in *Anabaptism and Mission,* ed. Wilbert R. Shenk (Scottdale, Pa.: Herald Press, 1984), 178–87.

24 Takashi Yamada, "The Anabaptist Vision and Our World Mission (II)," *Mission Focus* 4, no. 4 (March 1976): 7–14. Reprinted in *Anabaptism and Mission,* ed. Wilbert R. Shenk (Scottdale, Pa.: Herald Press, 1984), 188–201.

25 Marlin E. Miller, "The Gospel of Peace," *Mission Focus* 6, no. 1 (September 1977): 1–5. Reprinted in *Theology for the Church:*

Writings by Marlin E. Miller, ed. Richard A. Kauffman and Gayle Gerber Koontz (Elkhart, Ind.: Institute of Mennonite Studies, 1997), 3-12; also reprinted in *Mission and the Peace Witness: The Gospel and Christian Discipleship,* ed. Robert L. Ramseyer (Scottdale, Pa.: Herald Press, 1979), 9-23.

26 John Driver, "Mission—From a Believers Church Perspective," *Mission Focus* 7, no. 1 (March 1979): 1-6. See also John Driver, "A Missionary Community," chap. 6 in *Community and Commitment* (Scottdale, Pa.: Herald Press, 1976).

27 The Mennonite Board of Missions, "A Theology of Mission in Outline," *Mission Focus* 6, no. 5 (May 1978): 9-13; also printed as a pamphlet by MBM.

28 Hans Kasdorf, "Toward a Mennonite Brethren Theology of Mission," *Mission Focus* 16 (March 1988): 1-6.

29 Wilbert R. Shenk, ed., *Anabaptism and Mission* (Scottdale, Pa.: Herald Press, 1984).

30 Wilbert R. Shenk, ed., *The Transfiguration of Mission* (Scottdale, Pa.: Herald Press, 1993).

31 Calvin E. Shenk, ed., *A Relevant Anabaptist Missiology for the 1990s* (Elkhart, Ind.: Council of International Ministries, 1990).

32 R. Pierce Beaver, "Missionary Motivation through Three Centuries," in *Reinterpretation in American Church History,* ed. Jerald C. Brauer (Chicago: University of Chicago Press, 1968), 113-51; Johannes van den Berg, *Constrained by Jesus' Love: An Inquiry into the Motives of the Missionary Awakening in Great Britain in the Period between 1698 and 1815* (Kampen: J. H. Kok, 1956); J. A. de Jong, *As Waters Cover the Sea: Millennial Expectations in the Rise of Anglo-American Missions, 1640-1810* (Kampen: J. H. Kok, 1970).

33 Gerald H. Anderson, *The Theology of Missions: 1928-1958* (Ann Arbor, Mich.: University Microfilms, 1960), 343.

34 Jürgen Moltmann, *A Theology of Hope: On the Ground and the Implications of Christian Eschatology* (London: SCM Press, 1967); Peter L. Berger, *A Rumor of Angels: Modern Society and the Rediscovery of the Supernatural* (Garden City, N. Y.: Doubleday, 1969).

35 Henri Desroche, *The Sociology of Hope* (London: Routledge and Kegan Paul, 1979); originally published as *Sociologie de l'espérance* (Paris: Calmann-Lévy, 1973).

36 David A. Shank, "The Shape of Mission," 72-73.

37 Cf. the bold use made of this paradigm by John G. Gager, *Kingdom and Community: The Social World of Early Christianity*

(Englewood Cliffs, N. J.: Prentice-Hall, 1975), chap. 2.

38 Desroche, *Sociology of Hope,* 112.

39 Cf. Marlin E. Miller, "The Gospel of Peace"; and John Driver, "A Community of Peace," chap. 5 in *Community and Commitment* (Scottdale, Pa.: Herald Press, 1976).

40 Two studies that link atonement and mission demonstrate how theology is enriched when it is grounded in mission: John Driver, *Understanding the Atonement for the Mission of the Church* (Scottdale, Pa.: Herald Press, 1986); and C. Norman Kraus, *Jesus Christ Our Lord: Christology from a Disciple's Perspective* (Scottdale, Pa.: Herald Press, 1987). Both books were written in missionary contexts.

41 Cf. Wilbert R. Shenk, "The Great Commission," in *Mission Focus: Current Issues* (Scottdale, Pa.: Herald Press, 1980), 41–46, for a brief study of the varying emphases of the five versions of the Great Commission. These enrich and enlarge the scope of Christ's command. The biblical vision of the church as God's missionary agent is explored richly in John Driver, *Images of the Church in Mission* (Scottdale, Pa.: Herald Press, 1997). We need to reclaim this biblical foundation.

42 Franklin H. Littell, "The Great Commission," chap. 4 in *The Origins of Sectarian Protestantism: A Study of the Anabaptist View of the Church* (New York: Macmillan, 1964).

Wilbert R. Shenk is a professor and missiologist living in Pasadena, California.

Book Reviews

The Journey Toward Reconciliation, **by John Paul Lederach, Scottdale, PA and Kitchener, ON: Herald Press, 1999.**

Reviewed by Bernie Wiebe

John Paul Lederach has worked as a mediator in a great variety of contexts on all the continents of the world. Conflicts within smaller units like local churches in his home area of Virginia to major ideological and political disputes in Latin America, Northern Ireland, South Africa, and in the Basque region of Spain, have challenged Lederach's insights and beliefs to the core.

Journey Toward Reconciliation is an attempt to reflect analytically upon those experiences and then to do some integrative projections about their meaning. His method is communication by telling stories. It seems a bit sad to me that he chose to focus so extensively upon an Anabaptist readership with these stories. While John Paul justifies this because he feels "accountable to them" (15), these "stories" seem totally relevant to a much broader audience. And there are many in today's world who hunger for the stories told in this significant book. To be fair to Lederach, he does add that he wants to be "transparent" about his faith and also to engage in a "dialogue across faith traditions" (15).

The stories in *Journey Toward Reconciliation* range from the gut-wrenching experience of having his firstborn daughter Angie's life threatened in Nicaragua, taking the "heat" for the USA in a context where

American foreign policy had contributed to the violence Lederach now wanted to address in terms of reconciliation, the shock of seeing a "violent" colonel appear with a 10-year-old daughter who wore metal braces on her legs—maybe violent but nevertheless a caring father, his own personalizing the peacemaking process through use of the metaphors truth, mercy, justice, and peace as actual person participants in that process, meeting the warlords in Somalia, a visit to the genocide museum in Phnom Penh, his agonies at being invited to teach peacemaking at the War College in Carlisle (PA), discovering that Mennonite churches have their own Ten Commandments on how to deal with conflict in the church, to a story about working "through" disillusionment based on experiences in Northern Ireland and with Justapaz in Colombia, to a concluding story about Sam Doe's dream for Liberia. Each story carries a significant message for one who has the patience to listen and to learn. These stories by themselves are worth the price of the book and all who read them will not easily forget them.

There are several important contributions that John Paul makes in this book:

First, the complex "Big Picture" of conflict/violence and of peacemaking/reconciliation.

Lederach tells how he continues to learn more about first establishing what "enemy" means (chapter 2), including the biblical teachings in the Old Testament along with his experiences of encountering "enemies." Lederach concludes: "Living faithfully in the face of enemies is only possible with a deep spiritual connection to God's love and a willingness to live as vulnerably as Jesus did" (41). Secondly, in joining the journey toward reconciliation, Lederach says he has begun to see "beyond conflict resolution" (51) to reconciliation. While I was unable to understand fully why or how he separates the two, it appears that he is looking for a more holistic way of responding to conflicts, i.e. go further than conflict *resolution* into building new relationships. This he illustrates quite meaningfully with a methodology he has developed, based on Psalm 85 (53). He gets four key people to take on the roles of justice, peace, mercy, and truth. He then presents them in a conversation of how in a specific conflict these four can somehow come to harmony. It is an intriguing method that has a lot of potential, especially in church conflicts.

I have to wonder whether John Paul tries too hard to make Psalm 85 be an adequate key for mediation. In my own experiences, I have had to include the elements of self-esteem, patience or tolerance, growth, transformation, encounter, as essential "characters" in the process (he does add "hope" [p. 761]). It is here that Lederach reinforces his insight that reconciliation is a "journey," usually not the destination. Although I do get the feeling that at times he sees the journey getting to the destination eventually, both socially and spiritually. In my own experience, that has been very rare. I have come to see reconciliation on a continuum. It is indeed a journey, but it may move people only in the right direction and, when we are done, they may still only (but very significantly) be a few incremental steps into that direction. Occasionally I set people before the continuum line from crisis to resolution and ask them how far they believe they have journeyed. It has been extremely helpful.

Lederach's insight about the paradoxes on this journey are significant for the journey at all stages.

Second, for Mennonites, John Paul does an excellent service by revisiting some of our traditional approaches to conflict and then giving us reflections from his experiences. This makes us take another look at the place of tears and of anger (1-43); how to deal with "sinners" (49) and that we might discover God more readily if we could follow the way Jesus related to sinners. It is helpful when he reminds us that too readily we have applied "monochronic" approaches where we need to use polychronic ones (78ff).

It is one of the few times John Paul wanders into academic discourse; but it is essential for us to see the dynamic nature of both conflict and reconciliation "energies." John Paul says that traditional Mennonite "two-kingdom theology" (92) has often kept us from being involved in the "messy" dilemmas of today's world. He encourages us to examine our "unspoken Ten Commandments of Conflict in the Mennonite Church" (101ff) as not having helped us to be mediating influences at many critical points. One way to facilitate the process of changing our attitudes is to recognize that all of us are created in the image of God (as the Quakers say: there is a "thatness" of God in each person); yet it is also apparent from the Bible that conflict was present "in the beginning" (112). Nowhere does the Bible suggest that conflict itself is evil; instead, it is natural and creative. It becomes evil only when we are unwilling to learn from it. And, while this book is not a "how to" manual, he then reviews with the readers once again the details Jesus expresses in Matthew 18 on how we are to deal with conflict.

Third, Lederach's concluding chapter talks of "the dream" about what the future might hold. He dares to think we can expect hope out of disillusionment—it has happened in Northern Ireland, in South Africa, in the former Soviet Union. This will come only with the "groans of creation in all its parts—Romans 8:22-23" (189). We need to embrace the paradoxes. "We are shackled by a lack of imagination and dreaming that things can be otherwise . . . " (202); and Lederach challenges all readers to take up the journey of reconciliation by keeping our "feet on the ground and our head in the clouds."

The greatest strengths of *Journey Toward Reconciliation* are two. It is a deeply authentic attempt at analysis and reflection based on actual experience and an unshakable commitment to the Christian faith. This then helps John Paul Lederach paint *for* us a genuine piece of art that includes the realities of violence and disillusionment, but these are overshadowed by highly dynamic images of revelation, hope, and the quality of prophetic projection sending us forward to eagerly engage the world's presenting conflicts.

Journey Toward Reconciliation is a book from which all of us can learn. Anyone interested in more appropriate responses to conflict *will* be moved to fresh and energizing hope that will empower our efforts in this direction. I recommend it highly.

Bernie Wiebe teaches at Menno Simons College, Winnipeg, Manitoba.

Women Against the Good War: Conscientious Objection and Gender on the American Home Front, 1941-1947, by Rachel Waltner Gossen, University of North Carolina Press, 1997.

Reviewed by Kimberly Schmidt

When future historians of Mennonites study the historiography of the 20th century, what will they conclude? Of course, this type of conjecture is impossible to answer, but no doubt Rachel Waltner Goossen's book on women's experiences in Civilian Public Service will stand out as a fresh and distinctive approach to the telling of Mennonite history. Goossen's emphasis on the female story and on social history methodologies is still new in Mennonite historical circles. She, along with a few other historians, is just beginning to scratch the surface of Anabaptist and Mennonite women's history.

Goossen aptly employs social history methodologies. Her use of interviews, questionnaires, letters, diaries, photographs, and other archival resources produces a complex and tightly woven narrative about Mennonite, Quaker, Brethren women, and others who, because of religious beliefs and humanitarian convictions, objected to World War II.

We learn about Edna Ramseyer, a college professor when World War II started. She encouraged young women at Goshen College to train themselves for work at CPS camps. Many such women, known as C.O. Girls or COGs, completed the training and went on to work and live in CPS camps.

We also learn about wives and sweethearts of C.O. men. Many of these women followed their husbands when they were transferred from camp to camp. Their stories are about providing for and raising small children on their own while their husbands were contained in the camp setting. Many women, even those with small children, had to become wage earners because government compensation for CPS men was greatly reduced from the amount allotted to men in the armed services. Taking care of children and maintaining households on negligible incomes were common memories in Goossen's account.

But Goosen's story is not just about how women contributed to CPS camps, supported their husbands, sweethearts, and brothers, and "made do" on limited incomes. Her "cultures of nonconformity" analysis is interwoven with a gendered critique of both American culture and church structures. Nonconformist C.O. women challenged both church and societal prescriptions about proper feminine behavior.

C.O. women were nonconformists in the larger American culture because they advocated a pacifist stance instead of wholeheartedly supporting the war. They were also nonconformists in church circles. Many C.O. women wanted to substantially contribute to the work of the church and to CPS camps, and yet church administrators were more interested in employing women to boost the morale of men in the camps. Their work was not taken seriously by the church. In terms of training women for work in the camps there was an emphasis on nursing and nutrition, areas considered suitable for women. At a time when women were stepping in to fill men's vacated places on farms and in factories, and as a result truly redefining women's work, it seems that church leaders were mainly interested in tapping women's work but only if they remained safely within a female sphere. World War II did not produce a Mennonite equivalent of Rosie the Riveter, at least not among C.O. women.

As with many good histories some questions remain unanswered. Goossen claims that the CPS experience was transformative for women. We hear from interview material how crucial the experience was, but it is unclear how being a CPS woman made a long-term difference. Did the CPS experience produce female leaders in our church? One wonders, for example, if CPS women were more likely to pursue work outside the home after the war. How many of the women that Goossen questions had professional careers? Or were CPS women, like the population as a whole, eager to raise families and become homemakers after the war? This is not a criticism of the decision to stay at home with small children. It is simply a question about how far the culture of nonconformity was carried. It seems that the CPS women's nonconformity did not include a sustained challenge to gender role expectations. In a similar vein, Goossen says that the CPS experience caused women to form lifelong commitments to numerous peace and social justice movements, but few examples of such commitments were offered.

One also wonders about the day-to-day lives of the women with small children who had to work outside the home. How did they manage far away from home communities, without the help of extended families, and on small incomes? One CPS mother noted how she set up housekeeping in a "New Hampshire CCC barracks with snow sifting across our bed during the winter" (p. 60). The culpability of church administrators who expected female support for CPS men but did not lend aid to CPS wives and children is mentioned but remains largely unexplored.

Goossen also mentions how female support networks flourished around many of the camps. Did a women's culture evolve in these situations? It seems so because often help was found in the oddest of places. Especially intriguing was the story about the women who helped each other even when one's husband was a CPSer and the other's was in the armed services (p. 47). These practical women set aside ideology in order to help one another. The hints of more of these stories were tantalizing, and perhaps Goossen has the material and resources to pursue this "women's culture" topic in more detail. This research agenda and similar topics will surely be addressed at greater length as Goossen and others continue to devote themselves to the discovery and analysis of women in history.

Kimberly D. Schmidt, Hyattsville, Maryland, is an assistant professor of history.

Do I Still Have a Life? by John M. Janzen and
Reinhild Kauenhoven Janzen. Lawrence, KS:
University of Kansas (Publications in
Anthropology #20), 2000.

Reviewed by John A. Lapp

This is a remarkable book. John M. Janzen, professor of anthropology and director of the Africa Study
Center at the University of Kansas, and Reinhild
Kauenhoven Janzen, professor of art history at
Washburn University, Topeka, Kansas, have written
what will surely be a primary source book for
understanding what happened to the people of
Rwanda and Burundi during the disastrous war and
genocide six years ago.

While in the Great Lakes region of Central Africa
for less than three months at the end of 1994 and
early 1995, the Janzens interviewed widely and collected stories, photographs, and children's artistic
representations of life before the deluge of violence
and after. They include several thoughtful reflections
by survivors.

Before examining the book further, a personal
comment: Since the Janzens volunteered to represent
Mennonite Central Committee in this ministry of
reconciliation while I was executive secretary of
MCC, I cannot claim to be a disinterested reviewer.

Many readers will remember the terrible news in
the spring of 1994 when reports of massive killing
and the enormous flight of refugees from Rwanda
dominated the Western media. MCC administrators

were appalled but not sure we had a role there.

United Nations agencies were on the scene, as well as more than 150 independent relief organizations. MCC had no established relationships in Rwanda. Some executive committee members felt MCC was overextended.

North American Mennonites and Brethren in Christ felt differently. They were deeply moved by the reports of death and suffering. Spontaneously, with the expectation that MCC would respond, they called the offices and began sending funds. The constituency conscience is wonderful to behold.

MCC decided to send a five-person team to see if people on location could define a niche for yet another agency. The team was told that any program proposal should include the participation of the large Mennonite churches in Zaire (now the Congo) and that contacts should be re-established in Burundi, where MCC worked three decades earlier. There were an estimated 2 million refugees in Zaire, a half million in Tanzania, and several hundred thousand in Burundi.

The team reported the need was great. They found refugee camps that were poorly served by the United Nations and other agencies. They reported that the Quaker churches in Burundi and Baptists in eastern Zaire would welcome MCC assistance.

The team discovered enthusiasm among Zairean Mennonites for participating as partners in a program of relief and evangelical witness. They suggested shipping large quantities of food and clothing. They especially urged that the MCC response include personnel who could help a traumatized people begin the process of healing and reconciliation.

The Janzens, who had long Africa experience and spoke French fluently, offered to assist in the MCC response.

But *Do I Still Have a Life?* is not the story of MCC involvement. It is what the authors call an ethnography, a description that "highlights the voices of individuals in the contexts of their stories during and after the war." Some of these people provided rich reflections on the character of the churches, the process of ethnicization, the fate of cultural institutions, the role of clan, tribe, and family.

The authors studied the anthropology of war or genocide. Here the stories were traumatic and deeply painful. The Janzens learned that careful listening is therapeutic. They listened to voices carrying tragic burdens and questions. They made it possible for tellers to "regain their humanity and understanding [and even] to contemplate solutions." They observed that the "voices we heard and the stories we recorded were more like a sacred trust of the private agonies and the almost unspeakable memories individuals shared with us."

The Janzens do some analysis along the way but especially in their concluding sections on healing the wounds of war and justice as a precondition for peace. Readers will marvel at the empathy, patience, the capacity to hear contradictory assessments, and yet to understand the depth of fear, hurt, confusion, abuse, woundedness, disappointment, and despair. They are reporting from "the killing fields," a phrase used to describe an earlier genocide in Cambodia.

It is impossible to capture the rich detail of this volume. There is just enough political analysis and historical reference to put the upheavals of 1994 in context.

The description of the behavior of the church is very frank. The big churches—Roman Catholic and Anglican—were "declared dead" by many Rwandans. Decentralized religious communities with strong congregational life were not as torn apart by ethnicity and violence. The Janzens found hope, renewal, and remarkable personal stories of faith and heroic action in all churches.

"Do I still have a life?" is a question posed by a refugee and former soldier of the Rwandan army. The Janzens met the refugee, Bugingo, in December 1994. They maintained a connection until as recently as October 1999. He eventually returned to Rwanda and spent two years in prison. He struggles to become a full-fledged citizen without participating in the continuing injustices of Rwandan society.

The question of having a life permeates this volume. Whether in a refugee camp or as part of a fearful minority in the capital cities of Rwanda or Burundi, the questions have to do with purpose and meaning. Such a life is only possible in a context of societal stability and mutual respect between ethnicities. It is painfully clear that repeated rounds of violence have not resolved the fundamental issues in Rwanda or Burundi. The question continues.

We can be grateful to the Janzens for immersing themselves in a culture of violence, disruption, vengeance, reprisal, and war. They found love, forbearance, mutual caring and concern, peacemakers and resistance to violence, which gave them grounds for hope.

Insights into the human situation as presented here will require similar fluency in local languages and disciplinary expertise blended with empathy, understanding, and commitment. These qualities made it possible for the Janzens to communicate a clear and eloquent message: "We encourage you to build a society based on justice and equality, and there will be peace. Allow God to change your hearts and practice the *'alphabetisme de l'amour.'"*

John A. Lapp, of Akron, Pennsylvania, is a former executive secretary of Mennonite Central Committee.

From Anabaptist Seed, by C. Arnold Snyder.
Kitchener, ON: Pandora Press, and Scottdale, PA:
Herald Press, 1999.

Reviewed by Mikha Joedhiswara

We should thank C. Arnold Snyder for making it
possible for us to speak about our "historical core" of
Anabaptist-Mennonite identity in a simple and clear
way. His book, *From Anabaptist Seed,* provides us a
common historical point of reference. It tries to
understand our Anabaptist-Mennonite teaching,
church ordinances, and the practices of daily living
in the light of Anabaptist-Mennonite history in the
sixteenth century. Yet we cannot ignore our present
points of reference as we look at our historical beginnings and examine how those beginnings affect our
Anabaptist-Mennonite identity and action in the
world today.

C. Arnold Snyder uses a powerful metaphor, seeing the church as a plant and Anabaptist history in
the sixteenth century as a seed. "The seeds of that
harvest have been transplanted throughout the world
now for almost five hundred years," he writes.

For me it is better to see the Anabaptist-
Mennonite movement in the sixteenth century as a
plant, and the Gospel itself as a seed sown in the soil
of the sixteenth century context.

The Anabaptist-Mennonite churches of today could
not be like "potted plants" which have been transported without being transplanted. The gospel is a seed
sown in the soil of *culture*, time, context, condition,

and situation. Therefore, the plant of the Anabaptist-Mennonite movement in the sixteenth century bears the work both of the *seed* and the *soil*.

We should not begin with adjustments to a transplantation—like the transplanting of a grown tree from Amsterdam to Jakarta, or from Haarlem to Java, or from North America to Indonesia. Instead, we should begin with locating the living seed, then guarding, watering, and nurturing it as it roots itself *in the present or contemporary situation,* in *our context,* in t*he concrete experience* of the people and the concrete realities of today.

We need to read our "historical core" in the light of the present day, with compassion, with openness and acceptance, with repentance and with commitment.

The sixteenth century is a period when the church which is the one body of Christ had lost credibility. Within the church had grown a lot of doctrine, spiritual and theological insights, and forms of life which created a lot of conflict within the church. In fact, the church has handled conflict very poorly. This has led to divisions and splits in the unity of the church of Christ with all kinds of negative feelings and violent actions. Even for our history, the Anabaptist movement, after a nasty split in 1693, the Swiss Anabaptist group divided into "Mennonite" and "Amish" factions.

Because of sin and misunderstanding of the diverse gifts of the Spirit, the churches are painfully divided within themselves and among each other. The scandalous divisions damage the credibility of their witness to the world in worship and service.

Moreover, they contradict not only the church's witness but also its very nature.

For a long time, churches were not aware of the dangers of their partisan perceptions when they spoke about their identities. Each faction experiences and observes different data. Each is interested in different things. Each collects evidence to support their views and ignores or dismisses nonconforming data. Each faction selectively receives incoming data and selectively remembers what they want to. Each faction selectively recalls what they remember and revises their memories to fit their preferences.

We should be careful to see that the Anabaptist thought included "scripture and spirit" together, rather than as the Protestant references taught. They taught in "scripture alone" (that meant lack of spirit) and believed that the learned theologians were the ones who were "best fitted" to interpret Scripture. But, if we examine the Reformation and interpretation of Scripture, especially in the work of Martin Luther, it is clear that the protestors were eager to put the Bible into the hands of the people and to translate it into the vernacular. For Luther—

> Experience is necessary for the understanding of the word. It is not merely to be repeated or known, but to be lived and felt. But that does not mean simply that experience in religion brings comprehension of the Scriptures. It is essential that the Holy Spirit brings its illumination to the mind of the person who is searching the Christocentric meaning.

God must say to you in your heart, that
is God's word.

John Calvin also speaks about the "personal testimony of the Holy Spirit."

In the present century, churches need to come
together to discuss their agreements in faith and the
deep differences which have divided them for centuries. There is a growing awareness of an interde-
pendent and smaller world in which the Christian
churches are beginning to discover the need for
common mission and service. The calling of the
church today is to proclaim reconciliation and provide healing to overcome divisions. We need to overcome church-dividing differences and prepare the
way towards visible unity, thereby also supporting
this common calling to mission and service.

We need to develop Anabaptist-Mennonite identity which will include interchurch conversations, the
bilateral and the multilateral, in order to be comple-
mentary and mutually beneficial, to proclaim the
oneness of the church of Jesus Christ, and to call
churches to the goal of visible unity in faith and the
eucharistic fellowship, expressed in worship and in
common life in Christ, in order that the world may
believe.

What we should do now in order to develop our
identity is not only to make a comparative method
but also to perform theological dialogue which seeks
to bring out agreements and convergences and to
struggle with controversial issues by starting from a
common biblical and christological basis, mutual
understanding, and mutual recognition.

Our context today has challenged and assisted the churches to overcome their doctrinal differences, to share their diverse spiritual and theological insights and forms of life as a source of mutual enrichment and renewal, and to reappropriate and express together their common heritage in faith, life, and witness.

I pray that the Holy Spirit, as promoter of *koinonia*, gives to those who are still divided the thirst and hunger for full communion. I pray that we grow together according to the wish and prayer of Christ that those who believe in him may be one.

In the process of understanding our identity, let us also pray, work, and struggle for unity. The Holy Spirit may comfort us in pain, disturb us when we are satisfied to remain in our division, lead us to repentance, and grant us joy when our communion flourishes.

Mikha Joedhiswara is a professor in Salatiga, Indonesia.

Mennonites in Canada, 1939-1970: A People Transformed. Mennonites in Canada, Vol. 3, by T. D. Regehr. Toronto: University of Toronto Press, 1996.

Mennonites in American Society. 1930-1970: Modernity and the Persistence of Religious Community. The Mennonite Experience in America, Vol. 4, by Paul Toews. Scottdale, PA: Herald Press, 1996.

Reviewed by Pamela E. Klassen

Reading these two books in conjunction invites comparison along several axes. First and most obviously, these books chronicle the similarities and differences between Mennonites in Canada and the United States before and after World War II. But they also invite comparison on the grounds of methodology and even national identity. How do the approaches of intellectual history (Toews) and social history (Regehr) bring different kinds of experience to the fore? How do Canadian and U.S. narratives of national identity find their way into histories of Mennonites in those two countries? After briefly describing the two books, I will try to offer some answers to these questions, from the perspective of a Canadian scholar of Mennonite history who spent five years in graduate school in the U.S.

T.D. Regehr's account takes as its central question the transformation of Canadian Mennonites from a largely rural people to a more diverse group that includes among others, urban business people, award-winning authors, and rural farmers. The dust jacket foreshadows the narrative of urbanization, as a black and white city skyline seems to descend upon an image of two people sitting on a horse-drawn wagon. Regehr's telling of the story, however, is not a simplistic tale of urbanization triumphing over rural community. Instead, by incorporating stories of particular individuals grappling with the transformations of "modernity," as well as broader perspectives on the political and economic contexts of Canadian life, Regehr provides a complex portrait of diverse Mennonite experiences.

Regehr divides his narrative into an introductory section and four thematic sections that treat the significance of World War II, the economic contexts of urbanization, education, and the arts, and changing notions of religious mission. Throughout he demonstrates sensitivity to how larger currents in Canadian life affected Mennonite fortunes. For example, in order to provide a wider context for the June 10, 1940 visit by Mennonite leaders to Prime Minister Mackenzie King leaders concerning alternative service, he gives not only the Mennonites' viewpoint but also that of the prime minister. According to Regehr, June 10 was "one of the worst days in the war for Canada, and particularly for the prime minister" (42). The confusion over conscientious objection that followed was in part due to a meeting in which the prime minister was distracted by what he considered to be more serious concerns, namely the accidental death of the minister of national defense and Italy's entry into the war.

Regehr's choice of themes accentuates his ability to think of Mennonite history in terms of many strands of Canadian history, as his attention to economic forces, political shifts, and social change demands that he consider particular ways that Mennonites interacted with the wider culture.

Paul Toews's account of the Mennonite experience in America is markedly different from Regehr's. Though Toews also considers the transformations of modernity to be central to the story of U.S. Mennonites, he does not share Regehr's path to understanding these transformation. The focus of Toews's approach can be summed up in his own words: "The most important redefinition of Mennonitism and the most persuasive guarantor of continued Mennonite distinctiveness was the articulation of a new system of ideas" (341). For Toews, ideas, mainly in the form of theology, are the key to the "persistence of religious community." He gives the status of a manifesto to Harold S. Bender's essay, "The Anabaptist Vision," asserting that it reinvigorated Mennonite identity and provided Mennonites with "a new sense of particularity and mission" (341). When Toews does venture into discussion of how such ideas were made concrete, he focuses for the most part on the activities of the burgeoning Mennonite Central Committee, the structure of different church conferences, and the development of Mennonite educational institutions.

Toews structures his narrative within thirteen chapters that are a roughly chronological account of shifts in peace theology, church structures, and various ways that U.S. Mennonites interacted with "the world"—or at least, what they constructed as "the world." Most of his chapters begin with an anecdote or depiction of what Robert Kreider felicitously described as the "patriarchs of the church" (238). The cover of Toews's book—three young girls blowing up balloons at a relief sale—is somewhat at odds with his focus on the patriarchs. Instead, the lives of girls and women as told in their own words are mostly absent from the book.

That Regehr and Toews find different foci for their narratives can be partly attributed to their methodological approaches. Regehr uses the tools of social history—letters, diaries, census figures, and, most important, a commitment to finding historical data in the lives of even the most humble of people—to craft his narrative of Mennonite experiences of modernity. In particular, he seems to have benefited from the work of scholars of Mennonite women's history, as his acknowledgment of the contribution of Marlene Epp attests. Toews uses some of the same sources as Regehr, but is guided throughout by the approach of intellectual history, as he documents the lives and thoughts of the prominent intellectuals and church leaders of the mid-twentieth century in his depiction, perhaps rightly titled, of "the" Mennonite experience (in the singular).

The different methodological approaches of these two authors affects everything from the importance they attribute to the analysis of gender to their willingness to set Mennonite history in wider contexts. So, for example, while Regehr documents the early impact of feminism on Canadian Mennonite women by turning specifically to Laverna Klippenstein's questioning of the "intrinsic value in zwieback" (190), feminism, even as a system of ideas, is virtually absent from Toews's portrait. In addition to setting Mennonites in the wider context of the Canadian political system, which Toews also does to some extent in the American case, Regehr spends considerable energy documenting the relationship of Canadian Mennonites to grassroots politics, like the prairie cooperative movements. The economic detail provided by Regehr shows the complex, "secular" links that bound Mennonites to their Canadian society. Both books, however, could have benefited from a more direct discussion of Mennonites and class identity.

Regehr's methodology also seems to allow him to venture more comfortably into some of the most sensitive and controversial aspects of a Mennonite social history. For example, his exploration of sexuality among Mennonites ranges from a discussion of Jacob Janzen's innovative attempts in the 1940s at what I would call "sexology" to frank acknowledgment of the ways women were more harshly punished than men for engaging in premarital sex (212, 220). Regehr frames his discussion of topics like sexuality in his very helpful "personal prologue," in which he describes his own grappling with his Mennonite identity and the notion of scholarly objectivity. Ironically, he closes the prologue by taking Bender's "Anabaptist Vision" as his cue, and insisting that "spiritual and carnal, sacred and secular aspects of life were not necessarily in conflict with one another" (xxi). Toews, in using the same text as his base, does not include such intimate, yet profoundly political topics in his inquiry.

Their different use of sources also contributes to the very different ways that the two authors conceive of religious experience—something that must be central to any history of the Mennonites. In terms of revivalism, Regehr shows how the Brunk revivals of the 1950s were experienced differently by the Swiss Mennonites in Ontario and the Russian Mennonites in the West. More specifically, he argues that, for some Russian Mennonite young people, these revivals provided liberation from a culture bound to the language and ways of the "old world," but that, for others, revivals were a source of shame, terror, and social ostracism (210-11). Toews's exploration of the significance of revivalism draws a portrait of revivalistic fervor in more general terms, and discusses theological critiques of revivalism from church leaders such as *Gospel Herald* editor Paul Erb and Pacific Bible Institute president Reuben Baerg. Personal diaries of the joys and traumas of revival help Regehr develop a multifaceted portrayal of revivalism for the layperson, while Toews concentrates on the official reactions to revivalism as a theological phenomenon.

Perhaps the differences in the two accounts—Regehr's with its attention to the laypeople and the leaders and Toews's with its focus on the prominent voices in American Mennonitism—reflect something of the reality of Canadian and American narratives of national identity. At the risk of over-generalizing, I suggest that Canadians are not as familiar with the "patriarchs" of their history as Americans are (or claim to be). For example, finding a Canadian who could name the first three prime ministers would be a difficult task. Though some may lament this as historical ignorance, it may also speak to a different sense of what stories are important in a country's past.

Stories of the struggles of social movements (like that which initiated universal health care) and stories of the sources of our disunity (battles between French and English) might lie closer to the surface of Canadian memory. Compared to Americans, Canadians have certainly had to be more aware of fragmentation, given the "two solitudes," and more suspicious of particularism, given the legacies of British and American influence. The closely textured social history of Regehr's account of Mennonite life and the focus on intellectual and church leaders of Toews's history may well reflect these differing narratives of national identity. Although focus on the elites may be a necessary aspect of presenting any community's history, it can obscure the sources of conflict and voices of resistance within those communities.

A particularly valuable aspect of both books lies in their use of photographs. Especially in Toews's book, the photographs effect representations of many of those who are, for the most part, silent in the text. One of the most intriguing photos is that of Martin Luther King, Jr. on a visit to Goshen College (256). Toews discusses Mennonite responses to King and to the civil rights movement, but this photo made me want to know even more: What did King think of Mennonites? Might there be some diaries or letters in which he makes mention of his visit to Goshen? Both books could have tied the photographs more directly to the text, thereby using the photographs as important historical sources in their own right.

Both books provide important bases for new research on Mennonites in the twentieth century. They attempt the difficult task of chronicling almost four decades of Mennonite history—decades with a broader diversity of sources available to the historian than those available to the authors of any of the earlier books in these respective series. Working from the offerings of these two surveys, contemporary Mennonite historians have much to consider. I hope that they will grapple with some of the most difficult questions in the construction of twentieth-century "Mennoniteness"—for example, questions of gender and sexuality, ethnicity and religious experience. I hope that they will not only ask how Mennonites construct their identities within their own communities, big or small, but also how being Mennonite shifts in relation to the changing world and the changing "others" in that world.

Pamela E. Klaasen is associated with the University of Toronto in Ontario.

Mennonite Education in a Post-Christian World: Essays Presented at the Consultation on Mennonite Higher Education, Winnipeg, 1997, by Henry Huebner, ed. Winnipeg, MB: CMBC Publications, 1998.

Education for Peoplehood: Essays on the Teaching Ministry of the Church, by Ross T. Bender. Elkhart, IN: Institute of Mennonite Studies, 1997.

Theological Education on Five Continents: Anabaptist Perspectives, by Nancy R. Heisey and Daniel S. Schipani, eds. Strasbourg, France: Mennonite World Conference, 1997.

Reviewed by Rodney J. Sawatsky

What is the essence of Mennonite education? When are Mennonite schools, colleges, universities, and seminaries truly Mennonite, or perhaps better said, truly Anabaptist Christian? Questions of this order are unfortunately too rarely addressed in spite of our massive investment in Mennonite educational institutions. Perhaps the answers are considered self-evident when these institutions are primarily viewed as inner-directed or sectarian mechanisms to maintain a particular Mennonite ethos or Mennonite denomination from one generation to another.

But most Mennonite schools and colleges are becoming much more outward-directed and are looking for a more embracing and engaging identity. A more prescriptive and less preservative perspective

for Anabaptist Christian education becomes increasingly imperative as we move beyond our traditional
ethnicities and consider the education agendas of our
newer "third-world" churches, or as we invite non-
Mennonites to attend or teach in our Mennonite
schools, or as we interact with other Christian contexts and seek to share the Anabaptist approach to
Christian education. Here we can learn from the
Reformed version of Christian education, where
faith and learning are integrated throughout all disci-
plines in the formation of a coherent and consistent
worldview. Today this model is no longer the pre-
serve of schools in the Reformed tradition but has
entered the vocabulary of most Protestant and some
Roman Catholic schools and colleges in North
America. Our question might best be enriched to
ask: where do we locate the Anabaptist-Mennonite
charisma which would complement the gifts and
insights of other Christian traditions in pursuing the
education of the entire body of Christ?

The three books here reviewed help answer such
questions. *Theological Education on Five Continents:
Anabaptist Perspectives* evidences in its many brief
commentaries and longer essays the need to move
beyond a group maintenance model for Anabaptist
Christian education. Two contributions to this report
of the Consultation on Theological Education in Five
Continents, held just prior to the Mennonite World
Conference in Calcutta in 1997, are especially helpful. In her short essay, Lydia Harder proposes an
educational strategy that would educate Christians,
in good Anabaptist fashion, to be "in" but not "of"
the world. Building on an essay by Walter

Brueggeman, she suggests, most creatively, that our schools should teach students to be bilingual: to speak a communal language of faith (nurture) and a foreign language of engagement with the larger world (mission). Truly bilingual Anabaptist education would reduce the tension between these two common emphases in Mennonite education without losing the rightful voice of either one.

In a less strategic and more synthetic address, Daniel S. Schipani brilliantly details his theses: "We engage in theological education for the sake of the church in the world in the light of God's reign." As Anabaptist theology requires, the church here remains central but, unlike more separatist Anabaptism, it is the church in the world for the world. Anabaptist theological education, accordingly, is church-based and will prepare students for a ministry in which they will, in his terms, enable for worship, equip for community, and empower for mission. Schipani has formulated a solid foundation for Anabaptist theological education which, I believe, ought to inform all levels of Anabaptist-oriented Christian education.

The building blocks for much of Schipani's synthesis are evident in the work of his predecessor in Christian Education at the Associated Mennonite Biblical Seminary, Ross T. Bender. (And Bender is fully bilingual in Harder's terms, although we are not always sure which language he is speaking.) In *Education for Peoplehood: Essays on the Teaching Ministry of the Church,* Bender engages philosophers of education, such as Piaget, and issues in education, such as indoctrination. He addresses every dimension of Christian education as important, from the home, to Sunday school, to conversion, to the teacher, and on to theological education. Especially in his role as Dean of AMBS, Bender developed insights into Anabaptist education as recorded in this volume and in his earlier work, *The People of God: A Mennonite Interpretation of the Free Church Tradition* (Herald Press, 1971), which will benefit succeeding attempts to address the essence of Mennonite education.

Mennonite Education in a Post-Christian World is perhaps the most suggestive work in identifying the Anabaptist-Mennonite charisma in higher education. In this collection of essays, Gerald Gerbrandt helpfully outlines the geography of Mennonite higher education, including the differences between US and Canadian schools, while Joseph Lapp adds an autobiographical perspective on the nature of Mennonite education. These two Mennonite college presidents are descriptive of current Mennonite education and defer to their colleagues for the normative agenda.

Very important, the normative essays overwhelmingly, though largely implicitly, appeal for a third way in Anabaptist-Mennonite education: a way beyond both sectarian and Enlightenment models. Unlike too much Mennonite identity literature, these essays rarely negate other Christian perspectives and claim Mennonite superiority, but rather they self-critically and humbly suggest criteria for Anabaptist education relevant well beyond Mennonite schools. A coming-of-age might be discerned here and/or a selective embrace of the postmodern critique of Enlightenment objectivity, for every author assumes that Mennonite schools are first and foremost Christian institutions premised on the normativity of Jesus Christ. No one argues that in order to be truly legitimate as excellent schools they must in some way be neutral on matters of faith and values. The primary question asked is rather, What does it mean to be a truly Christian school?

The post-Christian world is an identified dynamic primarily in the essay by Nancy Murphy, an Anabaptist who is not a Mennonite. Building on the work of Alasdair MacIntyre, she argues for "the legitimacy of tradition-based educational systems in general, and thus of Mennonite higher education that is thoroughly steeped in its formative texts." This postmodern apologetic for Christian schools that has gained wide currency is very useful, although not without problems because of its perspectivalism. To MacIntyre's analysis Murphy adds what she perceives to be a Radical Reformation remedy to the profound distortions to knowledge and morality caused by power, or in Nietzsche's language, the will-to-power. The Anabaptist practice of communal discernment or power-renouncing practices, she maintains, are the best means to limit power and its distortions.

Murphy's proposal is most stimulating and deserves further conversation. We want to ask, for example, how Murphy defines power? At times she seems to confuse nonviolence with powerlessness. But surely the Anabaptists did not renounce power even if they refused violence, for they were fully aware of the power of suffering, not to speak of the power of the resurrection. If Anabaptist education is to empower for mission, as Schipani argues, it must be power-full, not power-less.

For the empowering potential of Anabaptist Christian education, we must look to three excellent, mutually reinforcing essays by Dale Schrag, Ted Koontz, and Tom Yoder Neufeld. All three would probably agree with the plea in Denny Weaver's essay that Mennonite colleges should teach peace throughout the entire curriculum. But their prior concern is the basic Christian ethos of Mennonite schools that undergirds lives of peace, love, and service. To this end, Schrag recalls Erasmus's rich understanding of the importance of teaching for piety in all Christian education. Yoder Neufeld reminds us of the centrality of the Scriptures in Anabaptist education, introduces the richness of the Wisdom literature as personified in Sophia for our educational task, and insists on the imperative of personal engagement with the formative texts of the Anabaptist tradition.

In combination, these three Mennonite educators suggest three defining characteristics of Anabaptist education. Firstly, they emphasize the centrality of worship. The whole enterprise must be worshipful; it is educating for piety. Secondly, they identify the centrality of teachers in Anabaptist schools, teachers who should be "measured not only by their skills at communication and publication, but by their love for God, by the warmth and intimacy of their friendship with Christ." It is argued that teachers must be partisans for the Christian gospel, and even pastors to their students. Thirdly, they call Mennonite schools to be saintly ". . . windows through which others see the joyful, new making power of Christ's gospel exemplified in their very 'being'—not only in their mission or their words, but in the shape and quality of their shared life." Our schools are called to incarnate or enflesh the Gospel structurally as well as personally. Indeed, I would add in agreement that the incarnation is the primary theological motif characterizing Anabaptist Christian education.

At first blush these three characteristics may not seem all that uniquely Anabaptist, and perhaps they are not. The uniqueness of Anabaptist schools might best be located in their faithfulness to Christ. For surely if these three dynamics were the heartbeat of all Mennonite schools, colleges, universities, and seminaries, they would be profoundly nonconformist institutions in relation to the surrounding culture. Educating truly nonconformist men and women, what else could be more Anabaptist?

With the assistance of excellent works such as the present books under review, the very important question regarding the Anabaptist educational charisma is being answered! The challenge now is to move beyond definition to incarnation.

Rodney J. Sawatsky is President of Messiah College, Grantham, Pennsylvania.

Changing Frontiers in Mission, by Wilbert R. Shenk.
Maryknoll, NY: Orbis Books, 1999.

Reviewed by Harold D. Lehman

Changing Frontiers in Mission brings the perspectives
of theology, history, and culture to the broad topic of
Christian mission. The New Testament church set the
pattern for missionary witness to the world.
Undergirding God's redemptive mission are the veri-
ties of God's reign, Jesus the Messiah, the Holy Spirit,
the church, the world, and the fulfillment of all
things. The church's witness in mission is expressed
in varieties of proclamation and service, word and
deed, individual conversion, and social concerns.

Two centuries ago the modern missionary movement began with attempts to *replicate* the homechurch
within another culture. There were efforts to make
the Scriptures available in the vernacular. The mission
rapidly became institutionalized. Little attention was
given to understanding the host culture. Because the
mission was frequently associated with Western conquest and colonization, the themes of "Christianity,
civilization, and commerce" became descriptive of this
early era of overseas mission work.

The second historical model of mission was *indigenization.* Again the Western missionary was the primary agent in bringing Christianity within another culture. Very early the goal for the mission church was to
become self-financing, self-governing, and self-perpet-
uating. But frequently this led to an unhealthy dependence on the "home" missionary society or board.

More recently the *contextualization* model recognizes the dynamic of the "host" culture, seeking to make the mission witness both "culturally authentic and authentically Christian." New religious movements are a fruit of the modern missionary movement in cross-cultural settings. Two case studies are presented: the United Evangelical Church in the Chaco of Argentina and Paraguay and the Dida Harrists of Cote d'Ivoire.

The major frontiers for mission in the 21st century will lie within our own Western culture, with its emphases on rationalism, secularism, science, and technology. Faithful mission in the future needs to recognize the recovery of Jesus Christ as incarnate, working as a minority church within a dominant socio-political setting.

The essays in this book seek to put mission into its proper framework with theology, to portray the successes and failures of missionary strategy in varied cultural settings and historical eras, and to establish the rationale for mission both now and in the future.

Wilbert Shenk is a recognized theorist and historian of Christian missions. The book is a collection of his published essays from missiology journals, with two formerly unpublished chapters included. It is a scholarly work directed primarily to academics. The insights and information within this book are so important that I hope the author someday puts this work in more popular form for a wide lay readership within our congregations.

Harold D. Lehman writes from Harrisonburg, Virginia.

Golden Apples in Silver Bowls: The Rediscovery of Redeeming Love, translated by **Elizabeth Bender and Leonard Gross, edited by Leonard Gross. Lancaster, Pennsylvania: Lancaster Mennonite Historical Society, 1999.**

Reviewed by Walter Klaassen

This translation and publication of *Golden Apples in Silver Bowls,* by any measure a major accomplishment, is simple, readable, and accurate. The collection (over 500 pages in the 1702 edition) of martyr accounts, confessions, letters, and prayers was first published in 1702, republished in 1742, and in a new edition at Ephrata, Pennsylvania, in 1745. The editor of the collection is credibly identified as Jakob Guth from Hilsbach in the Palatinate, although he is nowhere identified in the book itself. Using materials published earlier, Guth sought to help the Swiss Brethren respond to the spiritual challenges of the early eighteenth century.

Following an excellent introduction by the editor, the translation opens with the two original indexes. The first documents are Michael Sattler's letter to the church at Horb, the record of Sattler's trial and death, and his parting hymn, all of 1527. A collection of the writings of Thomas von Imbroich, including his confession of faith, seven letters to his wife, and one to a friend, constitutes section II. Then follows the touching "Last Testament of Soetgen van der Houte" to her children, and the record of her martyrdom (1560). Eleven letters of Matthias Servaes

and a reflection on martyrdom by Konrad Koch
(1565) constitute section IV. Section V, the largest, is
the edited version of the Dordrecht Confession of
Faith (1632/1702). Section VI offers a number of
prayers, eighteen of them by the Dutch Anabaptist
Leenhaerdt Clock, and VII, an instruction on singing
and the translation of the discipleship hymn "Mir
Nach, spricht Christus Unser Held," written by a
seventeenth-century Roman Catholic, and much
beloved by General Conference Mennonite congregations in Canada and the United States.

The Swiss Brethren had just endured the trauma
of the Amish schism when the book was first published in 1702. The editor was, in a sense, responding to the division by reminding his readers of the
common Anabaptist martyr and confessional tradition. While he could easily have found other Swiss
Brethren martyrs along with Sattler and Imbroich
(one thinks of Felix Mantz, Georg Blaurock, or Hans
Haslibacher), he chose to include Dutch Anabaptist
martyrs. While he could have appealed to his people
with a reminder of the Swiss Brethren Brotherly
Union of 1527, he chose rather to edit the Dutch
Anabaptist Dordrecht Confession of 1632. *Golden
Apples in Silver Bowls* seems, therefore, to have had
an ecumenical purpose as an antidote to schism.

It appears to this reviewer that, given the major
place allotted to Dutch Anabaptist documents, the
editor's repeated emphasis that the book reveals
notable differences between Swiss and Dutch
Anabaptism is somewhat overdrawn. The additions
and deletions from the Dordrecht Confession appear
to reveal matters of relative emphasis more than

underscoring basic differences. The original editor's antipathy to harsh church discipline may have been directed as much to the schismatic Amish as to the Dutch Anabaptists. In any case, we need to be reminded that not nearly all Dutch Anabaptists, even in the sixteenth century, agreed with the harsh views of the later Menno Simons and others concerning church discipline.

The introduction to the translation notes the influence of Pietism on Swiss Anabaptism, a theme which accounts for a second motive for this collection of writings. The book's emphasis on the inner life of the Christian, its evident purpose as spiritual edification, and particularly the addition to the Dordrecht Confession of an article on the Holy Spirit, reflect a response to Pietism with its emphasis on inner holiness. The Swiss Brethren could therefore also claim this emphasis as a part of their spiritual life. The addition brought the Dordrecht Confession into harmony with Thomas von Imbroich's emphasis on the Holy Spirit (p. 135). The subtitle, "The Rediscovery of Redeeming Love," sounds more Pietist than Anabaptist.

Thomas von Imbroich, leader of the Swiss Brethren along the Rhine in the 1560s, easily dominates the volume with his confession and letters. Most of the confession is concerned with his defense of the baptism of believing adults and a refutation of infant baptism. As with so many Anabaptists, he exhibited a truly amazing knowledge of Scripture. While he addressed mostly his Roman Catholic opponents, he also addressed Martin Luther on the subject of faith, although without mentioning his name.

Particularly notable about Imbroich is the absolute equality he accords his wife in his letters to her. There is not a trace of the husbandly condescension we find in the letters of Matthias Servaes, who refers to his wife as "my child." Imbroich always includes himself in the many admonitions. His profession as a printer of books probably explains his unusually informed writing. He refers, for example, to the mythical unicorn with its magic powers as a symbol of Christ. One has the impression that he wrote as much to bouy himself up as to help his fellow believers. While in prison and fated for death, he knows himself to "stand unbound and free" (p. 105), classical phrasing for a prisoner of conscience.

Soetken van den Houte appropriated for herself the Song of Mary (Magnificat) as an expression of the mercy and generosity of God. Jesus, she wrote, "esteemed the humility of Mary, and wanted to be born of her" (p. 159). This reference to the high status of Mary was relatively scarce in Anabaptist writing.

The prayers of Leenhaerdt Clock bear a strong sense of the awesome transcendence of God and at the same time the familiar intimacy of a childlike approach to the father. Maintaining this tension between transcendence and immanence should be an important goal to some of those modern Mennonites who have recently released the tension by neglecting the vision of God "high and lifted up." Moreover, we could do worse than actually using Clock's communion prayers (pp. 269-270) today.

The little "Instruction on Singing" was evidently written by someone familiar with details of church history. The answer to the sixth question of whether the early Christians sang in their meetings is given with a free rendering of the words of Pliny, the Roman governor of Bithynia in a letter to the Emperor Trajan in 112 A.D. These Christians "were accustomed to meet before daybreak, to recite a hymn antiphonally to Christ" (p. 289). The psaltery, referred to in the ninth question, and mentioned in Psalm 33:2, was in fact a ten- or twelve-stringed medieval instrument. It also bore a mystical meaning in biblical interpretation, revealing truth about the nature and being of God, some of which the writer repeats. Ten, he writes, is the perfect number. "Therefore Christ is our psaltery on ten strings" (p. 290). Though not out of place in this collection, there is nothing specifically Anabaptist about this short piece; it could have come from some educated Pietist source.

This first complete English translation from German of an important testimony to the spirituality of the Swiss Brethren is a significant addition to our knowledge of these Anabaptists. We still need an answer to Robert Friedmann's question, noted in his *Mennonite Piety Through the Centuries* (1949), as to why the original book had such restricted success. It virtually disappeared among European Mennonites and had no equal in North America after 1745. It may be hoped that this new publication of an ancient work will have a longer life.

Walter Klaassen writes from Vernon, British Columbia.

Film Ratings and Video Guide, 2000

WHAT MENNONITES ARE THINKING, 2000

The following capsule reviews rate movies which have shown in theaters (some are foreign films with very limited release) from an adult perspective on a scale from 1 (pathetic) through 9 (extraordinary), based on their sensitivity, artistry, integrity, and technique. These listings include a number of movies from the second half of 1999.

An Affair of Love—A study of intimacy between strangers. Can two persons, previously unknown to each other, have an affair without developing any feelings for each other? Exquisitely acted. In French. (7)

Alice and Martin—Events throw them together, but the young man with a secret in his past and the woman devoted to her violin inch toward each other. A powerful love story and psychological drama. In French. (6)

All About My Mother—Swerving between soap opera and melodrama, this colorful tale follows a woman who has seen her son killed in an auto accident as she goes to tell his father, her estranged husband. In Spanish. (5)

Almost Famous—A wonderfully engaging movie about the coming-of-age of a 15-year-old rock journalist in the 1973 world of rock 'n' roll. Highly effective writing and directing. A real treat. (8)

American Beauty—Not a date movie. A merciless dissection of middle-class, suburban malaise. Superb characterizations of a man who has lost purpose, his shallow real-estate-agent wife who despises him, and their surly daughter and the strange boy next door. Dark depiction of the desperation of what passes for "normal" in America. (7)

Angela's Ashes—A Hollywood detachment and gloss robs this story of both its passion and its compassion. An Irish-Catholic family struggles to survive in extreme poverty. (5)

Any Given Sunday—One of Oliver Stone's better pictures. Close-up, heart-pumping confrontation between football teams, between the aging coach and the young woman who's inheriting the team, and between cynicism and hope. Excellent acting and photography. Probably the best football picture ever made. (7)

The Art of War—An action picture about a secret agent working for the United Nations. Too many ideas and too much plot can ruin a story. (3)

Bedazzled—Another flat "sell-your-soul-to-the-devil" flick, without direction or soul. A social misfit wishes for acceptance. (1)

Being John Malkovich—A total failure. A puppeteer finds a portal into the mind of the actor. A clever idea, but the moviemakers aren't up to the challenge. Boring. (1)

Best in Show—A wacky quasi-documentary-style story about various participants in a dog show. Characters are colorfully eccentric and the script is both worshipful and irreverent toward the dogs and their owners. Very funny. (7)

Billy Elliot—An exhilarating, small movie about an extraordinary young boy in a northern England coal-mining town who wants to dance. He faces many obstacles, not the least of which is his coal-miner father's opposition. (7)

The Boiler Room—A greedy group of high-energy young males tries to get rich on a junk-bond scam. More like cheap TV than cinema. (2)

The Bone Collector—A crackling drama, terse with a touch of charm. The search for a sadistic killer leads a paralyzed policeman and his young colleague into the history of old New York. (7)

The Cell—A science fiction thriller about a therapist who is able, through new technology, to enter the dreamscapes of her patients. Can she surf the mind of a serial killer and save one of his victims? Visually stunning and imaginative, but overwrought. (4)

The Cider House Rules—A *David Copperfield* kind of story, set in a 1940s orphanage. A young orphan grows up under the influence of an eccentric doctor, learning about life. Later he leaves to learn even more. Somehow lacks soul and energy. (6)

The Color of Paradise—Set in Iran, this simple but inspiring tale unveils the world of a blind boy who is loved by everyone but his father. Movingly portrayed. (7)

The Contender—A hollow, spineless piece of political drama, wearing its causes on its sleeves. A senator has her past maligned when she is nominated for Vice President. (2)

Croupier—A young novelist, who likes to control his life and not take risks, gets pulled into a scheme to defraud a casino and starts to lose control. A brilliantly executed crime movie. (7)

The Cup—A gentle film about Tibetan monks exiled in India who become obsessed with the World Cup soccer competition. (4)

Dogma—Mix dull, misguided, and gross together. Two fallen angels scheme their way back to heaven. Cardboard characters. (1)

Double Jeopardy—A flimsy yarn about a woman seeking revenge. Not pretty. She believes she was framed for the death of her husband. Disappointing. (4)

Dr. T & the Women—A meandering yarn about a doctor and the women in his life. Too disjointed to ever feel sad. (2)

East is East—Likable tale about a Pakistani father, living in England with his British wife and unruly children. Whatever happened to tradition?! (6)

East-West—An engaging portrait about a Russian émigré physician who returns to Stalin's postwar police state with his French wife. Poignantly acted. (7)

The End of the Affair—An English author investigates a woman with whom he had an affair, only to discover her real reason for having broken off the affair. Based on the novel by Graham Greene. Would be perfect if chemistry worked better. (7)

Erin Brockovich—A plucky but borderline trashy mother takes on the big utility company. Efforts to exhibit Julia Roberts' physique get in the way of the story. (3)

For Love of the Game—Mediocre baseball picture about a fading star pitcher whose life is falling apart. Subject presents opportunities, but the movie strikes out. (3)

Frequency—A what-if psychological thriller about a young cop who connects with his dead father via ham radio. Strong acting delivers an enjoyable result. (6)

Galaxy Quest—A wacky comedy about the actors from a science fiction TV series being "recruited" by actual aliens who've been watching the show's reruns. Partly successful. (5)

Girl, Interrupted—A gritty portrait of the friendship of two young women in a Massachusetts mental institution in 1967. One is intelligent, high-strung, withdrawn; the other charismatic with an assault-like sociopathic persona. Well done. (6)

Girl on the Bridge—A gem, following the romance between a beautiful young woman contemplating suicide and the off-beat knife-thrower who pulls her back from the edge. In French. (7)

The Gladiator—A dramatic spectacle, set in ancient Rome, delivers a terrific result. A brooding Roman general, regarded as a hero, gets too close to the throne. Contrasts the glory of Rome and the gore of Rome. Can a good man, who has loved ones and honor taken from him, win against impossible odds? (8)

Gone in 60 Seconds—If you like cars and fast driving, you'll love it. A former car thief is dragged back into one last heist of 50 classics when his brother is threatened by the mob. Pulsates. (6)

The Green Mile—A gentle giant of a prisoner with a violent past has a touch of healing. Is it possible? Set in a Southern prison during the Great Depression, the story explores a measure of grace at the edge of death. (7)

High Fidelity—A witty film about a less-than-successful young man who operates a music store. He freely confesses his faults and his dreams, submerged in the "religion" of music. John Cuzack is superb. (7)

The Hurricane—A boxer fights to end his imprisonment while a young boy inspires a group of young people to join the campaign. Sterling performance by Denzel Washington. (7)

I Dreamed of Africa—Based on the true story of an Italian divorcee struggling to begin a new life with her young son and with her new husband in Africa. Her husband loves adventure more than she does. Shallow characterizations and disjointed story. (3)

The Insider—A riveting drama (based on a true story) about the risks a whistleblower faces when he testifies against the big tobacco companies. Also, the courage (and lack of it) on the part of the network television company who leads him out on the limb. Excellent acting. A fine movie. (9)

The Interview—A tense one-on-one drama, pitting an apparently innocent man against a good cop/bad cop team of detectives. Very original. So much fun to watch something that isn't predictable. (8)

Joe Gould's Secret—An eccentric, oddball derelict is discovered by a writer for *The New Yorker* magazine. Has its moments. A look at bohemian New York. (6)

Keeping the Faith—More successful than most films which deal with faith issues. Two best friends in New York grow up to become a rabbi and a priest. Enter their childhood (mutual) sweetheart. Well done. (6)

The Last September—A nostalgic portrait of the passing Anglo-Irish aristocracy. (5)

The Legend of Bagger Vance—A golden ambiance polishes the vistas of this would-be fable set in Depression-era Savannah. It's all about a likeable young man who was a star golfer before the war, and his reluctant decision to make a comeback. Seems stilted. *Tin Cup* was so much better. (5)

Love and Basketball—An engaging story about two basketball players who are quite good—a girl and a boy. The focus on their lives instead of the Big Game is refreshing. (5)

Mansfield Park—A young woman is plucked from her poverty and plunked down among her wealthy (but so unwarm relatives). Based on Jane Austin's novel. Witty and romantic. (7)

Meet the Parents—A really fun movie about a somewhat timid male nurse who visits the parents of his girlfriend. Her father has a Godfather complex and her mother's overbearing. Very clever and enjoyable. (7)

Mifune—An offbeat comedy, set in Denmark, exposing a big fat lie told by a successful businessman who's newly wed. He adds layers of deception as he tries to keep his new wife from discovering his humble beginnings. In Danish. (6)

Mission Impossible 2—Visually, it's fun. An action picture, featuring an agent (unless his sunglasses are actually the lead) pursuing a stolen killer virus. Weak plot. (4)

The Muse—Half-amusing. A screenwriter with writer's block seeks the help of a woman with a touch of magic and expensive tastes. Funnier in Hollywood than in the rest of the world. (4)

Music of the Heart—Meryl Streep shines in this warmhearted story of a mother of two whose husband leaves her. A friend persuades her to teach violin to inner-city kids. Based on a true story. A bit too sweet. (6)

Not One Less—A poignant story, set in China. The teacher in a poor rural school takes a leave of absence and a 13-year-old girl is asked to be his substitute. He tells her she must have the same 28 pupils when he returns a month later. Not one less. We see the young girl flounder about, uncertain, but determined. In Mandarin. (7)

Nurse Betty—An amusing yarn which attempts to mix slapstick with dark comedy and falls short. A young delusional woman, obsessed with the doctor in her favorite soap opera, tries to live in her fantasy world in L.A. Very funny by spells. (6)

O Brother, Where Art Thou?—A major disappointment for fans of the Coen brothers. Hapless and clueless, three prisoners try to make their getaway in Southern territory. Simply never gets going. Slow and meandering. (4)

The Patriot—A beautiful epic set in South Carolina during the French and Indian War. Sweeping vistas, stilted dialogue, and unfulfilled characterizations. A freedom fighter wants to farm peacefully, but gets pulled back into battle. (5)

Pay it Forward—A story with heart, albeit, a bit manipulative. A student, as a class project, decides to start to "pay forward" good deeds, on a pyramid basis. Well meaning and engaging, if you give in to the orchestrated tone of it all. (6)

The Perfect Storm—The six-man crew of a swordfishing boat get caught in the "mother of all nor'easters." Lots of water. Great water and storm photography. But the story never had enough of an anchor to make us care. (5)

Reindeer Games—A caper picture about mistaken identity. An ex-con is nabbed to help with a casino heist. Miscast. Misfires. (2)

The Replacements—A ho-hum flick, full of cliches about football and life. Replacement players during the NFL strike struggle for momentary respect. (4)

Return to Me—A widower woos a waitress, but later discovers that she is the transplant recipient of his late wife's heart. Tender and predictable. (5)

Ride with the Devil—A powerful saga about a band of irregular soldiers who support the Confederate cause. Young men growing up in a world that is coming apart, the decisions they face, the dilemmas they live with. (7)

Rules of Engagement—A military courtroom drama about the deaths of 83 unarmed civilian demonstrators in Yemen. Disappointingly wooden. (4)

Saving Grace—An entertaining tale, set in an old-fashioned English hamlet. A widow discovers she is left with many debts and becomes persuaded that growing marijuana might just be the solution. (7)

Sleepy Hollow—Site gags and over-the-top dramatics can't save this modern version of "The Legend of Sleepy Hollow." (2)

Small Time Crooks—Woody Allen finally delivers another hilarious film. Full of funny one-liners and comic situations. An ex-con dishwasher and his would-be-entrepreneur wife decide that robbing a bank will solve their problems. (7)

Snow Falling on Cedars—A major disappointment. Beautifully photographed scenics in the snowy Northwest seem to frost over the whole film. Chilly drama about a reporter covering the trial of the husband of his childhood sweetheart. Has the elements of a classic, but unfortunately the director never gets it out of the freezer. (4)

Space Cowboys—An amiable though hard-to-believe tale of four aging astronauts dispatched to repair a satellite before it crashes to earth. Enjoyable. (6)

The Story of Us—A glib, fractured yarn about a divorce and the inevitability of it all. (2)

The Straight Story—A marvellous film, following a 73-year-old Iowa man who drives his garden tractor (he doesn't have a license) to Wisconsin to visit his dying brother. Simple but strong, tender but true. Can reconciliation happen before it's too late? Slow, charming, and unforgettable. (8)

Sunshine—An engaging picture of three generations in a Hungarian family, and the price they pay for their Jewish heritage. Richly told. (7)

The Talented Mr. Ripley—A neurotic young man will go to any lengths to take over the lives of others. Set in beautiful Italy, this dark, uneven tale falters in its own morass. (6)

The Tao of Steve—A humorous, laidback former philosophy major pontificates on the fool-proof method of seducing women—until a smart young woman challenges him. Funny and endearing. (7)

Three Kings—An exhilarating action picture, set at the end of the Gulf War. Three U.S. soldiers learn of a stash of gold bullion looted from Kuwait by Saddam's troops. They decide to try to take it for themselves. Funny and dark, part war flick, part message film. (6)

Three Seasons—A goodhearted study of contemporary Vietnam through the impressionistic interweaving of four different storylines. (6)

Topsy-Turvy—An entertaining and knowing portrait of the backstage drama—the beginning ideas, the development, the preparation, and the presentation of a comic opera. Gilbert and Sullivan's *The Mikado*, to be exact. Highly polished, opulent examination of the artistic process. (7)

Tumbleweeds—A mother who seems attracted to the wrong men keeps moving from marriage to marriage with her 12-year-old daughter in tow. A tender but tumultuous mother-daughter relationship. (6)

U-571—An action movie about a disabled Nazi sub during World War II, and the Allies attempt to capture its "Enigma" code. Engrossing story, but shallow by comparison with "Das Boot." (4)

Up at the Villa—Uneven yarn about murder, romance, and intrigue set in Fascist Tuscany. (2)

The Way of the Gun—A quirky, violent story about desperate outlaws who kidnap a pregnant woman. Gets too convoluted in the end. (4)

Where the Heart Is—A quirky tale about a young woman who delivers her illegitimate baby in a Wal-Mart where her boyfriend abandoned her. The ensuing tale about celebrity and survival is warm and a bit hard to believe. (4)

Where the Money Is—Has its moments, but never really gels. A bank robber fakes a stroke and hides in a nursing home. (3)

The Whole Nine Yards—A contract-killer comedy which runs out of gas before its contract's up. An understated hit man moves in next to an overwrought dentist. (3)

Wonder Boys—Oh, the temptations of a famous writer/professor, unable to finish his second novel, when he stumbles onto a brilliant but socially inept student writer! Cleverly written; superbly acted. It's one funny, heartbreaking literary weekend. (7)

The World Is Not Enough—Predictable James Bond flick, chasing criminals, terrorists, and pretty girls. (4)

Merle Good of Lancaster, Pennsylvania, is a writer, dramatist, publisher, and a co-editor of this volume. He has been reviewing films for nearly 30 years.

Our Sponsors

For 25 wonderful years, we have welcomed intelligent questions.

Among our features, open year-round to the public:

- "20 Questions," an interactive museum developed around the 20 most asked questions about the Amish and Mennonites.

- The People's Place Book Shoppe, specializing in books about the Mennonites and the Amish.

- The People's Place Quilt Museum, featuring exhibits of antique Amish and Mennonite quilts.

- "Who Are the Amish?," a dramatic three-screen documentary about the Amish.

- The Village Pottery, featuring the finest work by more than a dozen Mennonite-related potters and ceramic artists.

- Come and visit us. Or check our website at www.thepeoplesplace.com.

THE PEOPLE'S PLACE

25 Wonderful Years

Route 340, P.O. Box 419
Intercourse, PA 17534
(In the heart of the
Old Amish settlement.)
Closed Sundays.
800/390-8436
Fax: 888/768-3433

One-Stop Resource!

Books about the Mennonites

- Biography
- Fiction
- History
- Peace/Justice
- Children's Books
- Family Life/Parenting
- Marriage
- Poetry/Music
- Cooking
- Meditation
- Women's Studies
- Humor
- Quilts/Decorative Arts
- Missions
- Grief
- Gift Books
- Leadership

Reliable. Readable. Reputable.

Cumulative Indexes

(Includes 1998, 1999, and 2000 collections of
What Mennonites Are Thinking*)*

By Scripture Reference

ORDER FORM

 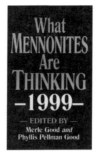 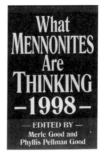

If you would like to order single copies, or if you would like to order any or all of these three books in quantity, please fill out the form below.

Quantity   *Price*   *Total*

_____ copies of **What Mennonites Are Thinking, 2000**   @ 11.95 each: _____

_____ copies of **What Mennonites Are Thinking, 1999**   @ 11.95 each: _____

_____ copies of **What Mennonites Are Thinking, 1998**   @ 11.95 each: _____

_____ TOTAL COPIES   Subtotal: _____

Quantity discount you qualify for: _____

PA residents add 6% sales tax: _____

Shipping & Handling
(add 10%, $3.00 minimum): _____

TOTAL: _____

The following discounts apply:

single copy — no discount
2-5 total copies (assorted) — 10% discount
6-10 total copies (assorted) — 15% discount
11-20 total copies (assorted) — 20% discount

Prices subject to change.

(Please fill in the payment and shipping information on the other side.)

METHOD OF PAYMENT

❐   Check or Money Order
      (payable to Good Books, in U.S. funds)

❐   Please charge my:
      ❐ MasterCard   ❐ Visa   ❐ Discover
\#   _____

exp. date _____

Signature _____

Name   _____

Address   _____

City _____

State/Province _____

Zip/Postal Code _____

Phone Number _____

SHIP TO: (if different)

Name   _____

Address   _____

City _____

State/Province _____

Zip/Postal Code _____

Mail order to:

   Good Books, P.O. Box 419, Intercourse, PA 17534-0419
      Call toll-free 800/762-7171
      Fax toll-free 888/768-3433

Prices subject to change.

·

About the Editors

Merle Good has authored numerous articles, books, and dramas about Mennonite and Amish life. Among his better known writings are Op-Ed essays in *The New York Times* and *Washington Post*, dramas *Today Pop Goes Home* and *Going Places*, children's books *Reuben and the Fire, Reuben and the Blizzard,* and *Reuben and the Quilt*, a novel *Happy as the Grass was Green*, and photographic essays *Who Are the Amish* and *An Amish Portrait*.

Phyllis Pellman Good has also authored many articles and books about Mennonite and Amish life. She served as Editor of *Festival Quarterly* magazine for 22 years. Her books include *Perils of Professionalism; A Mennonite Woman's Life; Amish Children; The Best of Mennonite Fellowship Meals* (her cookbooks have sold more than a million copies); *Quilts from Two Valleys: Amish Quilts from the Big Valley, Mennonite Quilts from the Shenandoah Valley;* and a children's book *Plain Pig's ABC's: A Day on Plain Pig's Amish Farm.*

The Goods have teamed together on numerous projects through the years. They are executive directors of The People's Place, The Old Country Store, The People's Place Quilt Museum, and Good Books, all based in the Lancaster County village of Intercourse. Among the books they have authored together are *303 Great Ideas for Families* and *20 Most Asked Questions about the Amish and Mennonites.* The Goods live in Lancaster, Pennsylvania, and are the parents of two young adult daughters.

338